To Jack

With love from

Sheam, Gina and family

Christmas 1983

'COLLAR THE LOT!'

HOW BRITAIN INTERNED AND EXPELLED ITS WARTIME REFUGEES

PETER AND LENI GILLMAN

Q

QUARTET BOOKS

LONDON MELBOURNE NEW YORK

First published by Quartet Books Limited 1980
A member of the Namara Group
27 Goodge Street, London W1P 1FD

Copyright © 1980 by Peter and Leni Gillman

ISBN 0 7043 2244 7

Printed in Great Britain at The Anchor Press Ltd
and bound by Wm Brendon & Son Ltd,
both of Tiptree, Essex

Contents

Illustrations

Renée Goddard (*photograph: Barbara Bellingham*)
Clive Teddern
Henry Teltscher (*photograph: Peter Gillman*)
Karl Wehner (*photograph: Peter Gillman*)
Bruno Fehle (*photograph: Peter Gillman*)
Serafino Pini (*photograph: Peter Gillman*)
Gerhard Mitchell (*photograph: Peter Gillman*)
Uwe Radok (*photograph: Peter Gillman*)
Erwin Frenkel (*photograph: Peter Gillman*)
Peter Jacobsohn
Frank Eaton (*photograph: Peter Gillman*)
Nobby Fulford
Winston Churchill (*BBC Hulton Picture Library*)
Mr and Mrs Neville Chamberlain (*BBC Hulton Picture Library*)
Sir John Anderson (*BBC Hulton Picture Library*)
Lord Halifax (*BBC Hulton Picture Library*)
Sir Nevile Bland (*BBC Hulton Picture Library*)
William Cavendish-Bentinck
Lord Swinton (*BBC Hulton Picture Library*)
Captain and Mrs Maule Ramsay (*BBC Hulton Picture Library*)
Anna Wolkoff (*Keystone Press*)
Tyler Kent (*Keystone Press*)

'Enemy aliens' registering (*Fox Photos*)

Arriving at camp (*Fox Photos*)

Huyton (*Fox Photos*)

Work at Huyton (*Fox Photos*)

Washing at Huyton (*Fox Photos*)

Women arriving (*Fox Photos*)

Isle of Man (*BBC Hulton Picture Library*)

Collinson's Café, Port Erin (*photograph: Leni Gillman*)

Marching on Isle of Man (*BBC Hulton Picture Library*)

Two views of a Canadian camp (*courtesy Clive Teddern*)

Arandora Star in Venice (*courtesy Blue Star Line*)

A public room and a cabin on the *Arandora Star* (*courtesy Blue Star Line*)

Gunther Prien (*Imperial War Museum*)

U-boat (*Ullstein Bilderdienst*)

Dunera (*John Fairfax and Sons Ltd, Sydney*)

Extract from Sydney *Daily Telegraph* 7 September 1940 (*courtesy Sydney Daily Telegraph*)

Major Julian Layton

Camp money (*courtesy Henry Teltscher*)

Italians clearing bomb sites (*BBC Hulton Picture Library*)

Internees leaving Britain (*Imperial War Museum*)

Acknowledgements

We received information, guidance and practical assistance from a large number of people. In particular, we should like to thank:

Lord William Bentinck; Sir John Betjeman; Betsy Blatz; Stanley Burton; Ann Chisholm; Alec Clague; Richard Cohen; Elaine Davenport; Michael Davie; Mona Douglas; Sol Encel; Millicent Faragher; Michael Foot; Martin Gilbert; Lord Gladwyn; Cameron Hazlehurst; Ronnie Howe; Derek Humphrey; Alexandra Johnson; Professor R. V. Jones; Dr Louis de Jong; Phillip Knightley; Eric Koch; Professor François Lafitte; Julian Layton; Kenneth Low; Ian McLaine; Dick Nelson; Tom Ormonde; Gordon Phillips; Chaim Raphael; Liz Rees; Rob Rohrer; George Rosie; Michael Seyfert; Sir David Scott; Thomas Snow; Leland Stowe; Tony Terry; Sir Dick White.

Our conclusions are, of course, our own.

We are also grateful to the following libraries and archives, with special thanks to the staff members we have named:

Australian Archives, Canberra (Jenny Stokes)
BBC Hulton Picture Library (Marjorie Willis)
Home Office records department (R. G. Pearson and Miss White)

Imperial War Museum (Terry Charman and Dr Peter Thwaites)
Lambeth Palace Library
London Library
Manx Museum Library (Mrs Killey)
Naval Archives of the Ministry of Defence (R. M. Coppock)
Public Record Office
Sunday Times Library (Fred Sayers)
United States National Archives, Washington (Ron Swerczek, Diplomatic Branch)
Wiener Library (Janet Langmaid)

We should also like to thank our valiant typist, Maimie Clifford, assisted by Hilary O'Connell.

'COLLAR THE LOT!'

Introduction

In the summer of 1940, a young Oxford graduate named François Lafitte was commissioned to write a book about internment in wartime Britain. Internment had reached its peak in the wake of the invasion scare, and it was a subject about which Lafitte, a radical and humanitarian, felt strongly. He completed his task in six weeks and corrected his proofs by candlelight in a London air-raid shelter while bombs fell outside. His book, *The Internment of Aliens*, for which he was paid £50, was published as a Penguin Special in November 1940. It remained the best account of the subject for the next forty years.

The year 1940 had seen violent debate over internment and there was no shortage of public statements for Lafitte to draw on. Lafitte also gathered the testimonies of internees anxious to describe their plight. But Lafitte faced the enormous handicap of being unable to examine government records and files. It was not until 1972 that some of these files were opened to the public: some, but not all. Anyone writing about internment today has the major advantage of access to much material beyond Lafitte's reach. But, even forty years after the event, a barrier of official secrecy still shields important parts of the story of internment in Britain during the Second World War.

In 1958, Britain's Public Records Act laid down that government records should, as a general rule, be 'available for public inspection' at the Public Record Office, or elsewhere, after fifty years. In

1967, the waiting period was reduced from fifty to thirty years. And as an act of convenience for historians, the government decided in 1969 that all records of the Second World War should be released by 1972. The main Public Record Office is a magnificent air-conditioned building by the side of the Thames in the London suburb of Kew. In theory there should be no difficulty in establishing from the records held there the truth about internment in 1940.

There is, of course, a catch. The thirty-year period is far from mandatory, being qualified by the following phrase: '*or any other period, either longer or shorter*, as the Lord Chancellor may, with the approval, or at the request, of the Minister or other person . . . prescribe'. There are procedures to be followed when documents are withheld: the Lord Chancellor's office must approve this action, the Public Record Office may scrutinize the documents in question. And, in 1970, the Lord Chancellor's office cited the grounds on which documents might be withheld. The definitions spoke of information acquired in confidence where disclosure would be a breach of faith, and disclosure that would embarrass individuals or their descendants. They also included 'exceptionally sensitive papers the disclosure of which would be contrary to the public interest, on security or other grounds'. This definition is so broad that it appears to permit a ministry to withhold those documents that it wishes to withhold. That, at any rate, seems to be so in the case of internment.

The ministry most vital to the story of internment is the Home Office. It helped to devise policy and lay preparations for internment before the Second World War began. It was the key protagonist in a bitter Cabinet struggle over internment during the spring of 1940. In the summer of that year, it assumed almost complete responsibility for internment. Yet the Public Record Office contains virtually no Home Office documents on the subject that are open to the public.

It is not necessarily the end of the road if a ministry has declined to open its documents after thirty years. The Public Records Act permits access to closed documents for the purposes of scholarly research, and we applied to the Home Office for permission to examine its internment files on this basis. On 23 March 1979 we spoke to Mr H. G. Pearson, Departmental Record Officer at the Home Office building at Queen Anne's Gate, London. Mr Pearson was encouraging. He explained that the Home Office liked to give access 'fairly freely' and that, although internment was 'a sensitive area', he was sure that the Home Office could help. Indeed, we always found Mr Pearson and his assistants friendly and anxious to please. But it was soon clear that they were labouring under the immense difficulties of a tiny staff and an enormous work-load.

On 24 March 1979 we sent Mr Pearson a detailed letter explaining exactly which episodes we wished to examine. We quoted titles and references of Home Office papers we knew of, and the dates and authors of Home Office correspondence we had seen in other files. We also tried to avoid asking for material which might be barred on the grounds of embarrassment to living people or their descendants. Our application was generously dealt with 'out of turn'. Even so, more than five months passed before we were invited to visit the library at Queen Anne's Gate.

There we were shown twelve files, nine of which had never been revealed before. We have made copious use of these files, largely in Chapter 3, and catalogue them in our source notes, starting on page 301. But the new documents referred only to the period from April 1938 to August 1939. And the three remaining files covered nothing earlier than July 1940. The central period in the story of internment is embraced by the dates September 1939 to June 1940. Of that period we were permitted to see nothing at all.

We contended to Mr Pearson that there were good grounds for believing that the Home Office had been badly misrepresented over internment and that its position was far more reasonable and liberal than its critics have argued. But the decision, it became clear, was not Mr Pearson's to make. We eventually learned that it was the Immigration and Nationality Department of the Home Office that was refusing to release the files. In a letter dated 26 November 1979, Mr Pearson wrote that the files had been withheld under the clauses that referred to potentially embarrassing material about individuals, and to sensitive papers whose disclosure would be against the public interest 'on security or other grounds'. We offer speculation elsewhere in this book as to what those 'security or other grounds' might be. In the absence of better particulars from the Home Office, it remains a guess.

Fortunately, we found other routes past the Home Office's barrier of silence. The largest set of documents on internment in the Public Record Office emanates from the Foreign Office, whose internal minutes and correspondence with other ministries, including the Home Office, contain much useful information, although even here some files are missing. In addition, there are files from the Dominions Office and War Office which illuminate important aspects of the story. We also discovered useful records in the National Archives of Australia, Canada, and the United States, including a large set of Home Office instructions on internment which were sent to the US State Department in February 1941, of which we have made extensive use. All these documents we have cited in our text and/or source notes.

We also received assistance and guidance from a number of people mentioned in our text and listed on page ix. We interviewed a small number of people who asked not to be named, including several former members of military intelligence and MI5, and we gratefully acknowledge their help.

Our most bountiful source was, of course, former internees themselves. Almost all we approached were happy to help, and made prodigious efforts to search their memories on our behalf. We were especially fortunate that their recollections were often invaluably supported by documents, diaries and letters, which were also made generously available to us. It should be clear from our text who helped us in this way, but we should like to thank formally here all those who assisted us and in many cases showed us exceptional kindness and hospitality.

They are:

Sir Hermann Bondi; Richard Broh; Frank Eaton; Bruno Fehle; Gus Fehle; Erwin Frenkel; Renée Goddard; Felix Gutmann; Peter Jacobsohn; Theresa Kermode; Jimmy King; Hans Margis; Dorothea Marx; Klaus Marx; Michael Mellinger; Gerhard Mitchell; Serafino Pini; Uwe Radok; Frank Stampfl; Clive Teddern; Henry Teltscher; Karl Wehner; Hellmuth Weissenborn.

We dedicate this book to them.

1 A Midsummer Morning

Nobby Fulford, an English sailor from Southampton, was asleep in his cabin when the explosion came. It was like a brief, angry growl and the ship shuddered in unison. Fulford sat up, breathing hard, and found the cabin plunged in darkness. He gingerly stretched out a foot, but the floor seemed to have disappeared. From somewhere in the blackness he was being sprayed with a warm, tacky liquid. It felt like oil.

After eighteen years at sea – ten on this ship – Fulford knew by instinct that he must get out. He groped his way from the damaged cabin and aimed for the stairs that led to the working alleyway – the crew's passageway that ran through the bowels of the ship. Somewhere ahead was the flickering beam of a torch. He made towards it and found that it was wielded by the chief engineer, directing men to safety. Fulford had intended to head for the main saloon in the stern via the ship's pantry and galley, but the officer warned him not to: that was where she was hit, that was where she was settling. He knew the chief was right. His bare feet could already feel the incline in the alleyway floor.

Fulford worked his way forward and upward through the stricken liner, to emerge on to an open deck, his eyes blinking in the early-morning light. The ship's bugler handed him a lifejacket and he hurried to his lifeboat station on the top deck. Passengers were crowding on to the promenade deck below, some fully dressed, others in pyjamas. He helped to slide the boat from its

1

davits until it was level with them and they clambered on board. When the boat was full, Fulford helped to lower it to the Atlantic swell fifty feet below. A rope flailing from the davits whipped into his stomach, and he gasped.

Fulford heard a shout from the ship's bridge and looked up to see the ship's master, Captain Edgar Moulton, beckoning to the men around him. A friend of Fulford named Jimmy Hutton ran up the companion-way to the bridge. At that moment the ship lurched; the deck steepened, and Fulford was sure the end was near. He ran to the edge of the deck and jumped. As he tumbled through the air he felt he had leapt from the top of the sky.

When he hit the water his lifejacket was driven hard under his armpits and into his face, cutting his chin. His first feeling after-wards was pleasure that the sea was not especially cold. But then he remembered how the suction from a sinking ship is supposed to engulf all those around her. He started to swim as far away as he could.

Serafino Pini, an Italian restaurant owner born near La Spezia, had spent an uncomfortable night on the floor of 'D' deck, high in the ship. The explosion jolted him awake and he could hear cries and running feet. He thought at first that the ship had been struck by a mine, but then he heard men shouting that she had been torpedoed. He hurried out to the main deck, where someone gave him a lifejacket. He ran towards a lifeboat but it was full. He saw another tip up as it was lowered, spilling its passengers into the sea. Pini looked over the rail into the water and hesitated. As he glanced around him, his eyes met those of Captain Moulton on the bridge. 'Don't be afraid,' Moulton called. 'Jump!' Pini grasped a rope hanging from a davit and slid down it. As he reached the water, a falling passenger crashed into him and something jabbed into Pini's eye. He tried to reach a lifeboat, but it was carried away in the choppy water around the liner's hull. Planks and other debris bobbed up and down in the oily sea; he heard shouts in various languages from the water around him. When he tried to swim, his lifejacket somehow kept pushing him on to his back. He was relieved to see the distance between him and the liner gradu-ally opening up.

Erwin Frenkel, who was Austrian, the son of a rabbi in Vienna, was lying on a palliasse when the torpedo struck. He told the man on the neighbouring mattress to get up, but he seemed reluctant, so Frenkel pulled on shorts and a shirt and made his way to the main deck. He saw men scrambling for the lifeboats and looked down at the water. A passenger came to the rail beside him, wearing a collar and tie and an elegant pair of gold-rimmed glasses. He, too, looked over the side and announced: '*Ja, das Schiff sinkt!*' He climbed on to the rail and performed a perfect swallow-dive into the water. Frenkel was encouraged to follow, and jumped. He soon found a life-raft and clambered on board. The man who made the swallow-dive was already there. His collar and tie were sodden and askew, but his gold-rimmed glasses were intact.

Uwe Radok, a young German engineer, whose home had been in East Prussia, had woken at six o'clock that morning. His brother Rainer had left the cabin to join the queue for bread outside the ship's mess. When Uwe heard the explosion, he turned to his other brother, Jobst, and said: 'That's it. Let's get out!' They met Rainer just outside the cabin, and the three found themselves a lifejacket each. Passengers were milling in confusion; some were climbing into lifeboats, others rushing to and fro. The ship seemed solid enough to Uwe, but when he looked over the side he could see how far the water had risen. He told Jobst and Rainer: 'We have no future here.'

Moored to the hull below they could see a lifeboat that was less than half-full. A rope ladder hung into the water, dangling free on account of the list which the ship had already developed. Several Italian passengers with suitcases clung to it, apparently afraid to descend. Uwe started down the ladder first. He passed the Italians on the inside, and dropped into the water. But when he tried to swim to the lifeboat, it moved away with the ship. Jobst came next; he was a strong swimmer and managed to reach the boat. Rainer, arriving last, could not do so and he and Uwe floated away together. They came upon a wooden ladder and tried to climb on to it, but it sank under their combined weight. Then they saw a lifeboat heading erratically away from them, rowed inexpertly by some of the passengers. They swam after it and were pulled on board. The boat, which was piloted by a member of the ship's crew, steered from survivor to survivor and hauled them from the water; Uwe and Rainer were relieved to see Jobst wave from another boat. One of the last to be saved was a boy clinging to a sack of straw. Finally the boat was full and the crewman said he could save no more. They still passed men struggling in the water, their heads dipping up and down as they tried to stay alive. Then their heads went under for the last time. Uwe had not known that men could die so quickly.

The *Arandora Star*'s time had almost come. The Atlantic had been surging through the hole blasted by the German torpedo, pulling her inexorably down by the stern. Now her bows rose more steeply and she began to turn over to starboard. The men who were in the water around her remember different aspects of that climactic moment. Lifted by the swell, Nobby Fulford momentarily glimpsed Captain Moulton and his officers still on the bridge, and imagined Jimmy Hutton was still with them. He also saw men trying to scramble up the steepening decks. From his life-raft, Erwin Frenkel saw steam and debris burst from the portholes in a final explosion which threw some men clear of the ship. Others still hung to ropes along the side, but a giant plank swept them from their holds. Uwe Radok, half a mile distant in his lifeboat, saw the liner's bows almost reach the vertical and men tumble from the decks like dolls. Then the *Arandora Star* slid almost gently from his sight, leaving only wreckage and debris and the bodies of men. From the throats of those who were dying came a sound like strange music, a sing-song noise Radok had last heard from geese among the reeds on the edge of the Baltic Sea.

Some two dozen lifeboats and rafts were now spread across a widening area of the ocean. Nobby Fulford was pulled on to a boat and soon afterwards saw the body of the *Arandora Star*'s chief engineer float by. Serafino Pini had also reached a lifeboat and was hauled on board; as he sank down he saw that three men in the boat had already died. There were eight men on Erwin Frenkel's raft and one of the pontoons on which it floated was punctured. The raft was beginning to list and Frenkel wondered how long it could stay afloat. The crewman in charge of the Radoks' boat told them that the *Arandora Star*'s radio operator should have had time to dispatch a distress call and that help would be on the way. Uwe Radok scarcely heard this. In his mind he could hear the bird-song noise men made when they drowned. It would stay with him for the rest of his life.

The 15,000-ton former luxury liner *Arandora Star* had sailed from Liverpool on 1 July 1940. Bound for Canada, she carried 374 British men, 712 Italians and 478 Germans. It was her most extraordinary complement in her twelve years at sea.

The British consisted of 200 officers and men of the British army; and 174 members of the *Arandora Star*'s crew, including Nobby Fulford, most of whom had sailed with her in entirely different circumstances before the war. Most of the Italians were expatriates, who had lived in Britain for much of their lives. The Germans comprised the strangest mixture, from Nazis to Jews, businessmen to revolutionaries and socialists. Some were fervent supporters of the Third Reich; others were refugees from Nazi persecution who had left friends and relatives in German concentration camps. Some were merchant seamen who had been taken from their ships by the Royal Navy. Some did not consider themselves German at all, but Austrian, and had fled their country after Hitler annexed it in 1938. Each of these groups was represented among the *Arandora Star*'s survivors on that blessedly mild morning in July 1940. Each was represented, unevenly, among those who died.

How men from such diverse backgrounds were thrown together in this abrupt and dramatic manner is one of the questions this book attempts to answer. It can only be done through the telling of another, larger story, which concerns the decision of the British government to arrest 'enemy aliens' throughout the country. More than 25,000 were interned and many thousands were deported across the Atlantic or to the far side of the world. Some found themselves on the *Arandora Star*.

The story begins during the First World War, when Britain interned almost 30,000 foreigners and chaos and suffering ensued. In 1939 the government announced that this action would not be repeated. We follow the wavering course of that decision until it collapsed under a wave of panic and hysteria in the spring of 1940. Political leaders like to blame their most shameful acts on the people in whose name they govern. In this case, it was not the people but the leaders who were gripped by an unreasoning fear, which they turned on the most vulnerable group in Britain. Conveniently dubbed enemy aliens, most had fled for their lives from Nazi Germany and wanted only that Britain should triumph in the war.

As we have indicated in our introduction, the story is easiest to trace when least controversial. There is ample evidence from many sources for what occurred until Britain declared war. From then until the following spring, the debate on internment was conducted in Cabinet, for which full records are also available. But in May 1940, it disappears almost entirely from public view. That is the period when arguments and motives were at their most disreputable and the manoeuvres at the heart of government most sinister. But enough has surfaced to establish a framework of events whose gaps can be filled by inference and the occasional guess. What is revealed is a phase when power in Britain was secretly concentrated and arrogantly disbursed. The sinking of the *Arandora Star* lifted that secrecy and broke that power. It also caused the policy of internment and deportation to be reversed. The story does not end there, for that turning-point came too late for the thousands whose lives had been altered by being deported, and the hundreds who had drowned.

Some of the names in the story are unfamiliar, others well-known. There is the Joint Intelligence Committee, which at the crucial period committed every mistake to which intelligence-gathering bodies are prone. There is MI5, headed by a field-sports enthusiast, which used its unaccountability to behave with ruthless inefficiency. There is the Home Defence (Security) Executive, with untrammelled power over life in Britain, headed by a Tory political boss whose deputy had been immersed in political intrigue for twenty years.

Some of the public figures may emerge in a new light. The Home Secretary, Sir John Anderson, has been vilified as one of the instigators of mass internment; the reality is different. The Foreign Secretary, Lord Halifax, flits briefly and ineffectively past. Neville Chamberlain demonstrated his unswerving loyalty to the man who had just deposed him by enacting deportation with the utmost dedication. Finally there is Churchill himself, watching internment broodily, intervening to maintain its impetus, and uttering the words which led to the tragedy of the *Arandora Star*.

The story opens with a government spokesman in 1939 admitting that internment during the First World War had been a disaster. It would not, he promised, happen again.

2　The Health Resort

On 24 October 1939, when the Second World War was less than two months old, Viscount Cobham rose in the House of Lords to answer a question about internment. Cobham, who was fifty-eight, had just been appointed Parliamentary Under-Secretary of State for War. His qualifications included active service in the Boer War and the First World War. He also came from a prominent cricketing family, the Lyttletons, and was treasurer of the MCC. The question, posed by Lord Mancroft, was hardly a tough one; Mancroft cited the government's 'humane and sympathetic' approach to the matter, and Cobham was undoubtedly grateful for his tribute to the government's sense of fair play.

Cobham had already explained to the assembled lords that the government had decided not to indulge in mass internment. Encouraged by Mancroft's generosity, he now amplified the background to the government's thinking. It had been much guided by what happened during the First World War, when a large number of aliens had been interned on account of 'spy fever'. This had been especially strong after the *Lusitania* was torpedoed in 1915, and the government very much hoped that the same thing would not recur. Cobham was optimistic. 'In fact,' he said, 'it is not likely to happen, as there are far fewer enemy aliens, especially of military age, in this country now than there were at the commencement of the last war, in spite of all the refugees. The figure I have been given as likely to be interned as enemy aliens is somewhere between

1,000 and 1,500, as against a figure of over 29,000 during the last
war.'

Cobham's speech was by no means the only policy statement on
the subject of internment made during the early days of the Second
World War. On 4 September, the day after the war began, the
Home Secretary, Sir John Anderson, also answered questions in
Parliament. Anderson had been in his post for twenty-four hours,
and was less forthcoming than Cobham; none the less, he enun-
ciated what he was later to describe as a 'liberal internment policy'.

It did not seem to matter at the time that different ministries
should be pronouncing policy on the same subject. The statements
were roughly similar and the division of responsibility between
Home Office and War Office seemed clear enough. The Home
Office decided who should be interned; the War Office guarded
the internment camps. It was more notable that, from the War
Office, Viscount Cobham should refer so frankly to the excesses of
internment policy during the previous war, excesses which both
ministers now trusted would not be repeated. Such candid admis-
sions fall rarely from the lips of government spokesmen, and the
statements by Cobham and Anderson were also remarkable in that
they left very little room for manoeuvre. They become more understandable, however, when the nature of internment during the
First World War is considered. This can be done by an examination of the Home Office files on the subject, released to the Public
Record Office fifty years after the event, supported by the account
of one German civilian who spent four years behind barbed wire.
The story they reveal is of breathtaking indecision and vacillation,
with changes of policy occurring with bewildering frequency. Their
effects were hardly as devastating as the regular slaughters taking
place on the other side of the English Channel; yet they shed
depressing light on the nature of Britain's war leadership. They
also did much to shape Home Office attitudes of the future.

On 8 August 1914, three days after Britain entered the war, a
conference of senior government officials was held at the War
Office in Whitehall. In the words of Sir Edward Troup, Permanent
Under-Secretary at the Home Office, the officials decided to intern
'only those aliens who were regarded by the Police as dangerous,
or likely to become dangerous'. On 4 August, before Britain was
officially at war, the police had arrested 'twenty known spies'.
These were Germans who had been assiduously shadowed for

some time by a new section of the War Office, the Special Intelligence Department, set up in 1909 under a thirty-six-year-old captain, Vernon Kell, and later to become known as MI5. Soon after the 8 August conference, the police rounded up 200 other people who had been 'noted as under suspicion or to be kept under special observation'. The Home Office was later to boast that these actions had 'broken up the spy organization which had been established before the war'.

The first of many fluctuations in internment policy occurred less than a month later. On 4 September, the Home Office and War Office collectively decided that Britain should now intern all Germans of military age – between seventeen and fifty-five. The purpose of this move was to deny the enemy their use for the duration of the war. On 7 September, the Home Office sent a circular to all chief constables, ordering this new group of Germans to be arrested. The trouble was, no one knew what this entailed. The Aliens Restriction Act had come into force on 5 August, requiring all aliens to register with the police. Even so, the Home Office could only guess at how many Germans there were of the relevant age in Britain, estimating the number as betwen 20,000 and 25,000. It was almost certainly too low, but the precise figure was of far greater concern to the War Office, who had the task of guarding aliens once they were arrested. And, from the War Office, loud cries for help were soon heard. On 13 September it entreated the Home Office to stop arresting Germans as it had run out of space to hold them. As Sir Edward Troup drily recorded, 'action on the Home Office circular was suspended'.

The new policy was as short-lived as the old. New pressures against the German population built up as newspapers and politicans competed in racist rhetoric to marshal support for a senseless war by representing the enemy as the most evil in history. Lloyd George appeared on platforms to speak of the barbarian flood, the sanguinary deluge, that had overwhelmed Belgium. Even he was restrained in comparison with those who spread propaganda about the massacre of babies, the rape of nuns, the village priest tied as a clapper to his church bell: no story, it seemed, was too ludicrous to be believed. The hysteria reached a new crescendo when three British cruisers, *Aboukir*, *Hogue* and *Cressy* were sunk in the North Sea on the same day, 22 September. They were torpedoed by a U-boat whose commander was astonished that he should come upon three such easy targets. In Britain it was argued that such a stunning reverse could only be the result of treachery.

The Home Office files reveal that the government made some attempt to stem the tide of anti-German feeling: they tell, for example, of the efforts made to challenge the words of Admiral Lord Charles Beresford, who told a recruiting drive in Aberdeen that the 'three cruisers were lost by information given from this country to the German Admiralty. The British people should insist that the Home Office prevent the British Army and Navy being stabbed in the back by assassins in the shape of spies. All alien enemies should be locked up!'

The Assistant Director of Public Prosecutions wrote a restrained and courteous letter to the admiral:

> As I feel sure that your Lordship would not have made such a statement without having evidence to support it . . . I am writing to ask if you will be good enough to confidentially impart to me the information upon which your evidence was founded, or the sources of it, in order that I may consider the evidence available with a view to taking an action against the offender or offenders.

Such gentle irony was wasted on the admiral, who in a blustering reply declared that the danger of 'alien enemy spies' was acute and was increased by 'a system enjoining that proof or evidence must be forthcoming that an alien is going to commit some treacherous act before he is arrested . . .' Soon afterwards the admiral made a new and more absurd claim in a letter to the press: 'Numbers of men have been caught red-handed signalling etc.: and have been discharged through not enough evidence.'

In vain the DPP's office asked the admiral: 'Would you kindly tell us what are the particular cases to which you refer?' By now the pressures had become irresistible. On 20 October, Sir Edward Troup recorded another shift in policy, citing three somewhat spurious reasons why it should change yet again. There was 'the altered military position on the Continent'. By this, Troup was referring to the first great slaughter of the war at Mons. There was the 'increased possibility of a hostile raid and of attacks by aircraft'. No such raid ever came, and the first aircraft attacks were not until 1915. There was 'the strong feeling against Germans roused by the atrocities committed by German officers and soldiers in Belgium'. It was true that there was 'strong feeling', even if the stories of atrocities themselves were false. But Troup's instructions were precise enough. The internment of Germans, Austrians and Hungarians should start again at once.

Among those caught up in the new wave of arrests was a young German student named Karl Wehner. Aged seventeen, from Frankfurt, he had come to England that summer. His father was a civil engineer from Silesia who had come to like the British through his business dealings with them and who wanted Karl to learn their language. Wehner was enrolled for a private language course at a college in Margate, Kent. One day in July, he had dressed in a three-piece suit and winged collar and tie and said good-bye to his father at Frankfurt railway station. When he arrived in London, he went to stay with a friend of his father in Stoke Newington, and was there on the day the war began. The English course in Margate was cancelled and Wehner was still in London during the battle of Mons, to see women weep as they read the casualty lists in the newspapers. His father wanted him to join relatives in the United States, but the Home Office would not grant him an exit permit. Soon afterwards police called at the house in Stoke Newington and arrested him.

Wehner spent his first night as an internee in a police cell. The following morning he was taken to Olympia, the cavernous exhibition hall in west London which was then a popular venue for travelling circuses. Wehner had seen a German troupe perform there just before the war, and thought he could detect the musty odour of sawdust and animals still lingering in the hall. Several hundred Germans were already there when Wehner arrived. Some were visitors like himself; others belonged to London's own German community, based around Charlotte Street, off Tottenham Court Road. Schmidt's had a grocery store there, later to become a restaurant; there was also a tidy community of butchers, bakers and barbers.

Conditions at Olympia were somewhat rough and ready. The internees were given food ladled from dixie-cans three feet high: a dead mouse pulled from one only briefly dampened their hunger. They slept on damp straw palliasses spread throughout the hall. They used the hall's public lavatories, and at first could do so in peace. But, after a dramatic escape through one of the windows, all the doors were removed. A guard regulated the queue, barking at each internee as he approached: 'Pisserashit?'

By early November, 1,500 men were held at Olympia, while the total detained throughout Britain had reached 10,000. They were housed in a bizarre variety of camps that included a disused jute mill and a skating rink. As the demand for space mounted, the War Office accepted help from all quarters. The National Sailors' and Firemen's Union of Great Britain asked the abbot of Beech House in Hampshire to take in a number of destitute German sailors who had been stranded in Britain when the war began. The War Office handed responsibility for their safe-keeping to the abbot, while the Sailors' and Firemen's Union unashamedly referred to the abbey as a 'concentration camp'.*

After several weeks at Olympia, Wehner was transferred to a liner named the *Royal Edward* that was moored in the Thames Estuary near Southend. A second liner, the *Saxonia*, also held internees, while a third, the *Ivernia*, was reserved for genuine prisoners of war – mostly German soldiers captured in France.

Among Wehner's new fellow-prisoners was a German tennis team who had been playing in a tournament in Australia. While sailing home on a British liner, they had been removed at one of the ports of call and brought to England instead. For most of the time the internees were confined below deck, guarded over by British Boer War veterans; the tennis players in particular found the lack of exercise irksome.

In other ways their treatment was generous, if very closely prescribed. Each internee was given a daily food ration that included 1½ pounds of bread, a ½ pound of meat, 10 ounces of vegetables, a ½ ounce of salt and $1/72$ of an ounce of pepper. Those who could pay 2s (10p) a day were fed a sumptuous diet that was changed daily. On Wednesdays, the choice for breakfast included porridge, bloaters, grilled steak, potatoes, bread and butter, tea and coffee. For lunch there were fresh herrings, cold meats, bread and butter and tea. The dinner menu offered soup, fried fish, roast pork, potatoes, root vegetables, stewed fruit and butter. Wehner could not afford this more luxurious fare, but he did benefit at Christmas, when local Quaker groups visited the three ships to share out extra food. That night, singers and entertainers among the internees on the *Royal Edward* staged a concert, and afterwards were rowed to the other two ships to perform their acts again.

Unknown to Wehner, further arguments about internment had

* Concentration camps were invented by the British to imprison Boer civilians in South Africa during the Boer War. The term had not yet acquired its true ring of horror.

been raging behind the scenes. Inhabitants close to some of the internment camps were vociferous in their objections. Protestors in Hampshire called a public meeting and handed out leaflets asking, 'Germans at Beech Abbey – Shall we have them – Shall we be protected?' To the dismay of the Home Office, Hampshire's chief constable sided with the demonstrators and made much of an incident when several of the seamen walked out of the abbey and became riotously drunk at a local pub. The police promptly incarcerated the seamen at a near-by army camp. A Home Office delegation reported that Beech Abbey was 'quiet and orderly', but the chief constable demanded that the seamen be more firmly supervised.

The continued rise in the numbers of internees persuaded the Home Office to join the War Office in a search for one dramatic solution to the problem of accommodation. Their eyes lit upon the Isle of Man. It held one camp already, a freelance enterprise owned by a farmer named Cunningham, who did his best to make a profit from the 10s (50p) a week which the government paid him to house and feed each internee. As the internees slept in tents, his costs were not high, but with the approach of winter Cunningham's Camp seemed hardly a desirable residence.

A Home Office team visited the island at the end of October to prospect for new sites. Near the hamlet of Knockaloe, it found a camp used by the Territorial Army in time of peace. It had a good water supply and was close enough to Peel Harbour for prisoners 'to be marched there direct'. There was one snag. The soil was heavy clay: the huts would have to be elevated from the ground and cindered paths laid. The Home Office estimated that to construct the camp could cost 'probably well below £5 per head, which compares most favourably with expenditure elsewhere'. There was another ticklish problem to overcome. Like most small islands, the Isle of Man cherished its independence dearly. As a semi-autonomous part of the United Kingdom, it directed its own domestic policy, though this right was partially curtailed in times of war. The Home Office dispatched a senior official to address a gathering of the island's authorities and dignitaries. He explained that the island 'would prove its unique value in rendering a great imperial service if it could be utilized for the purpose suggested'. His speech, the Home Office recorded, met 'with general approval'.

The camp was to be built – at a hoped-for profit – by the Isle of Man government itself. It ambitiously promised that the camp would be ready to take 5,000 internees by 11 November. The Home Office passed on the good news to the War Office, which soon began to ship internees to the island. The result was chaos. By the target date, huts were ready for only 750 men. Over 1,300 were squeezed into the camp, while a further 900 were passed to Cunningham's Camp, which had a theoretical capacity of 2,400 and now held 3,300. Chaos brought disaster. On 19 November, internees at Cunningham's Camp staged a protest demonstration in the mess hall against overcrowded conditions. The military guard – reservists from Lancashire and local volunteers – opened fire, and five internees were killed.

The Home Office sent a committee of inquiry to the island. Its report, presented within a week, made uneasy reading. The committee dutifully declared itself 'absolutely satisfied' that the guards had been entitled to fire. But it also pointed out that no order to fire had been given, and that no demonstrators had tried to escape or attack the guards. It judged the camp diet to be 'suitable, ample and palatable', but conceded that a recent incident had caused much disquiet. A supply of potatoes infested with wireworms had been used to make stew. 'Instead of the matter being immediately put right, as was undoubtedly practical, the fault was not remedied for nearly a fortnight and the prisoners were driven to complain, not only of the potatoes in question, but also of the meat which they erroneously thought was tainted in the same manner.'

The committee expressed the greatest concern over the over-crowding at the camp, caused by the 'necessity of providing accommodation at once for a larger number of interned aliens than the War Office could cope with', and it issued a strong warning about similar dangers at Knockaloe. It greatly regretted that the Isle of Man government had not told the Home Office it was unable to meet its target date, and recommended that the 'reception of aliens should be suspended until further orders'.

As an official document, the report was strong meat. But the Home Office could hardly have foreseen the reaction of the War Office. No less a personage than Lord Kitchener, Secretary of State for War and the nation's chief recruiting officer, demanded that the Home Office should release as many internees as possible. The Home Office demurred at yet another switch in internment policy, responding that since the arrests had been carried out by the local police, it was up to them to initiate any releases. In exasperation, Kitchener wrote to the Home Secretary, Reginald McKenna: 'I feel strongly that we must clear these camps quickly of those to whose release there is no objection . . . I must ask you to do all in your power to expedite the enquiries by the Police, which you say will not take many days.' Some 2,700 men were released the following month. They had to sign an undertaking which read:

> I hereby promise and undertake that I will neither directly nor indirectly take any action in any way prejudicial to the safety of the British Empire, or to the safety of her Allies during the present war.

Among those who signed was Karl Wehner. His father had already persuaded several of his British business colleagues to petition the Home Office on his behalf, and Kitchener's intervention clinched his release. He returned to Stoke Newington and wrote to ask his father what he should do next.

His father was a pacifist who was bitterly opposed to the Kaiser and the war. Above all, he did not want his son to be called up and sternly instructed him to stay in England.

Wehner tried to learn English as best he could, but the passions aroused by the war continued to distract him. One afternoon he was reading his text-books on a park bench when an open chauffeur-driven limousine pulled up. A woman wearing a plumed hat asked him: 'Young man, why are you not in the army?' Wehner spluttered that he was a foreigner, but she handed him a white feather. The gesture was lost on Wehner; only later did he discover that the feather was a symbol of cowardice.

Although several thousand men had been released the Home Office was determined not to be caught out again and ordered construction at Knockaloe to continue. By the end of February there was room for 2,000 men in two compounds of ten huts each, with work under way on three more compounds to increase its capacity to 5,000. The biggest headache was caused by the heavy soil, as the cinders that were laid for roads and paths soon sank into the ubiquitous mud. The sanitation consisted of pails that were emptied at most twice a day. Internees were allowed to receive food parcels from London, although they complained at the regularity with which camp guards, searching for contraband, sliced open the German sausages.

When the spring of 1915 arrived, it seemed that the number of internees was stable and the conflicts between the Home Office and the Isle of Man had been reduced to manageable proportions.

On 7 May came one of the psychological turning-points of the war: the 45,000-ton Cunard liner *Lusitania* was torpedoed off the south coast of Ireland and 1,201 passengers died. In Britain, German shops were ransacked, dachshunds were stoned, and on 13 May the Prime Minister, Herbert Asquith, announced that 'all alien enemies of fighting age' would be interned.

Karl Wehner was at home in Stoke Newington when the local police called again. This time he was sure that there would be no early release. He was sent to Liverpool by train, and from there by boat to the Isle of Man. As one of the first new arrivals at Knockaloe, he had the good fortune to be given a bunk. Many who followed were merely handed a palliasse and told to sleep on the floor. The Home Office ordered Knockaloe to be expanded to hold 20,000 men.

Wehner found the food at Knockaloe that summer adequate, though not matching the quality of the *Royal Edward*. Internees were encouraged to manage their own affairs, and, in addition to their daily food ration, were issued with 280-pound sacks of flour. If a compound accumulated ten such sacks, it could sell them back to the camp for £2 each and spend the proceeds on delicacies at the camp store. Some individual internees went further in their efforts to supplement the camp diet. One imported a load of black-market bacon which he hid in the compound wash-house, waiting for the right moment to offer it for sale. But foraging camp rats alerted the other internees, who commandeered the bacon and gave the would-be profiteer a sound thrashing. Another private venture also had an unfortunate dénouement. A group of prisoners toured the camp with a dixie full of stew which they advertised as veal, for sale by the ladle. At the camp parade the next morning, the camp commander announced that his dog had gone missing. Wehner noticed a number of internees turn a deathly white.

Wehner took a wry pleasure in observing the rich variety of nationalities and races conveyed to Knockaloe by the fortunes of war. There were Turks and Bulgars from Eastern Europe; from South Africa came some who had opposed the British in the Boer War. The most bizarre internees were Duala tribesmen, sent to Knockaloe after the British had captured the German Cameroons. Other Dualans later patrolled Knockaloe from the outside. When the British took over, they had volunteered to fight in France; but they were too short for the mud of Flanders, and were sent to perform guard duties on the Isle of Man instead. When they found they were guarding members of their own tribe, they downed arms and were replaced by British infantrymen who had been invalided home from France.

The flood of internees continued. By the end of 1915, the 20,000-man capacity of the four camps at Knockaloe had been reached, and passed. To compound the overcrowding, Knockaloe's second winter magnified the defects in the drainage and sanitation. The Home Office could not ignore these problems as it received a stream of reports about Knockaloe from numerous overseas delegations. The American Embassy was the most frequent visitor, and was generally kind about what it found. However, its officials observed in December 1915 that 'the rapid creation in the Isle of Man of such a town as the Knockaloe Camp, with a population of nearly 24,000, has raised many problems in housing, feeding, drainage, etc.'. Knockaloe's huts were 'not entirely weatherproof'. They saw 'luggage, boots and clothing entirely covered with mildew caused by rain blowing in under doors and through window joints'. In three days of their visit, they found 'almost the entire six-acre area of every compound covered with mud and rainwater'. On the fourth day, the whole area froze solid. But the Americans were pleased to observe that the Home Office had sent an architect to attend to the flooded compounds. The British Foreign Secretary, Sir Edward Grey, asked whether the American report should be published, but the Home Office – establishing a firm precedent – opposed the suggestion, as 'no good would be done'. It added glumly, 'We shall no doubt get it, or bits of it, back from Germany with demands for redress and we may as well wait till then.'

The forecast soon came true. In March 1916, the American Embassy forwarded a petition from the Austro-Hungarian Foreign Ministry at Vienna. Knockaloe held some 3,500 Austro-Hungarians who were aggrieved at their predicament, for their own government – the 'Dual Monarchy' – had been the only belligerent not to order internment. They were particularly galled that, while they languished on the Isle of Man, British enterprises in Austria-Hungary were flourishing. They complained especially of the rotting huts and the flooded compounds, caused by the island's appalling winter weather. The Americans took this point up. The British replied that the weather was hardly the government's fault.

The complaints as to the climate of the Isle of Man are based no doubt on the unfamiliarity of the conditions there to persons acquainted only with a Continental climate or accustomed to a tropical climate. It is true that the Isle of Man is subject at times to high wind and driving rain and that its climate, like that of the west of England generally, is damp at certain seasons, but it is by no means unhealthy and the Island is, in normal times, the favourite health and pleasure resort of great numbers of English people.

This bland reply was deceptive. The Home Office was only too aware of rumblings below the surface at Knockaloe.

In particular, the strain of looking after more than 20,000 prisoners was exposing a tangle of administrative responsibilities which had never been resolved. Thus Knockaloe was under the 'direction' of the Commander in Chief of Western Military Command, General Sir Henry Mackinnon. But all matters relating to the 'administration' of the camp – even the accommodation of the British soldiers guarding the internees – was the responsibility of the Isle of Man government. This fine distinction was further clouded by the proviso that the Isle of Man government was 'subject to the usual constitutional control of the British Home Office'.

Matters came to a head early in 1916 when guards discovered a large subsidence in a camp compound. It marked the collapse of an eighty-nine-yard tunnel from the camp theatre to the far side of the perimeter fence. But the camp commander, J. M. Carpendale, found that the internees' compound spokesman had ordered all work on the tunnel to cease in case the British closed the theatre. Carpendale was lenient, consigning the chief tunneller to the cells for fourteen days and demoting him from his position as hut captain. The Isle of Man government was furious. It told the Home Office that the would-be escapers should have been tried by a military court; the Home Office asked the War Office to dismiss Carpendale. The War Office defended him, but soon afterwards there was a real escape. Four prisoners broke through the fence at Knockaloe and stole a fishing boat in Peel Harbour, though they were recaptured before they could reach the open sea. The Manx government blamed Carpendale. Carpendale protested bitterly that the island government had provided only six men to maintain the fence, but he was dismissed. The Home Office, the War Office and the Isle of Man government tried once again to resolve the imbroglio. They optimistically agreed that the Isle of Man should be responsible for *discipline* among the internees, and the War Office for *guarding* them. A new camp commander, Lieutenant-Colonel F. W. Panzera, was appointed. He saw clearly where his duties – and his interests – lay. In October 1916, there was a minor demonstration at the camp, with a canteen broken into and a few stones thrown. Panzera immediately posted notices warning that these acts constituted mutiny, which was punishable by penal servitude for life, or death by shooting. One man was sentenced to three years' hard labour, though this was later quashed on appeal; another received twelve months.

Panzera's stern approach reduced controversy for a while. But then another visit by diplomats from the American Embassy led to a full-blown constitutional crisis. The Americans reported that Knockaloe was still badly drained and that the internees were unable to take proper exercise. This was the source of a long dispute between the Isle of Man and Whitehall. Internees had at first been allowed to make route marches under escort, but local inhabitants protested and the island's governor, Lord Raglan, ordered them to cease. The censors who read all internees' letters had told the Home Office that Knockaloe was in a 'state of unrest and indiscipline'. On reading the latest American report, one official raged that Raglan be dismissed. Raglan defiantly responded that he should have 'all executive control' over Knockaloe. The Home Secretary, Sir John Simon – who had replaced McKenna in 1915 – defused the crisis by arranging with Colonel Panzera that internees could take walks on the island 'if medically required'.

Further incidents showed that confusion remained over who was in charge. Local businessmen smuggled food into the camp in return for items manufactured by the internees: hand-made shirts were especially popular. When this black market was uncovered, a court of inquiry could not even decide who was supposed to suppress it. Then it was found that some British army guards were drawing double wages, being paid by both the War Office and the Isle of Man.

A new note of concern was beginning to enter visitors' reports. The Swiss Legation found 'a poor state of mind' among internees, for which it blamed the 'long period of internment, the enormous size of the camp, reduced rations, and the presence of sick and old among the prisoners'. It added that some internees presented a pitiful sight – 'it is easy to detect those who pass their time in

gambling, smoking or quarrelling'. A report in early 1918 concluded: ' . . . another winter of internment would probably mean
for many men ruined health for life.'

Wehner was twenty-one that spring. As he started his fourth
year at Knockaloe, he counted himself fortunate to be among the
several thousand internees who were permitted to work outside the
camp. He tended pigs and dug potatoes for a local farmer, and
was paid 1½d (½p) per day, with a further 3d (1p) a day being
paid to the Isle of Man government for his services. Wehner was
glad of the physical exercise and the temporary release, having
also observed the internees who were succumbing to 'barbed-wire
psychosis'. Wehner particularly noted a merchant sea-captain who
had discovered a vantage point at Knockaloe from where he could
glimpse the Irish Sea. He stood staring at the sea for hours on end.

In November 1918, the Armistice brought an end to the carnage
in Europe. It did not bring speedy release for those at Knockaloe.
The Home Office had assumed that most of the internees would
simply return to their former addresses in Britain, and was surprised when most opted to go home. The Home Office attended
to their travel arrangements in a leisurely manner, and in February
1919 Knockaloe still held 16,000 internees. Karl Wehner was
released at that time, and was sent by train to Harwich, where
feelings ran high. The harbour had been shelled from the sea, and
as he boarded a boat Wehner was assailed with stones and shouts
of 'Baby-killer!' The military guards rifled their possessions and
Wehner was one of the few on board to escape with his baggage
intact. There was further unpleasantness at the Hook of Holland.
A flotilla of Dutch craft came alongside to sell eggs and oranges
and the British guards promptly opened fire. The ensuing row
between the British and Dutch governments delayed disembarka-
tion for a frustrating twenty-four hours. Wehner finally reached
Frankfurt on 23 February 1919.

The numbers remaining in Knockaloe fell slowly: six months
after the war had ended, it still contained 1,400 men. It was finally
closed in September 1919. The Home Office and the Isle of Man
squabbled over surplus supplies worth £2,000 and who was to pay
for removing the railway lines that had been laid on the Douglas
quayside. The last 278 internees were transferred to a camp at
Islington, London. No one knew what to do with them, and the
Home Office files do not record their fate.

These benighted souls apart, the Home Office was understandably relieved when the last consignments of Germans, Austro-Hungarians, Turks, African tribesmen and assorted other nationalities had disappeared. The Home Office had hardly enjoyed the constant bickering with the War Office and the Isle of Man, or the complaints from delegations from half a dozen nations, or the witch-hunt atmosphere generated against all foreigners. After much indecision, a reasonably coherent policy had been devised by Christmas 1914. It had been overwhelmed in the panic that followed the *Lusitania* and divided responsibilities had led to confusion, discomfort, and the occasional disaster. Furthermore, the need to house and guard a large number of innocuous civilians had diverted precious resources from the prosecution of a ferocious war. Small wonder that government spokesmen in 1939 should state so boldly that they wished to avoid their predecessors' mistakes. In 1919, the Home Office had naturally hoped that the need for internment would not arise again. But, if it did, the most sensible moral from the First World War was that the Home Office should do its best not to become involved.

3   The Home Office Need Not Be Informed

In 1923, the Committee of Imperial Defence, mulling over the ghastly lessons of the First World War, met to consider internment. The committee, which was composed of senior Cabinet ministers and Britain's military chiefs, concluded that there was little point in depriving the enemy of a large number of able-bodied men if it took a large number of your own able-bodied men to look after them. It decided that the best policy towards enemy aliens in any future war would be to expel them. The Home Office was happy to concur. At the same time, the government 'War Book' – the official primer if war broke out – laid down that preparation for a limited measure of internment should still be made. The Home Office asked the War Office to prepare to accommodate 5,490 internees. The War Office agreed.

The first problem created for the Home Office by the rise of Adolf Hitler was that of refugees. The first concentration camps were opened within days of the Nazis taking full power in March 1933, and the panoply of a racist, totalitarian state was soon assembled. By the end of the year, 37,000 Jews had left Germany, many of them fleeing to neighbouring countries. Two thousand racial and political refugees came to Britain. Under Britain's alien legislation, the most important condition was that immigrants should not become a charge upon the state. Many of the early arrivals from Germany had family and business ties and no short-age of sponsors. At the same time, the Jewish community in Britain

promised to support all Jewish refugees in need, and the Home
Office accepted its guarantee.

In September 1935, the Nazis' Nuremburg Laws reduced Jews
to second-class beings in Germany, not citizens but 'subjects' of
the Reich. Jewish leaders had predicted that the number coming
to Britain might reach 4,000, but this was soon exceeded. Various
landmarks in the catalogue of Nazi horrors accelerated the flow:
the rise of Himmler's SS, the subversion of the courts, the spread
of concentration camps, the takeover of all scientific and cultural
endeavour by the state. In March 1938, German troops marched
into Austria and another 185,000 Jews came under Nazi rule. More
anti-Jewish laws were enacted and an ambitious bureaucrat named
Adolf Eichmann went to Vienna to speed Jewish emigration.

By that time 30,000 refugees had entered Britain. The Jewish
community warned that it could no longer provide automatic guar-
antees, and the Home Office persuaded the Foreign Office to
require visas for all new arrivals. British officials applied a battery
of tests, with the right of permanent admission resting on whether
the applicant would be 'an asset to the United Kingdom'. But
there were other ways of reaching sanctuary in Britain. Some
entered with visitors' permits. Young people could train for skills
they could use later in the Dominions. Britain also provided a halfway stage for those seeking to enter the United States. The US
State Department enforced stringent entry requirements and
applied a rigid quota system, and would-be immigrants could stay
in Britain while their cases were being processed or until they
reached their place in the queue.

On 9 November 1938, the nightmare deepened. That was *Kristallnacht*: the 'night of the broken glass' (literally, 'crystal night')
when the Nazis unleashed a night of terror throughout the Reich.
Synagogues were sacked, businesses and shops ransacked; 20,000
Jews were arrested and 100 killed. Afterwards, British Consular
offices were besieged and the capacities of the Home and Foreign
Offices overwhelmed. None the less, by September 1939 Britain
had accepted 55,000 refugees from Germany, Austria and Czechoslovakia, and even its critics concede that its response had been
generous and compassionate. When war came on 3 September
1939 the doors were closed, and only a trickle of refugees reached
Britain from Europe afterwards.

For fifteen years, following the decision of the Committee of
Imperial Defence, the Home Office had been content to leave the

question of internment to the War Office. In the spring of 1938, as Hitler annexed Austria and looked menacingly towards the Czech Sudetenland, the issue had to be squarely faced. The CID convened a committee to consider 'The Control of Aliens in War'. It was chaired by a Home Office man, and representatives came from a variety of departments that included the Secret Intelligence Service and MI5. The Home Office and War Office provided secretaries, and the first meeting was held at the end of March.

The committee first endorsed the long-standing view of the CID that, if war came, all enemy aliens should leave. No one had any idea how this might be achieved. The Home Office thought that 'guarded hints' might be dropped in the press and help sought from 'consuls of friendly states'. If these gentler tactics failed, the committee decided that all enemy aliens who had come to Britain after 1 January 1919 should be 'required to return to their own countries'.

The Home Office knew only too well that there was an enormous difference between the enemy aliens of 1914 and those of 1938. There were several thousand Germans, such as businessmen, in residence, and a similar number who had married or put down roots in Britain, many hoping to become naturalized. But they were far outnumbered by the 30,000 refugees in the country, most of them Jewish, with hundreds more arriving each week. Without doubt, these would resist most strongly any suggestion that 'they return to their own countries', and what might ensue if the government 'required' them to leave – in effect, imposing forcible repatriation – did not bear thinking about. When the Home Office proposed a system of appeals against deportation, the sub-committee readily agreed.

But what would happen to refugees who won their appeals against repatriation? Were they to be interned? No one seemed to know. As a precaution, the Home Office asked the War Office to increase its accommodation for internees from 5,490 to 18,000. Beyond that the sub-committee merely reported: 'It is not proposed to undertake an automatic internment of male enemy aliens immediately on outbreak of war, but we concur in the Home Office view that some measures of general internment would become inevitable at an early date.' This imperfect mix of piety and fatalism received the approval of the full Committee of Imperial Defence a week later.

The bureaucratic implications of the new policy were enormous.

The Home Office earmarked thousands of gas masks and ordered vast quantities of stationery and other paraphernalia, including 185 rubber stamps, 100,000 police and MI5 inquiry forms, 300,000 copies of various Home Office memoranda and 300,000 sticky labels. Apart from this, it was still hoping to remain aloof from the sordid details of internment. In September 1938, it received a set of instructions for camp commanders drafted by the War Office. As before, the War Office proposed to divide internees according to their social status. Candidates for Class 'A' were past or present army officers, senior government officials and those who 'might appear to chief officers of police to be of good social and financial status'. They could pay 4s 6d (22½p) per day to receive high-class food and accommodation, while all other internees would be placed in Class 'B'. (The latter group would also provide batmen for Class 'A', at a ratio of one between ten.) The Home Office filed the draft instructions with the note: 'This concerns internal routine and administration and Home Office need make no general observations.'

When a conscientious member of the Scottish Department wrote to query the camps' sanitation, he received a revealing rebuke:

> The Home Office is not concerned at all with the establishment and running of camps, but merely with the arrest of those to be interned, their conveyance to the camps, and their release from internment. It is true that during the last war, the Home Secretary was reluctantly dragged into general questions as to conditions in camps, but we hope (although somewhat faintly) that this would not occur again.

The Home Office continued to hope that the CID's policy of persuasion would prove effective. In September 1938, it wrote to chief constables: 'In the event of a war emergency . . . it is hoped that as many aliens as possible would leave the country.' To senior immigration officers it was a little more forceful: 'It will be the policy of HM Government to encourage aliens to leave the country, and in general therefore aliens who desire to do so should be permitted to embark.' The War Office meanwhile continued its search for a threefold increase in space for internees. It showed the same ingenuity as in 1914: among the premises it proposed to take over were a hospital, a Scottish castle, several country houses, four race courses and the Olympia exhibition hall again. By the summer of 1939 it had found twenty-seven sites, and it told the Home

Office that it was ready. But there were now over 50,000 refugees in Britain, and the Home Office had clearly given the whole matter much further thought.

On 23 August, a Home Office representative named M. G. Russell visited the War Office to view the list of twenty-seven camps it had prepared. Russell explained that the Home Office now felt there were considerable difficulties in treating refugees as enemy aliens, and he proposed a solution. Apart from the War Office's own proposed division by social class, there should be two main categories of camp: one for ordinary internees, the other for refugees. The War Office should run the internment camps proper, the Home Office the new refugee camps, though with War Office guards to prevent escapes. Russell, who conceded that his suggestion had come rather late in the day, said that the Home Office would like the War Office to run all the camps to start with, but would take over the refugee camps as soon as it could. Not without misgivings, the War Office agreed. Soon afterwards it sent the Home Office a revised list, with fourteen of the twenty-seven camps marked as refugee camps. It enclosed a helpful amendment to the camp commanders' instructions, to make clear the distinction between the two groups of internees: 'among the enemy aliens . . . will be a number who have been admitted on the ground that they are refugees from their native country for racial, religious or political reasons. . .' The War Office remained unhappy about the proposed 'dual control' of the refugee camps and warned that the question 'will want thoroughly thrashing out . . . should the present emergency pass'.

The Home Office was beset with misgivings too. It agreed that the division of camps carried appalling bureaucratic complications. Nor was anyone clear how many aliens should be interned, or when. Its officials' anxieties increased when they considered the special circumstances of one camp on the War Office list.

As part of the Jewish community's undertaking to support refugees in Britain, the Council for German Jewry had taken over a British army training establishment at Richborough, Kent, known as Kitchener Camp. (There was a Haig Camp next door.) In August 1939, the camp housed almost 3,000 Jewish refugees from Germany, all between eighteen and forty-five years old, many of them skilled or professional men and almost all hoping to emigrate to the United States or elsewhere. (It was hardly surprising that the eighty medical doctors among them should want to leave, as the British Medical Association would only permit those few who held Italian qualifications to treat even their fellow refugees in the camp.)

It seemed a simple ·matter to take over the premises as an internment camp with the occupants coveniently *in situ*. And support for this view came from a surprising quarter. Sir Robert Waley-Cohen, former managing director of Shell and chairman of the Kitchener Camp committee, telephoned the War Office to propose just such a move.

On 25 August, Waley-Cohen met Sir Alexander Maxwell, Permanent Under-Secretary at the Home Office, to repeat his suggestion. Maxwell, while intoning the ritual Home Office hope that general internment 'might not be necessary', agreed that in the event the government could indeed take over Kitchener Camp, 'lock, stock and barrel'.

Norman Bentwich, director of the Council for German Jewry, was also present at the meeting, and was evidently concerned in case Waley-Cohen had left a misleading impression of the Jewish community's attitude towards its charges. Later that day Bentwich wrote to Maxwell to remind him that the 3,000 men in Kitchener Camp were 'anxious to do any form of service for the country of their asylum'. The idea of converting Kitchener into an internment camp appeared to prey on Maxwell's mind too. After all, many of those inside had already been behind barbed wire in Germany. On 29 August, the Home Office told the War Office that, having reflected on Kitchener Camp, it now felt 'it would clearly raise all sorts of difficulties if the military attempted to take over the camp or to erect barbed wire in anticipation of an order for general internment'. Maxwell meanwhile made a note that there were 28,500 potential male enemy aliens of military age, refugees or otherwise, in Britain. There was room for only 18,000 internees.

During the morning of 29 August, Maxwell visited the Home Secretary, Sir Samuel Hoare, to resolve the impasse. He told Hoare that his officials could see only two alternatives. The first was 'wholesale internment with release after review' – and this, said Maxwell, would be expensive and troublesome, and would need to be delayed until enough accommodation was prepared. The second was an entirely new system, which Maxwell proceeded to outline. The Home Office should set up tribunals throughout Britain to consider the cases of all male enemy aliens over sixteen and decide 'whether any of them ought to be either interned or sub-jected to special restrictions'. The tribunals should be headed by barristers assisted by Home Office representatives, and should start work as soon as the war began.

Hoare was considered a reforming Home Secretary, and was held a moderate, among Conservatives at least, for favouring the abolition of flogging in prisons. Maxwell generously wrote later that Hoare was 'anxious to avoid any general measures of intern-ment as long, at any rate, as possible', though the Home Office files we have seen reveal no previous interest in the subject on his part. The system of tribunals was devised by Hoare's officials, who were undoubtedly grateful when, thanks to Maxwell's skilful pres-entation, Hoare opted for their scheme. Maxwell now had an important letter to write. It was to General Sir Vernon Kell, the head of MI5.

Kell, sixty-six, had remained in his post ever since he had been appointed to it as an army captain in 1909. His credentials then had been his background of hunting and shooting, and his experi-ence as an intelligence officer in Shanghai at the time of the Boxer Rising, from where he had doubled, without embarrassment, as a foreign correspondent for the *Daily Telegraph*. From his room in the War Office, Kell and his staff, largely veterans of the Regular and Indian Armies, had prepared the list of suspected spies who had been arrested in August 1914. It was through their efforts that twenty-two men and women were convicted as enemy agents dur-ing the Great War, and many of them executed. Afterwards Kell reckoned that only two agents had escaped: one being the solitary genius who had supposedly planted bombs on four British warships while in harbour, each exploding with much loss of life. His high success rate in the First World War did much to secure his repu-tation and professional longevity.

When peace came in 1918, Kell's staff was reduced. He saw his duty in being ready for the next conflict, and Soviet Russia was held to be the most likely adversary. As late as July 1937, Sir Samuel Hoare was minuted as telling the Committee of Imperial Defence that: 'The growth of communistic international organi-zations might involve us in some dangers from our own people in time of war, and it had been brought to his notice that most of the people working on behalf of the Comintern in this country were British nationals.' Kell prepared for the crisis by instigating an

enormous card index that he considered to be his proudest inno-
vation. Many cards bore the names of British nationals considered
to be agents of the Comintern, or potentially subversive in other
ways, the definition including hunger marchers, pacifists and those
who signed petitions opposing book censorship. Much of the
information came from the Special Branch at Scotland Yard.

By 1939, it was clear even to the CID that Germany and not
the Soviet Union was the most likely adversary in any future war.
Here Kell was on more familiar ground. Many of those uncovered
between 1916 and 1918 had posed as businessmen with a regular
excuse for foreign travel. It was easy to keep track of German
businessmen from the records of immigration officers, and Kell
began to compile a new list. He added the names of visiting or
resident Germans of known Nazi sympathies, and included a third
category whom it was natural for Kell to suspect, given his own
literary activities in Shanghai: journalists.

In the summer of 1938, Kell sent his list to chief constables and
immigration officers in sealed envelopes, only to be opened on the
eve of war. The Home Office instructed that, while most aliens
were to be encouraged to leave if war came, those on the MI5 list
were not. They were to be arrested.

It was on this account that Maxwell hastened to assure Kell
after his meeting with Hoare on 29 August. Maxwell described the
new tribunal system, but added: 'This scheme will not, of course,
interfere with the arrangements for interning at once any enemy
aliens whom you regard as dangerous.' As its instructions to the
police make clear, the Home Office was still hoping not to be
involved. The police should convey those on MI5's list 'as soon as
practicable to the nearest prison'; from there the prison authorities
should take them to the nearest internment camp. 'The Home
Office need not be informed.'

At 11 a.m. on Sunday, 3 September, Neville Chamberlain told
the nation that Britain was at war with Germany. The image of
families throughout the country listening to Chamberlain's halting
announcement on their cumbersome, pre-transistor wireless sets
has endured over the decades. Karl Wehner was not among them.
Interned for the third time in twenty-five years, he was already in
Brixton Prison.

4 Essex by the Sea

After his enforced four-year stay on the Isle of Man, Karl Wehner had made up for lost time in Germany by taking a doctorate in history at Frankfurt University. He then became a journalist with the Wolff Agency, rivalled only by Reuters for the speed and efficiency of its news gathering in Europe. In 1926, Wehner moved to Berlin and spent seven happy years on the *Berliner Tageblatt*. He also established himself as a creative writer, and had two plays broadcast by German radio. A third was being cast and prospects of a film were in the air when the Nazis came to power.

One of the ugly neologisms favoured by the Nazis was *Gleich-schaltung*: it meant absorption into the state, which the Nazis now applied to the worlds of science, the arts and literature. News-papers were expected to reflect the world through Nazi eyes, and the party gradually imposed its editors upon them. Journalists became skilled in the use of 'slave language' to convey their mean-ing through inference and analogy. When the Nuremburg race laws were passed, Wehner wrote about the fate of the American Indians; when Himmler increased his power, he described the behaviour of Tammany Hall politicians in the United States. In 1936, the year of the Berlin Olympics, the Nazis relaxed their hold a little. When foreign newsmen and visitors had gone, they moved against the *Tageblatt*, and Wehner knew it was time to leave. He came to London and worked anonymously on the night shift of a European news agency, with a promise from the proprietor that

31

he could become the chief European correspondent when the Nazis lost power. He and his wife bought a flat in Highgate.

Every month German journalists met for lunch at a Soho restaurant. The group's secretary was a Nazi who persistently asked Wehner to attend. Wehner went once, and discovered afterwards that the Gestapo were asking in London about his political attitudes and contacts in Britain. He did not attend again. On about 24 August 1939, the German Embassy in London instructed the journalists to go home. Wehner bought an air ticket and flew to Holland, where he kept a bank account. From there he did his best to wind up his financial affairs in Germany, and caught a plane to Croydon airport. His heart sank when an immigration officer forbade him to enter. 'I must come in,' Wehner protested, 'even if I'm interned.' The officer grudgingly stamped his passport with permission to stay until 31 December 1939.

On 1 September, General Kell decided that it was time for MI5 to act. Wehner was at home with his wife in Highgate when two young plain-clothes policemen called. They told him he was being arrested under the Defence of the Realm Act,* gave him time to pack a suitcase, and took him to Highgate Police Station for the night. In the morning he was driven to Brixton where he was locked in a gloomy cell somewhere deep in the prison. He could hear a prisoner complaining loudly next door: it proved to be a fellow journalist named Leonhard Singer, a former correspondent of the *Hamburger Fremdenblatt* who had been sacked when the paper was Nazified. Wehner had been due to have lunch with him that day. Wehner was alarmed to discover a cardboard label bearing the letter 'D' on his door. He supposed it meant 'Deportee', but a warder told him it stood for 'Detainee'.

After a few days, Wehner was moved to Hammersmith and found himself back in Olympia, the exhibition hall where he had begun his first internment twenty-five years before. Some forty Germans were already there. Many, like Wehner, had been arrested in the forty-eight hours before the war began, and there were several well-known journalists among them. One was Dr Alex Natan, who had written for trade-union papers before fleeing Germany in 1933. A champion athlete, he had worked in Britain as a track coach and had taught PT to the Middlesex Regiment of

* When Britain was actually at war, the 'Royal Prerogative' was used instead. See page 119.

the British army. Arrested on 2 September, he had been brought to Olympia by taxi and was loudly complaining that he had been made to pay the fare himself.

Olympia also held a sprinkling of minor German aristocrats, including Albrecht Montgelas, a Bavarian count, who was London representative of a large German brewery, and Baron Constant von Pillar, a tall, handsome man of almost sixty who was born in Estonia and had fought in the Tsar's army *against* Germany in the First World War, and was director of the shipping company Norddeutscher Lloyd. The most colourful was the Bavarian Putzi Hanfstaengl, who had been an intimate of Hitler and had been appointed liaison officer to the foreign press in 1933. He soon acquired a strong distaste for his boss, Josef Goebbels, and settled in London to await the moment – as he told all and sundry – when Hitler fell and he could assume his due role as head of the Fourth Reich.

Of the forty taken to Olympia, seventeen declared themselves anti-Nazi and a dozen more Jewish. Another dozen were active members of the Nazi party or its off-shoots. The proportions were probably similar among the 350 of MI5's suspects arrested throughout Britain and taken to clearing centres at Lewes, Bedford, Bristol, York, Leeds and Edinburgh, where Donaldson's School for deaf-and-dumb children had been hastily vacated. After a few days, all except the Scottish contingent were consigned to the windswept seaside resort of Clacton in Essex. The train journey from Liverpool Street Station wound through much of East Anglia, calling at Cambridge and Norwich, and took seven hours. As he arrived, Wehner saw barbed wire being erected around his new home, whose former inmates had left only the previous day. It was a Butlin's Holiday Camp.

Karl Wehner found his first visit to a holiday camp somewhat bizarre. Billy Butlin had opened the Clacton camp two years before, the second in his bold experiment of providing cheap, regimented holidays for the British working classes. (The first was at Skegness, a hundred miles further up the east coast.) Butlin advertised a week's holiday for a week's pay. In September 1939 the pioneering wooden huts, surrounded by flower beds, still had a vestige of newness about them. There was an arcade of shops, tennis courts, a soccer pitch, an open-air swimming pool: 'Everything the exuberant imagination of a bank-clerk could dream of,' as one internee patronizingly put it. For Wehner, the most incongruous touch was the Pirates' Grotto, with its skeleton whose eyes were supposed to flash. That, combined with the ubiquitous barbed wire, created for Wehner an unsettling ambience of *danse macabre*.

The internees were housed in pairs in the wooden huts, neatly equipped with two-tiered bunks, wardrobes, mirrors and wash-basins. They ate somewhat stodgily in the camp dining-hall, two hundred yards away across a field that soon became a quagmire. Soldiers armed with fixed bayonets escorted them to and from the dining-hall and everywhere else. When one man hammered on his door to be let out to urinate in the night, guards ordered him to perform in the middle of the lawn and shone torches on him as he did so. The camp commander, Major Macdonald, followed War Office instructions to the letter. Smoking was permitted under supervision; Macdonald allowed it for forty-five minutes in the dining-hall twice each day. Letter writing was also closely con-trolled. Internees were allowed one sheet of War Office issue note-paper at a time. There were twelve lines to each side and they were forbidden to write between them. The writing had to be distinct and 'in the Roman characters if possible . . . in plain language, of which the meaning is clear'. As all letters were routed through the postal censorship in Liverpool, there were long delays. Wehner was inclined to accept this as mere inconvenience, but those expecting food parcels were less tolerant. By the time they arrived from Liverpool, perishable food had done just that. Major Macdonald could only suggest that relatives should send preserved food instead.

Soon after their arrival at Clacton, the ranks of the Nazis were swollen by a number of merchant seamen who had been seized on the *Pomona*, a banana boat which plied between Jamaica and Britain and had been caught in London on 3 September. The crew had tried to scuttle her but had been foiled. The captain, named Siebert, was short and fat, and – Wehner observed – 'a rabid Hitlerite'. His sympathies were shared by many of his crew.

The treatment of merchant seamen was to prove a tough bone of contention between Britain and Germany, and to involve other nations too: as First Lord of the Admiralty, Winston Churchill held punitive views on the matter. It mattered more to the non-Nazis at Clacton that Captain Siebert appeared to be acting as the spokesman for all the internees. Major Macdonald agreed to hold a ballot, and Baron von Pillar, the Estonian shipping director, was elected, with Siebert continuing to represent his crew. Later, von Pillar was replaced by Count Montgelas, considered by most to be a liberal and certainly no Nazi. Wehner regarded the election as an accurate reflection of the camp's sympathies. There were loud protests when a German pastor who had been interned conducted a service at which he prayed for a rapid German victory.

Life at Clacton soon settled into a round of eating, exercise, anxious conversation and sleep, and for Wehner it depressingly resembled his internment twenty-five years before. However, the internees were not left entirely to their own devices: almost every day small groups went to London by train for interrogation by MI5. Some rode with the morning commuters, embarrassingly squashed among them with their armed guards. Wehner was more lucky, travelling in mid-morning with an MI5 officer who had the internees brought one by one into his first-class compartment for preliminary questioning.

In London, Wehner was taken to Scotland Yard. There an MI5 officer named Captain Stevens* asked if he would work for the British Secret Service. Wehner regarded the question as a trap. He felt that if he agreed, Stevens would assume that he was already working for the *Abwehr* (the German intelligence service). He said 'No', told Stevens he considered himself anti-Nazi rather than anti-German, but offered to help the British war effort by writing propaganda. Wehner was alarmed to hear violent shouts from a room near-by.

From his wife Johanna, Wehner learned later of other efforts by MI5 to discover if they had links with the *Abwehr* – and perhaps to entice them into working for British intelligence. On one occasion, a man on a bus tried to start a conversation with Mrs Wehner – quite unlike the English, she thought. He remarked that she seemed to be foreign, and that he worked in a 'government factory'. Soon afterwards a policeman called and asked Mrs Wehner to come to Highgate Police Station. There a plain-clothes officer accused Mrs Wehner of trying to seduce an officer in the Royal Navy. When she said this was a lie, she was allowed to go home.

* Captain Stevens had a brother, Major R. H. Stevens, who was one of the better-known names of British intelligence, though for unfortunate reasons. Major R. H. Stevens, together with a colleague in military intelligence named Captain Payne Best, was abducted by the German Secret Service from the Dutch border town of Venlo in the early days of the war. Their kidnap was known ever after as the Venlo Incident.

Wehner assumed that the bus passenger had been a rather ineffective MI5 *agent provocateur*. He came to the same verdict about the woman who helped his wife to cross the road and later called uninvited for a cup of tea. She said that her husband had been on the *Royal Oak*, the British battleship which had been torpedoed in Scapa Flow in October 1939 with the loss of over 800 lives. It was a shattering blow to both British morale and the reputation of British counter-intelligence. Wehner guessed that MI5 had been trying to discover if he or his wife knew anything about the incident.

At Scotland Yard, however, Captain Stevens behaved towards Wehner in a straightforward and courteous manner. Wehner was sent back to Clacton, not knowing what impression he had left and wondering how long he would be interned on this occasion. His apprehension was increased when a new internee arrived with a rucksack packed as if for an expedition, right down to a needle and thread. He told his astonished audience that he had been interned for the duration of the First World War and was preparing for a similar spell this time. 'Not again,' Wehner thought.

In May 1940, General Kell declared that if Germany did have a network of spies in Britain on the eve of war, MI5's swoop had smashed it. Later he boasted that the German Secret Service had been compelled to start the war 'blind'. In the world of intelligence, bold assertions such as these can be made in the safe knowledge that any evidence to the contrary will be slow to surface. Even so, Kell's boast is substantially correct.

The first indication that this was so came in 1972 with the publication of *The Double-Cross System in the War of 1939–45*, an extraordinary account of how British counter-intelligence had controlled the entire German espionage system in Britain, capturing all its agents and turning many around so that they sent home a mixture of trivial and misleading information. The author of the book was Sir John Masterman, who had been a member of the 'XX' or Double-Cross Committee that controlled the operation. Masterman wrote that Germany had obtained considerable routine intelligence about Britain through the normal operations of its London Embassy until September 1939. But the *Abwehr* had been much hindered by Hitler's view of Britain as his natural European ally. Until 1937, it had been forbidden to plant undercover agents in Britain and had been badly handicapped by the delay. No agents had survived after September 1939, and the *Abwehr* had made its main effort in the autumn of 1940, when it attempted to land agents by parachute and from small boats. All, it seems, were captured, and either executed or put to good use.

Masterman was well aware of the breath-taking scope of his claim, and added that no one on the Double-Cross Committee had believed during the war that it was the case. But post-war scrutiny of captured German documents proved it to be true. The claim was further substantiated when the writer Ladislas Farago examined *Abwehr* files in Washington twenty-five years after the war. Farago discovered reports from two *Abwehr* agents who had made frequent and productive visits to Britain in 1938 and 1939. One was a Pomeranian named Fritz Block who had a business in Holland and started visiting Britain on spying missions in 1938. He submitted 130 reports, which included photographs of airfields in the home counties and the north-east, information about Tyneside shipyards, and details of gun emplacements in Dover. The second agent was a photographer named Friedrich Kaulen, who was recruited in January 1939 and made three trips to Britain as a tourist. He discovered three RAF airfields of which the *Abwehr* had been ignorant and supplied considerable data about anti-aircraft defences in western England.

But neither agent stayed in Britain when war began: the MI5 swoop was defective only in that both managed to leave Britain at the eleventh hour – Block from Croydon airport on 29 August, Kaulen by steamer from Holyhead on 2 September. Farago discovered that three agents did remain, two brothers and a woman in Bournemouth. They appeared to have contributed little and all three were soon arrested. One was turned round, the other two interned.

Finally, Farago considered the Welshman named Johnny Owens, who was recruited by the *Abwehr* and turned round by the British under the codename 'Snow'. Farago asserts that he was of more value to the Germans than to Britain. But the profit-and-loss account of double-agents is always hard to evaluate, and, all in all, Kell's boast has been vindicated.

5   Of Dubious Repute

On the day war was declared, Britain acquired a new Home Secretary. In a pre-planned shuffle, Chamberlain gave Sir Samuel Hoare a seat in his War Cabinet as Lord Privy Seal and replaced him at the Home Office by Sir John Anderson.

As *The Times* delicately phrased it, Anderson was 'not in his first youth'. He was fifty-seven and had spent almost his entire career not as a politician but as an administrator. The son of an Edinburgh businessman, he began as a clerk, second class, in the Colonial Office in 1905, moving to the National Insurance Commission in 1912 to help enact the famous '9*d* for 4*d*' scheme devised by Lloyd George. In the First World War he used his administrative gifts to solve an urgent medical crisis among the British troops. Venereal disease was having a field day among Kitchener's army in France, and the most effective cure, a secret arsenical compound called 606, was manufactured in Germany, which naturally refused to release this strategic material. Anderson shored up the gap in Britain's defences by persuading the British drug companies to perfect their own cure.

This success eased Anderson's inexorable rise through the echelons of the civil service. In 1917, he became secretary to the Minister of Shipping; 1919, chairman of the Board of Inland Revenue; 1920, Under-Secretary at Dublin Castle, Britain's seat of government in Ireland. It was a bloody time, when Sinn Fein fought on for a united Ireland and the British unleashed the Black and Tans. Anderson emerged unscathed to become Permanent Under-Secretary at the Home Office, achieving the highest rank in the civil service at the age of forty.

Anderson remained in the same post at the Home Office for ten years. He served seven Home Secretaries in that time, and saw the General Strike through in 1926, when he headed an emergency committee to keep the country's vital services running. He was an aloof man who disdained friendliness towards those above him or informality towards those below. One incoming Home Secretary greeted him warmly, only to be rebuffed with the words: 'I have been brought up in a profession which has taught me that it is wrong to give expression to emotions, either of pleasure or sorrow, on occasions such as this.' He worked hard, with punctual but unvarying hours, from 10.15 to 1.45 each morning, 2.45 to 6.15 in the afternoon, and hardly ever took files home.

As a civil servant, Anderson was a functionary pure and simple, concerned only with the art of administration, not at all with the content of the policy being administered. Although responsible for prisons, he showed no interest in penal reform. He was a cautious minute writer, reluctant to commit himself to paper. His inclination was to operate efficiently within existing limits. His biographer, John Wheeler Bennett, concluded that when he left the Home Office after ten years, it bore no more imprint of his personality than when he arrived.

In 1932, Anderson was elevated to the governorship of Bengal. His Irish experience served him well in the fight against those seeking independence: he imposed collective fines on districts which sheltered terrorists, and survived an assassination attempt at Darjeeling racecourse. (Anderson pardoned the culprits from the gallows.) He returned to Britain in 1937, and was asked to take over an even more contentious position, as High Commissioner for Palestine, then rent by the bitter struggle between Arabs and the Jewish settlers who sought their land. Anderson took the course of discretion and decided instead to run for Parliament. He was loth to commit himself to any political party and was spared the dilemma when a seat fell vacant for the Scottish universities. His main opponents were the Scottish Nationalists, and Anderson won with ease.

Soon after his arrival in the Commons, Anderson was tempted again with an offer of employment as chairman of Imperial Airways (precursor of BOAC and British Airways). He was still toying with the prospect when Chamberlain turned to him during Munich, appointing him Regional Commissioner for London and the South-East in the event of war. When the crisis passed he stood down, but was soon invited to help Britain prepare for the coming conflict. In October 1938, Chamberlain asked him to join the Cabinet as Lord Privy Seal, with the task of organizing air-raid precautions (ARP) and civil defence in the Home Office.

Anderson was a tedious speaker in the House of Commons: his instincts as a minister were to protect his flanks, and he was grudging in the information he offered to MPs. During one opaque peroration, a Labour member, recalling Anderson's spell in Bengal, called out: 'Don't talk to us like a lot of niggers!' Yet it was in this period that his name received its most lasting endowment. He was anxious to provide British householders with protection in their gardens from air-raids, and the structure of earth and corrugated iron designed to his specifications was named the 'Anderson shelter'. Anderson ensured that it went into prompt production, and by the outbreak of war 1,500,000 homes had been supplied. It was Anderson's proudest achievement, and he was greatly put out when he saw how the shelters were used during the 'Phoney War'. The great British talent for improvization discovered that the bank of earth around each shelter provided the perfect well-drained soil required for the cultivation of vegetable marrows.*

On 4 September, it fell to the new Home Secretary to make the first announcement to the House of Commons about internment. It was typical Anderson: a dry recitation in passive terms of the policy to be introduced, mechanically intoned. When he declared that refugees from Czechoslovakia would not be treated as enemy aliens, the Labour MP Hugh Dalton shouted: 'This is reparation for Munich' – a reference to Chamberlain's ceding of the Czech Sudetenland to Hitler in 1938. Anderson carried on without a pause. MPs looking for some declaration of humanitarian principle were disappointed, and Arthur Greenwood rose at the end of Anderson's speech to phrase the words for him. He asked: 'Am I to take it that the policy of His Majesty's Government is to draw a sharp distinction between those who are the victims of the system we are now fighting and those who may be properly under

---

* Later in the war Anderson's successor, Herbert Morrison, gave his name to the 'Morrison shelter', an iron frame designed to sit under dining-room tables indoors.

suspicion?' 'That very accurately describes the spirit that we have endeavoured to introduce into this statement,' Anderson gratefully replied.

Later in the war, when the ashes of internment were being raked over, Anderson was to declare that this opening announcement represented 'what I think can fairly be described as a liberal policy', adding: 'It was in accordance with the best traditions of the country' and had given him 'personally the greatest satisfaction'. These remarks, made in August 1940, were the first public revelation by Anderson of any such attitude. Whatever thoughts he officially committed to paper remain secret, for the Home Office has declined to release any files for the ten-month period that starts with his appointment as Home Secretary and ends in July 1940. There are brief indications that Anderson had some feelings on the subject to be gleaned from his letters to his father, which we shall refer to later. However, at the start of the war it seems that Anderson's main concern was to ensure, as always, that the new tribunal policy was administered as smoothly and efficiently as possible.

There were to be 120 tribunals set up across Britain. Their chairmen* were drawn largely from the legal profession – barristers, JPs, the occasional judge. They were paid the delightfully idiosyncratic sum of 2½ guineas (£3.67½) for each half-day session, with travelling expenses to cover either the first-class rail fare, or petrol for 'four-wheeled motor cars over 10 h.p.' at 4d (1½p) per mile. To aid chairmen in their task, and to ensure that all possible human inconsistencies were ironed out, the Home Office issued a comprehensive series of printed and duplicated memoranda, covering every aspect of the tribunals' work, from the travelling expenses cited above to how an enemy alien's loyalties should be judged.

Even these documents, widely distributed at the time, have been withheld by the Home Office today. Fortunately, they were also sent to interested parties overseas and sets may be found in the US National Archives in Washington and the Australian Archives in Canberra. One of the most important was an eight-page memorandum 'for the guidance of persons appointed by the Secretary

---

* In the non-sexist use of the term: we know of no tribunals chaired by women.

of State to examine cases of Germans and Austrians', to help decide whether an alien was to be interned.

The tribunals had to place enemy aliens into one of three categories:

Category 'A' – for those to be interned.
Category 'B' – for those who were not to be interned but were still subject to restrictions.
Category 'C' – for those who could remain at liberty.

The Home Office then described the main types of enemy alien:

First there were refugees, who had left their homes because they were 'subject to oppression by the Nazi régime upon racial, religious or political grounds. . . They will be hostile to the Nazi régime and ready to assist this country rather than to assist the enemy.' They should therefore be placed in Category 'C'.
Secondly came those who had lived in Britain for some time and who had 'definitely thrown in their lot with this country'. If they could produce 'evidence of character, associations and loyal intent', they, too, should be placed in Category 'C'.
Thirdly came Germans and Austrians who were to be expected, given the opportunity, 'to help their own countrymen or hinder the war efforts of this country. Such persons may be men or women of good character who, if they acted in a manner prejudicial to this country, would do so from a sense of loyalty or duty to their own country.' Tribunals should be especially wary of past or present army officers and civil servants, or those 'with special knowledge of aircraft, marine or transport services, or of chemistry, mechanics, engineering and the various munition services'. On the face of things, they qualified for Category 'A' – internment.

So far so good. However, the Home Office warned the chairmen not to apply the categories too rigidly. A refugee could be interned because he or she was of 'bad or dubious character and repute', or had 'criminal convictions or criminal associations'. Nor should the Home Office's 'loyal German' necessarily be interned – although if not, the chairman had to tell the Home Office why.

To permit chairmen some discretion, the Home Office had provided the compromise Category 'B'. Its restrictions included a ban on travelling more than five miles, or owning cars, cameras or large-scale maps. If aliens were performing 'some useful business or service', that provided an extra reason for not imposing travelling restrictions and placing them in Category 'C'. The Home Office provided an official to help tribunals through this maze of considerations. The Ministry of Labour also sent an official to help the tribunals decide whether an alien should be given a work permit.

The tribunals met in secret. Aliens were not allowed to bring a lawyer, but they could be accompanied by a 'friend'. The tribunals could accept information from a variety of sources: aliens could offer letters or testimonials from the welfare agencies or from 'reputable British subjects'. Secret information, on the other hand, might be offered in the alien's absence by the police or Home Office. Among this would be data acquired when refugees entered Britain, often vouched for by refugee and welfare organizations. It would also include information from Special Branch or MI5. Although the memorandum was generally liberal in its tone, it concluded with a stern warning against undue leniency.

> There will be some cases in which pleas of hardship and distress will be put forward to the tribunal. While it is desired to avoid any unnecessary hardship to individuals, nevertheless the interests of the individual cannot in present circumstances be a primary consideration; they must be subordinated to considerations of national security.

There was a war on, after all.

The tribunals began their work in the first week of October 1939. The local police, who provided the tribunals with a clerk, also sent aliens a letter summoning them to a hearing, usually held in a prominent building such as a school, council chamber or the town hall. To begin with, there was some confusion and considerable inconsistency between the tribunals, particularly over the compromise Category 'B'. The tribunals in Reigate and Leeds gave most aliens a 'B'; in Croydon and Manchester, they almost universally favoured Category 'C'. Some tribunals put unemployed aliens into 'B', telling them to come back for a 'C' when they had found a job. The chairman in Sutton, Surrey, put anyone with a car into Category 'C': the rest were classed as 'B's. (He told them that if they had to drive at any time, they could apply for a 'C'.)

The proportion of 'B's was so high in the first two weeks –

François Lafitte, in *The Internment of Aliens**, suggested that it was almost 50 per cent – that the Home Office called the tribunal chairmen to a conference to explain its instructions more clearly. On 21 October, Maxwell issued supplementary instructions to widen the definition of 'refugee': they were not merely those who had been in 'concentration camps or subjected to actual physical ill-treatment', but 'those who were prevented from carrying on their professions or occupations and earning their living, and were deprived of the protection of their own Government'. Where Germans had left their country early on in the Nazi régime, and had not been 'subjected to any actual oppression', the chairman should decide whether they could have 'reasonable grounds for anticipating oppressive treatment'.

The ratio of 'B's fell, and, at the same time, the hearings were educating the tribunal officials. Six chairmen were so horrified by what they learned of Nazi cruelty that they wrote a long letter about it to *The Times*, published on 1 October. But prejudices remained. Many women refugees had found employment as domestic servants: one tribunal placed all such women in Category 'B'. (The trustworthiness or otherwise of domestic servants is a recurring theme in the story of internment.) Other tribunals placed a political interpretation on the clause about 'dubious character or repute', and interned refugees who were socialists or communists, including veterans from the International Brigade in Spain. One married couple had to explain that they were not communists merely because they had supported the Weimar Republic. The historian H. N. Brailsford took up the case of a Jewish socialist who had edited an anti-Nazi weekly in Vienna and later fought in Spain, who was interned. Another to suffer the same fate was the German socialist Karl Olbrisch, a former member of the Reichstag, who was arrested in 1933 and spent four years in prisons and concentration camps before escaping to Czechoslovakia.

The tribunals worked fast. By the end of November they had considered 35,000 cases and ordered internment in 348 – just less than 1 per cent. The proportion declined as their work proceeded. By March 1940, it was 600 out of 71,600 cases. The final total of cases considered was 73,800. Of these, 64,200 were placed in Category 'C'.

The tribunals also had to record whether an alien was a 'refugee

* See Introduction.

from Nazi oppression' – a genuflection to the distinction the Home
Office had hoped to establish between refugee camps and others.
The tribunals conferred this title on 55,460 people – 75 per cent.

In general, those who passed safely through the tribunals' hands
recall least about their proceedings. It is the 1 per cent whom the
tribunals interned who have most cause to remember what happened on that vital day.

6 A World of Its Own

Peter Jacobsohn left Berlin with his mother on 27 February 1933, the night of the Reichstag fire. He was sixteen and Jewish. His father, Siegfried Jacobsohn, had died when he was ten, leaving to him and his mother the liberal magazine, *Die Weltbühne* (the 'World Stage'), of which he had been proprietor and editor. *Die Weltbühne* had campaigned courageously against secret German preparations for rearmament and its new editor, the pacifist Carl von Ossietzky, was imprisoned for treason by the Weimar government in May 1932. He was released in December and defiantly returned to edit *Die Weltbühne* just as the Nazis were taking the last steps to complete power. *Die Weltbühne* had been a strident opponent of the German right and Ossietzky had long been on the Nazis' list of enemies. He was arrested on the morning after the burning of the Reichstag and dispatched to the prison of Sonnenburg, soon converted into one of the first concentration camps.

Mrs Jacobsohn was a far-sighted woman who had already considered possible lines of escape. She had founded a parallel magazine in Austria, *Die Neue Weltbühne*, and after Ossietzky's arrest she and her son hurried south to Vienna. She was also an Anglophile. She had been to finishing school in England and regarded the country as her spiritual home. She had business contacts there, too, having translated *Winnie the Pooh* and the Dr Dolittle series of children's books, and published them with much success in Germany. She sent her son to an English school in Switzerland for a year, and in August 1934 took him to London. They moved into a house in Hampstead, off Haverstock Hill.

Jacobsohn studied in London for a year, and then went to work in the public relations department of the British Shell company. He became friendly with another of Shell's employees, the future poet laureate, John Betjeman. After a time he moved to the advertising company of Colman, Prentis & Varley, working in the market research department for 30s (£1.50) a week. Despite its reputation as a pioneer of persuasive techniques, the company liked to preserve the genteel trappings of English life. Jacobsohn was delighted to receive tea and cakes punctually every afternoon, dispensed from a trolley by an immaculate butler.

Back in Germany, Carl von Ossietzky was still in the Nazis' hands. He contracted TB in Esterwegen concentration camp and was moved to a prison hospital in Berlin. In London, Jacobsohn helped to produce a passionate pamphlet which publicised his treatment and proposed him for the Nobel Peace Prize. Edited by Amabel Williams-Ellis and published by Gollancz in 1936, it was endorsed by an impressive array of British intellectuals, including Bertrand Russell, H. G. Wells, Aldous Huxley, J. B. Priestley, and Leonard and Virginia Woolf. It was backed by a similar campaign in other countries, and Ossietzky was awarded the Nobel Prize in November. Hitler was so enraged that he banned Germans from receiving any future awards. Ossietzky died in 1938.

When the war began, newsprint rationing brought a reduction in advertising and Jacobsohn lost his job at Colman, Prentis & Varley. He went to work on a farm in Berkshire in return for board and lodging and a few shillings a week. He thought it was a safer place to be if London was bombed; he milked the cows and rode into London on the farmer's lorry once or twice a week.

In October 1939, Jacobsohn received a summons to attend a tribunal in Reading. He asked his former Shell colleague, John Betjeman, who lived near-by, to speak on his behalf. 'This will be very easy,' Betjeman assured him. 'I know the chairman.' Jacobsohn was too confident; the chairman was a JP who, Jacobsohn felt, regarded him as one of the juvenile delinquents he was more used to dealing with. He was placed in Category 'B' and Betjeman had to restrain him from slashing the chairman's tyres. The 'B' was not too serious in itself, but Jacobsohn promptly disregarded the restriction on travel by going to stay with a friend in London. When he tried to register with the local police he was arrested. A

friend of his mother secured his release, but soon afterwards two
plain-clothes policemen called and told him he was to be interned.

Jacobsohn was sent to the Oratory School in Brompton Road,
Chelsea, which had been converted into a classifying centre.
Between sessions with several coldly polite interrogators, he waited
in a long airless basement which contained two rooms equipped
as dormitories and a third as a recreation room. There were several
dozen other internees who played cards or ping-pong or took
cramped walks in the narrow yard outside. In some annoyance,
Jacobsohn waited to learn his fate.

Franz Eichenberg, a tall, imposing lawyer of thirty-seven, came to
England in 1936. For Eichenberg, flight from his fatherland was
an ironic choice. He had fought for Germany on the Western Front
in the First World War, crewing the giant cannon that shelled
Paris from up to ninety miles away. Eichenberg was wounded in
the back by a shell splinter, and as he lay in a field hospital, Kaiser
Wilhelm had awarded him the Iron Cross.

Eichenberg practised as a lawyer in Hamburg after the war.
Recovered from his injuries, he became a keen soccer player too.
Until 1933, he viewed the rise of Hitler with mere distaste. The
Nuremburg race laws altered his view. The Reich Citizenship Law,
and subsequent decrees, spoke of those who were one eighth or one
sixteenth Jewish. Although he had been baptized a Lutheran,
Eichenberg had mostly Jewish ancestry. As arrests of Jews and
political dissenters mounted, Eichenberg decided to leave Germany, as he said candidly later, while the going was good. He
considered the United States, but had no one to act as his sponsor,
so, in the spring of 1936, he made a reconnaissance trip to England
instead.

In Norwich, Eichenberg was introduced to a businessman who
was looking for a partner in a firm distributing Calor Gas. Eichenberg wound up his practice in Hamburg and went back to Norwich
with his wife that autumn. He was lonely for the first year, but
gradually made friends and became a respected local figure. He
played soccer again, for a local side sponsored by the Norwich
City league team. He watched Norwich play league matches, travelling to away games in the Midlands in his trusty Austin 7.

Early in October 1939, the police told Eichenberg that he had
two weeks to prepare for his tribunal. The hearing lasted several
hours, and Eichenberg was asked to explain the symbols he used

in games of postal chess with his wife's brother in France. The chairman also asked about his parents, who were still in Germany, and suggested that someone might approach Eichenberg one day and offer to 'protect' them in return for services to Germany. Finally the chairman told Eichenberg: 'We must intern you for your own safety, your parents' safety, and the safety of England.' Like Peter Jacobsohn, Eichenberg was sent to the Oratory School in Brompton Road.

Erwin Frenkel arrived in London from Vienna in May 1938. He was a headstrong young man of seventeen, the son of the chief cantor at the synagogue in Leopoldgasse. Frenkel shared his father's musical talents and had trained on the piano and organ from the age of six. He joined his father's choir at seven and became a soloist at eight. Apart from a year in Czechoslovakia, he had been educated in non-Jewish schools. By Jewish standards, the Frenkel home was an observant one, but not over-strict. Since his Barmitzvah, Frenkel had acquired a liking for non-Jewish girl friends.

When the Nazis arrived, they extended the Nuremburg race laws to Austria. They included a decree (the Law for the Protection of German Blood and German Honour) that forbade 'extra-marital relations between Jews and members of the national community of Germany or kindred blood'. Frenkel's mother was afraid that if he was stopped in the street by the Gestapo or the SS, his fierce temper would land him in trouble, and she implored him to leave Austria.

Frenkel wanted the whole family to emigrate together. In May, the Chief Rabbi of Vienna secured exit permits from Adolf Eichmann for sixty families, and offered one to the Frenkels. But Frenkel's father felt that his duty lay with the synagogue, and Frenkel's mother persuaded him to leave alone. He obtained a visitor's permit from the British Embassy and went to Vienna airport one day late in May. He had two suitcases and 20 marks, all that the Nazis allowed Jews to take out of the Reich. His mother said good-bye with tears running down her face.

'We'll never see you again,' she told him.

'Of course you will,' Frenkel replied, but his mother was right.

In London, Frenkel rented a bed-sitter above a milk bar in New Cavendish Street, close to the BBC. He lived with an Austrian girl who was working as a maid, and made a bare living playing a piano in a pub in Finsbury Park. He was summoned to a tribunal in October. Armed with testimonials from several London rabbis, he was confident of a successful outcome, until the chairman asked if he was living off the immoral earnings of his girl friend. Frenkel spluttered hopelessly in reply, and deduced afterwards that he had been denounced to MI5 by a rival pianist who wanted his job in Finsbury Park. He protested that the allegation was untrue, but was classified 'A' and interned.

Not all Germans in Britain had come to escape the Nazis. Bruno Fehle was a businessman who had worked in Denmark since 1923 and transferred to London in November 1935. Aged thirty-six, he became the managing director of the British subsidiary of a German optical company. He liked England, admired the British sense of 'fair play', and respected their way of doing business on trust. He brought his wife Irmgard and their two sons, Gus, aged three, and Rolf, aged one. The family rented a semi-detached house in Hillside Gardens, Edgware.

Fehle was a patriot but disliked the Nazis. Even in Britain it was hard to escape their influence. The Fehles enjoyed the German community's social functions at London's Porchester Hall, where the German Ambassador, Leopold von Hoesch, was a regular guest. In 1936, von Hoesch was replaced by Joachim von Ribbentrop and gatherings became political rallies, with Nazi uniforms, swastikas everywhere, and beer and sausages the only sustenance served. The Fehles stopped attending.

Business for Fehle's company remained good until 1939, when a Jewish boycott of German firms affected his trade with West End opticians. In the summer Fehle was so worried at the accelerating European crisis that he travelled to his head office at Rathenow, fifty miles west of Berlin. The managing director told him: 'Don't worry – there will be no war. Hang on in Britain until things get better.'

Back in London, Fehle's misgivings deepened when his German wages clerk, who was a Nazi, announced that the party had called him home. Fehle sent two German tool-makers with him and decided soon afterwards that he and his family must leave. The Edgware police told him that he needed an exit permit. When he applied he was told that his wife and sons could leave but he could not.

On Monday, 4 September, the second day of the war, Fehle

telephoned the German Embassy for advice. He was told to go home as soon as possible. When Fehle asked how, the official replied: 'That's up to you.' The Edgware police told him to carry on working as normal. Fehle was already afraid he might be interned, but felt reassured by a promise from his British co-directors that whatever happened, his salary would be paid and his family cared for.

Fehle and his wife appeared before a tribunal on 30 November. Fehle said truthfully that he had never been a member of the Nazi party, but the chairman had one damaging item of evidence. In 1938, the German cruise ship *Wilhelm Gustloff* had visited London.* The Fehles accepted an invitation from the German Embassy to go on board, where they found that a ballot had been arranged as part of the plebiscite to approve the *Anschluss*, the unification of Germany and Austria. Fehle and his wife saw no harm in taking part and voted secretly in a booth. It was easy for the British to tell that the Fehles had visited the *Wilhelm Gustloff* as their passports had been stamped when they left the quayside. But when the chairman asked how they had voted in the ballot, Fehle became flustered and refused to say.

Fehle was struggling against the odds, anyway. He fitted the Home Office definition of a 'loyal German' too well and his position in the optical industry gave him 'special knowledge' of use to the enemy; his recent trip to Germany also told against him. These were probably the reasons why he had been refused an exit permit in August. The chairman told Irmgard Fehle she would be placed in Category 'B', but said to Bruno: 'I'm sorry, I have to intern you.'

From that moment Fehle was under close supervision. The police escorted him back to Edgware and allowed him to pack a suitcase. An officer watched him when he went to the lavatory in case he tried to escape through the window. Fehle said good-bye to his wife and children and was driven away down Hillside Gardens and out of sight.

Not all those interned in October and November even had the benefit of appearing before a tribunal, as the story of Uwe Radok and his two brothers shows. They came to Britain one by one,

---

* The *Wilhelm Gustloff* belonged to the KdF organization: the initials stood for *Kraft durch Freude*, or 'Strength through Joy', a semi-political body that arranged holidays for German workers.

Uwe in May 1938, his brothers in 1939. The Radoks also exemplify the dilemma faced by so many families who considered themselves loyal to Germany and were reluctant to leave their homes.

The Radoks came originally from a Jewish ghetto in Czechoslovakia. Uwe's grandfather emigrated to East Prussia in the 1860s and became a successful engineer in the town of Königsberg. In 1900, he decided that the family should become Protestants, and they were duly baptized. Uwe Radok's father married in 1912. He served creditably in the First World War, although the main battle honours were taken by his brother, who fought valiantly to prevent a Bolshevik takeover in the Caucasus and was awarded the coveted Star of Tamara. Uwe was born in 1916, the second of five children. (There were four boys and a girl.) After the war his father prospered as the director of a railway manufacturing company. He took an upright view of business ethics, refusing to play the stock market even though he understood it well: 'It's not proper,' he used to say.

The Radoks were a close family and the children shared their father's patriotism; like most Germans, they were indignant at the punitive terms of the Treaty of Versailles. But occasional clouds darkened the family's horizon. One day Uwe was told at school that, although his parents had been baptized, he remained a Jew by *Abstammung* – by 'descent'. That night he asked his mother, 'What's a Jew?' The subject became harder to ignore. In 1932, the main parties sent speakers to Uwe's school. Uwe liked the Social Democrat but noticed that when the Nazi raised his arm in a 'Heil Hitler' salute, half the class responded.

In 1933, Uwe went to the ancient University of Königsberg to study maths, physics and meteorology. That summer the students had to give service to the state, either in military training or on the land. Uwe wanted to help with the harvest, but his father secured him a place on an artillery course. Uwe won a shooting competition and was awarded a signed picture of Hitler. He brought it home and stood it in a closet with the face to the wall.

By now many of the family's friends were leaving Germany, and one suggested that the Radoks join him in New York. Uwe's father was unwilling to leave all he had worked for in Königsberg, and at the same time rejected the Nazis' new definition of who was a Jew. Uwe tried to carry on. When he transferred to Munich University, he was given a yellow student's card to show that he was

Jewish. Other students objected to his taking part in a course on aircraft design, and he received only grudging help from his tutor.

The strains on the family were beginning to tell. Uwe was turned down for several jobs in the aircraft industry. His father made strenuous efforts to help, first through his own business contacts, later by writing to Hermann Göring. They were all in vain. Uwe repeatedly told his father that he would not stay in a country which considered him and his family *minderwertig* – 'inferior'.

In March 1938, the family came together for the last time in Germany. Uwe's eldest brother, Peter Christoph, was in the German army, but he obtained leave and joined the family on a skiing holiday in Bavaria. They met in the Walsatal, a beautiful valley lying across the border of Germany and Austria. Soon afterwards Uwe decided to go to Britain. He obtained a visitor's permit and crossed into Holland on 14 May 1938. He sailed to England a few days later, and headed for Glasgow. He had friends there and applied for a job as trainee engineer with the construction company Sir William Arrol, builders of the Forth Railway Bridge. He was given a work permit at the end of August, which also allowed him to stay in Britain, and started to work at £2 15*s* (£2.75) a week.

Uwe lodged with a Scottish family in Rutherglen, paying 25*s* (£1.25) a week for his room, food and laundry. In the winter, his room was so cold that the window froze on the outside and at night he skipped in his room with a rope to restore his circulation. He had been a keen glider pilot in Germany, and he took up the sport again. He enjoyed flying above Loch Leven in Fife where eagles soared alongside and a ruined castle lay far below.

Uwe learned about *Kristallnacht* one dank and foggy evening in Glasgow. He dreamed of returning to Germany and assassinating Hitler. In the morning he wrote a long letter home, imploring his family to come to Britain. Uwe was relieved to discover that his parents had been away from home during *Kristallnacht*. Soon afterwards his brother Jobst, who was a year younger, joined him in Glasgow, and Uwe helped to find him a job as a trainee manager at a colliery in Fife. They discussed emergency plans for the future, and Uwe started to save £1 a week. He spent the evenings reading in a public library to improve his English, working steadily through the collected plays of Shakespeare. Uwe's youngest brother, Rainer, then nineteen, joined Uwe and Jobst in August 1939. Peter Christoph was still in the German army and Uwe's parents stayed in Königsberg with their daughter Gundula, who was eighteen. In

Britain, the three brothers decided that the family's best hope lay on the far side of the world, and they applied to emigrate to Australia. Permission was soon granted and Uwe booked passages for the entire family, apart from Peter Christoph, on the next available liner. It was due to sail in mid September.

The voyage was cancelled on the last day of August, the eve of war. For no very logical reason, the three brothers decided to leave Glasgow. Jobst told the others of a family he had met in Yorkshire, the Pennymans, who had invited him to return at any time. Mrs Pennyman was an upper-class socialist who had been a nurse in the First World War and had taken in refugee children from Spain during the Civil War. Her husband was a retired major from the British army, and they lived in a country house named Ormsby Hall. As Jobst described its spacious rooms, its sweeping drive and its acres of rolling farmland, it seemed like a haven of retreat. A gliding companion of Uwe offered to drive them to Yorkshire, and they set out at dusk on 1 September. The car's headlights were blacked out and they drove cautiously along the crown of the deserted roads. They arrived at Ormsby Hall at dawn. The following morning, Uwe, Jobst, Rainer and the Pennymans heard Chamberlain announce that Britain was at war. Mrs Pennyman turned the radio off abruptly when it started to play 'It's a Long Way to Tipperary', and in the afternoon the three brothers went out to help with the harvest. Mrs Pennyman told them they could stay at Ormsby Hall for as long as they liked.

One morning early in October, Major Pennyman told Uwe and his brothers: 'I'm afraid the police have come for you.' The police waited while Mrs Pennyman made the brothers a packed lunch, and then they were taken away. They spent the night in a disused garage in Lincoln and in the morning were questioned by an officer of MI5. Several days later they were put on a train for Devon.

In Butlin's Holiday Camp, Clacton, Karl Wehner was told he was going to Devon too. In the second week in October, the camp commander, Major Macdonald, called the internees on parade and announced that they were to be moved from Clacton *en masse*. Major Macdonald told them they had some choice in the matter, for the War Office had now set up two camps, one for Class 'A' internees, the other for Class 'B'. The groupings reflected not the Home Office categories, but the attempt by the War Office to

divide internees according to their social station, just as it had
done in the First World War.

The 'A' camp was at another holiday camp at Paignton, near
Torbay. But when Macdonald invited the internees to take advantage of its privileges for 4s 6d (22½p) a day, only a handful stepped
forward. Wehner was not among them. He and most of the others
were therefore consigned to the 'B' camp at Seaton, on the coast
thirty miles east of Paignton. It was a former holiday camp, too,
run until the war by Warners.

Wehner had heard nothing following his session in London with
MI5, and when he was told to pack his suitcase for the long train
ride to Devon, he gloomily complied. During the journey he heard
some surprising news. The officer in charge of the party had only
just opened that morning's mail, to discover that it contained
release orders for three internees. They were all journalists; one
was Wehner. After just one night at Seaton, Wehner caught a train
back to London, a free man.

By mid October, the tribunals had interned almost 300 people in
Britain. They were all sent to Seaton, apart from a handful in
Scotland who remained in the deaf-and-dumb school in Edinburgh. Among the first to arrive by train from Lincoln were the
three Radok brothers. They found that the camp occupied a most
unfortunate site. It stood in a low-lying meadow, close to the sea,
that rapidly became water-logged when it rained. The English
autumn was already showing it at a disadvantage. The huts were
built of thin boards which were showing marked signs of wear,
while the damp westerly winds searched out every crack or per-
foration. But after the garage in Lincoln, Uwe was delighted by
the open skies and the noise of the crashing breakers, even if the
sea remained unseen behind a hastily erected fence. Other newcomers were less charitable. Peter Jacobsohn, Erwin Frenkel and
Franz Eichenberg were all struck by the cold.

Peter Jacobsohn was feeling particularly sorry for himself. He
was convinced that the British upper classes were deluded about
Hitler and he recalled in disgust the liberal friend of his mother
who had told him: 'When all is said and done, you must remember
that Hitler is a gentleman.' Seaton's plywood huts, the pipes that
froze, the toilets that did not function, seemed part of the same
offensive treatment. His hackles rose when a large influx of prisoners arrived at the camp.

Under Churchill, the Admiralty was still pursuing an aggressive policy towards German merchant vessels on the high seas, and in mid November the navy had chased the passenger ship *Adolf Woermann* as she headed home from the Angolan port of Lobito. When the destroyer *Neptune* closed, her master, Captain Burfeind, scuttled her. The *Neptune* picked up 162 survivors who, just before Christmas, found themselves in a damp and cold British holiday camp in Devon.

Captain Burfeind seemed an honourable man: 'The kind who would shun Jews but who would not participate in mass murder,' Erwin Frenkel forgivingly said later. Those who had been at Clacton found the crew of the *Adolf Woermann* less objectionable than the *Pomona*'s, but still reckoned that they contained a sprinkling of Nazis, including one passenger whom they suspected of belonging to the Gestapo. When Captain Burfeind held an open-air service for the passengers and crew who had drowned, some Jewish internees let loose a barrage of jeers.

A dazed Bruno Fehle arrived at Seaton in early December. He was enraged at an act of betrayal by his British co-directors, who had reneged on their promise and had cut off his salary at the end of November. But he had been partly cheered up by a delegation from his work force which had delivered a package to the Oratory School containing 200 cigarettes and 50 cigars. He had been asked if he wanted to go to the privileged camp at Paignton, but felt in no position to finance such extravagance. At Seaton he, too, suffered from the biting cold.

Internees were permitted visits from their relatives, and Irmgard Fehle pluckily decided to take her two sons to celebrate Christmas with her husband. The long train journey to Devon on Christmas Eve lasted all day, and they spent the night at a virtually deserted hotel near the camp. The internees were given a substantial Christmas lunch and were astonished when they were waited on by the camp staff. Afterwards the dining tables were arranged in a double line, and the visitors allowed in. Mrs Fehle sat with her two children on one side, her husband on the other, and discussed what the family should do. Acutely anxious about their lack of money, Fehle told his wife that she and the children should go to live with her parents, who were then in Holland. Reluctantly his wife agreed. When the visit ended, Fehle did not know if he would ever see her, or his children, again.

Early in November a group of non-refugee internees had been

transferred to another new camp at Lingfield Race Course in Surrey. Uwe, Jobst and Rainer Radok joined them there just before Christmas. The Home Office had set up a committee to hear appeals against the tribunals' verdicts, and as the Radoks had not even been before a tribunal, they thought an appeal against their internment was justified. They were moved to Lingfield to be on hand for their hearing, which was held at the Oratory School shortly after Christmas.

Uwe Radok was questioned first by a single MI5 officer, whose technique consisted of allowing long silences to develop in the hope that his victim would feel obliged to fill them. Uwe found it most effective. He believed he had a good chance of release until his interrogator struck a devastating blow. He read out a letter from his father to Hermann Göring, appealing for his help in finding Uwe a job. Unknown to Uwe, his father had written that he had 'proved his loyalty' to Germany by undergoing military training. What exactly did that mean, the MI5 man gently asked? Uwe could only reply: 'We had to as students,' and knew that his chance had gone. He could not fathom how the British had got hold of the letter in the first place, beyond supposing that it had been filed at the German Embassy in London and the British had found it when they took the building over.* After his interrogation, Uwe appeared before the full advisory committee, presided over by the formidable barrister, Norman Birkett. One member asked if he would take British nationality if he had the chance, and Uwe thought it best to give an honest, if discursive, answer: 'I haven't really thought about it – it's not something you pull on and off like a shirt – I suppose that in the end I would.' Jobst, who was more straightforward, simply replied, 'Yes.' Neither answer helped. All three brothers were returned to Seaton, and several weeks later were told that their appeals had been turned down. (The committee received 162 appeals by March 1940, and ordered forty-five releases.)

By now the internees at Seaton had formed natural groups. There were the Jews; other refugees; non-Nazi Germans like Bruno Fehle

---

* One alternative explanation was that the British and German security services had been in the habit of exchanging information about 'undesirables' before the war. This suspicion was shared by Karl Wehner. If true, it would not be the only time that unlikely alliances have been struck in the intelligence and security world.

who had lived in Britain and were known as *Reichsdeutschen*; Nazis; and seamen. Each group had its spokesman, and Fehle was chosen to represent the *Reichsdeutschen*. Among his more mundane duties was to distribute toilet rolls. He noticed that one batch was stamped with the letters OHMS and a coat of arms. He generously took them back to the British officer in charge of supplies, who blanched and ordered them to be instantly recalled.

Count Montgelas had been moved to Lingfield, and Franz Eichenberg became camp spokesman, following an election in which he defeated an International Brigade veteran by a narrow margin. Eichenberg was worried that his tiny majority did not give him sufficient authority to represent the internees, but the camp commander, Colonel Friston, assured him that 'one was enough'. Eichenberg moved uneasily between the various groups, finding it impossible to overcome the suspicion that he was too close to the British, even though he leaned towards the Jewish refugees. When Captain Burfeind asked him to do more for his seamen, Eichenberg bluntly said it was impossible.

For a time there was an unspoken truce between Jews and Nazis, but it broke down when the Nazis beat up a young Jewish internee who had jeered at them. The Jews exacted prompt revenge in kind. Eichenberg was summoned by Colonel Friston and told that such private vendettas had to stop. He passed the word back but the truce was never fully restored.

In March, the War Office transferred the internees whom it regarded as Nazis to Derbyshire. The definition was somewhat lax, for it included Captain Burfeind and his crew, and Bruno Fehle; but Fehle was pleased to find that his new camp consisted of a mansion named Swanwick House that had previously been a convalescent home for miners. It held 300 internees. Swanwick House itself was occupied by the British officers and guards while the internees stayed in more modern buildings in the grounds. Fehle liked the food better than at Seaton; after meals he could brew his own coffee in the boiler room, where one of Burfeind's stokers placed his coffee pot briefly on the glowing furnace.

The transfer did much to restore peace to Seaton, and life developed a certain unvarying routine. To Uwe Radok, the camp was becoming a world of its own. He enjoyed the company of new friends and spent hours in abstruse discussion with the noted economist and statistician, Jürgen Kutchinski, who had belonged to the communist underground in Nazi Germany. As life at Seaton became increasingly predictable, the three brothers tended to go their own ways, for they were traditionally close only in times of crisis. Jobst worked in the camp's administrative offices and, like Franz Eichenberg, was regarded with some suspicion by the other internees. Uwe worked in the camp's canteen, washing up 900 sets of cutlery and plates three times a day.

One day the Radok brothers received dramatic news from Germany. Their father had been imprisoned in a concentration camp, but after four months of valiant effort, their mother had won his release, and they were both planning to leave Germany for South America soon. Their uncle had not been so fortunate. Despite the bravery which had won him the Star of Tamara in the First World War, he had been sent to the concentration camp of Theresienstadt, where he had died. Uwe sought consolation in the camp routine once more, pursuing an endless round of work, conversation and walks between the wooden buildings. He came to resent any break in the pattern, such as a search by the guards, as an unwarranted disturbance of the camp's equilibrium.

As the winter ended with few outward signs of war, it might have seemed that the world had forgotten about the internees at Seaton. Since the first week of September, however, there had been frantic activity behind the scenes over their fate. When the War Office and Home Office had drawn up their plans for internment, no one appeared to consider that other participants might feel entitled to hold views on the subject. One party which was now determined to make itself heard was the government of Germany. It was not at all interested in the fate of Jewish refugees who were interned in Britain. But it did care about *Reichsdeutschen*, like Bruno Fehle, who wanted to come home.

7 The Bargaining Counters

When war began, Britain and Germany had inevitably broken off diplomatic relations. But there are in the most bitter wars matters on which adversaries need to address one another. The intermediary through which Britain and Germany conducted their dialogue was the United States. The game of war is often one of tit-for-tat, where to apportion blame is a fruitless exercise. None the less the US State Department came to feel that, of the three nations which had carried out internment – France being the third – Germany had behaved in the most liberal manner. Faced with this opinion, placating the United States became for the British Foreign Office a very important and difficult task.

While the Home Office had decided at the eleventh hour against mass internment, it had still carried through its original policy of allowing Germans to leave, at least until 'Z plus 7' day, 9 September. In the ten days till then, 2,000 Germans left Britain. Apart from those actually interned, only 100 who wanted to go home failed to beat the 9 September deadline.

In Germany, the role of 'protecting power' for British interests was taken over by the United States. At the start of the war, the German Foreign Office told the American Embassy in Berlin that there 'was no German intention to intern British subjects'. Germany warned, however, that its policy would be 'governed solely by the attitude of the British government towards German citizens'. On 5 September it learned of the round-up of German suspects in Britain and responded by preventing British subjects from leaving the country.

Germany's attitude hardened when it heard what was happening in various outposts of the British Empire. In India, all German males over sixteen were arrested; Germans were held in Tanganyika. They were also detained in former possessions where Britain still had influence, such as Iraq and Egypt. As the Foreign Office itself acknowledged, it was 'in response to British pressure' that Cairo police arrested ninety Germans at the German Legation, as well as raiding the German Archaeological Institute and a German bank, and holding all inside.

Germany retaliated by arresting 100 British men and interning them in the ancient castle of Wülzburg in Bavaria. At the same time, it told the American Embassy in Berlin that it would let British subjects in Germany go home, provided that Britain did the same. From Berlin, the American chargé d'affaires, Alexander Kirk, sent an urgent telegram to Joseph Kennedy, the American Ambassador in London. Kirk reported: 'The Germans wished assurance not only that Germans in the United Kingdom would be allowed to depart, but that Germans in Egypt, Iraq, India, the Straits Settlements and other parts of the British Empire would also be allowed to regain their country without hindrance.' The German Foreign Office had evidently made a curiously frank admission about the clandestine activities each side might be involved in, for Kirk added that Germany would respect any 'special reasons' offered by the British for preventing 'a given German' from leaving. Germany was also keen to fix a precise date for an exchange of internees, otherwise negotiations 'might drag on indefinitely'. It was an accurate forecast.

Kennedy passed Kirk's report to the British Foreign Office on 25 September. Two days later, the fate of enemy civilians in each country was raised for the first time in the British Cabinet. It arose in the context of the treatment of merchant seamen, and evidently aroused some passion, for there were three separate discussions on the subject in the space of four days.

Winston Churchill, First Lord of the Admiralty, held characteristically forthright views. On the first day of the war, the crew of the banana boat *Pomona* had been removed from the London docks and interned in Clacton; the crews of enemy merchant ships, in port or on the high seas, were considered to be fair game. But Churchill also favoured taking prisoner German merchant seamen from *neutral* ships, which was quite another matter. From Lord Lothian, British Ambassador in Washington, came a warning of the dire consequences of going too far. It was a fundamental tenet of British foreign policy to enlist American sympathies, with the distant objective – hardly yet whispered – of drawing the United States into the conflict on Britain's side. If the navy stopped *American* ships on the high seas to arrest German seamen, the effect on American opinion could be disastrous.

Any restrictions irked Churchill. He declared that as a German destroyer had removed seven British seamen from a Swedish ship, Britain would retaliate by taking *two* Germans for each of the British, and if he was now to be prevented from searching American ships, he would try to find them on vessels of other nationalities. For this remark he was rebuked by Lord Halifax, the British Foreign Secretary. Halifax told the Cabinet that Germany had been within its rights under the rules of war to take the seven British seamen, as they were survivors from a torpedoed British ship – and he pointed out that the Admiralty had publicly confirmed this view. Churchill was determined to have the last word. He vowed that for each British seaman interned, Britain should take *three* Germans in revenge.

It was in a defiant mood that Churchill turned his attention to the general principles of Britain's internment policy. The Attorney-General, Sir Donald Somervell, told the Cabinet that no enemy aliens had been detained, apart from those 'known to be dangerous'. The minutes record that discussion ensued 'as to the wisdom of this policy which was different from that adopted in 1914'. One of those who challenged the new line was Churchill. When it was stated that official policy was to repatriate enemy aliens, Churchill intervened to dispute whether this should be so. He also asked what was happening to British subjects in Germany. The question was directed primarily at Lord Halifax. He said he did not know.

The internment by both sides had caught the Foreign Office in disarray. True, on 5 September it had asked the United States to 'assist a number of British subjects' who were stranded in Germany 'for various reasons such as ill-health, lack of transport, etc.'. But no one at the Foreign Office seemed to know how many British subjects there were in Germany; officials first advised Lord Halifax that there might be as many as 300. Not long afterwards, a Foreign Office minute recorded a higher figure: there were 200 British visitors and tourists alone who had been caught by the German exit embargo, plus a considerable number of 'Germanized British subjects . . . with interests and roots in Germany'. There were 500 of these in Berlin, and an undetermined number elsewhere. The International Red Cross, traditional protector of prisoners' rights in times of war, thought even more British were at risk, informing the Foreign Office that there were 3,000 British in Germany. But, for bureaucratic reasons, the Red Cross report went unheeded. The question of internees was being handled by the Foreign Office Consular Department, which was not sure whether it was its place to communicate with the Red Cross. Until the Foreign Office later set up a separate Prisoners of War Section, all letters from the Red Cross remained unanswered.

On 30 September, Halifax told the Cabinet, rather vaguely, that there were '200 to 300' British subjects in Germany and that '100 to 200' had been interned. He offered no details of their condition. From the American Embassy in Berlin, the Foreign Office was later to learn that the Germans were treating their prisoners reasonably. American officials made three visits to Wülzburg Castle in 1939, and felt that while life was 'undoubtedly unpleasant' for the 120 British – and eighty French – held there, there was 'no physical hardship of any sort'. They concluded that the Germans were 'making every effort to treat the interned personnel well'. But, after the flurry of interest at the end of September, no one in the British Cabinet asked about the British internees again in 1939 – not even Churchill, who had raised the question in the first place.

Even so, the Foreign Office shared Churchill's feeling that German prisoners should not be repatriated without an attempt to secure any benefits that were going. But its position was made more awkward by a new strand that was discernible in American policy on internment. The United States had first become involved in its role as protector of British interests in Germany. The American State Department now appeared to feel that an even-handed concern for civilian victims on both sides in the war would be a neat and uncontroversial demonstration of American neutrality. The appropriate sentiments were duly expressed in a telegram dated 29 September to the American Embassies in London, Berlin and Paris, from Cordell Hull, American Secretary of State since 1933. Hull asked his ambassadors to remind their hosts of the lessons of the First World War, when 'nearly all belligerents adopted the rigorous expedient of internment of enemy aliens', which had caused 'widespread and seemingly unnecessary suffering to thousands of innocent persons'. On 4 October, the American chargé d'affaires in London, Herschel Johnson, delivered a paraphrase of Hull's appeal to the British Foreign Office. Johnson added his own fear that a process of reprisals was already under way between Britain and Germany, but expressed his hopes that mass internment would not occur and that internees would be exchanged.

The Home Office could see no reason why the exchange should not take place. It still favoured its original policy of repatriation, and in mid October announced that MI5 no longer had any interest in the twenty-five German women arrested in September and held in Holloway; they could therefore go home. The German government had responded with alacrity to Hull's appeal, and on 24 October the US State Department pointedly sent the Foreign Office a copy of Germany's positive reply. The Foreign Office preferred to view the Home Office's unwanted prisoners as 'bargaining counters', which meant that its own response to Hull would require some skilful drafting.

On 29 October, Sir Alexander Cadogan, the mercurial and guileful Permanent Under-Secretary at the Foreign Office, wrote to his Home Office counterpart, Alexander Maxwell. Cadogan expressed himself with an honesty that is not customary in correspondence between rival ministries. 'We are working on the assumption that the surest way of getting British subjects out of Germany is to hold German citizens here and then exchange them,' Cadogan told Maxwell. 'At the same time, we wish to avoid the appearance of resorting to wholesale internment in any shape or form, so it would need to be understood that the need for retaining these people arises out of the attitude of the German and not of His Majesty's Government. . .'

The awkward fact the Foreign Office had to overcome was that the British had carried out internment first. None the less, in his own draft reply, R. M. Urquhart, an official of the Consular Department, noted that there was plenty in Hull's message that could be used 'to good advantage'. In particular, there was the American hope that mass internment would not be called for. 'Here we can really let ourselves go,' Urquhart observed. 'We can state very definitely that internment en masse has not been our policy and we can state principles which will fully correspond with American ideas.'

The American emphasis on avoiding reprisals gave the Foreign

Office the cue it needed to shove most of the blame for internment on to Germany. Strictly speaking, of course, only Germany had indulged in reprisals, for the simple, logical reason that Britain had acted first. The Foreign Office reply, dispatched by Lord Halifax to Kennedy on 24 November, was based on this central point. Halifax expressed his regret at having observed 'the same indications of a policy of reprisals on the part of the German government which attracted the attention of the Department of State and which showed that the Government of the German Reich have deprived of their liberty certain British subjects whom there was originally no intention and presumably at no time, any need to intern'. The British arrests, on the other hand, were merely 'such measures for the restraint of dangerous enemy aliens as may be directly necessary to secure the safety of the State'.

Halifax recited the details of the Home Office tribunals and said that 'similar reviews' were in operation – or being contemplated – in the British Empire, and that 160 Germans had already been released in India. Halifax dealt with the American proposal for mutual repatriation by ignoring it.

Despite the British omission, Cordell Hull was pleased with the British reply. On 28 November, he told the London and Berlin embassies that after a 'careful reading' of the British and German notes, he felt the two countries were close to agreement on several major points, including: no reprisals, no mass internment, and repatriation for those who wanted it. In London, Kennedy acted on his own initiative over repatriation, dispatching an official to press the Foreign Office further. The Foreign Office's own position had just been eased by an undertaking from the Home Office which had decided on further groups of internees who could now leave. The Home Office wanted to keep the Germans who were suspected of being spies, and those who had been in contact with the British arms industry or defence plans: all others could be released. They included those 'with special expert or technical knowledge which would be useful to the enemy'. Kennedy reported this to Hull, and it seemed that nothing would now prevent *Reichsdeutschen* like Bruno Fehle from going home. (A return to Germany was, of course, the last thing that Jewish and refugee internees wanted.)

The fact that repatriation did not take place for those British and German civilians who desired it was the result in large part of last-minute objections from Winston Churchill. As Churchill had threatened in September, the Royal Navy had been assiduously garnering Germans from merchant ships around the world. Three times late in 1939, for example, British warships had compelled Brazilian vessels to heave to while they removed the Germans on board. The navy did not limit itself to merchant seamen: on 2 December it had stopped the SS *Itape* and taken off twenty-two German passengers who had merely been travelling to northern Brazil. Diplomatic warnings against such moves continued, and in January 1940 came an incident which exploded into controversy. On 21 January, a British cruiser held up the Japanese ship *Asama Mahu* thirty-five miles from the Japanese coast and removed twenty-one Germans, some of them merchant seamen.

The Japanese government furiously denounced the British action and the United States was soon involved. Tension between Japan and the United States was increasing and the American Ambassador in Tokyo reported that the incident had given Japanese military extremists 'powerful ammunition'. The British Ambassador had advised caution, and the American Ambassador revealed that the British felt the Admiralty had 'badly mishandled the whole matter'. Under heavy pressure, the British government finally agreed on 5 February to hand back nine of the twenty-one captured Germans.

On 13 February, the German Foreign Office made a formal declaration to the American Embassy that it would guarantee that 'every British citizen who so desires will be granted permission' to leave Germany, the only proviso being that 'reciprocity is granted'. But Churchill was not about to concede any more of the navy's prisoners. Kennedy continued to pursue an agreement in London, but on 27 March told Cordell Hull: 'I am advised that the number of captured merchant seamen is continually growing and that the Admiralty is not disposed to release them.' Kennedy added that the Foreign Office was 'using this government's interest as an additional argument with the military authorities', but admitted that the chances of a general exchange had 'lessened perceptibly'.

In the end, the civilians allowed home came only from restricted categories, the United States persuading Britain and Germany to exchange women, children, and men over sixty. As a result, 100 or so from each side were exchanged by the spring of 1940 – the German women from Holloway promptly having their stories widely broadcast by Goebbel's Propaganda Ministry. In addition,

Germany released 400 Lascar seamen on condition they did not serve in warships afterwards, and several thousand Germans eventually reached home from the British colonies.

For the United States, the negotiations had been a frustrating experience, and on 1 April a memorandum to the Assistant Secretary of State, Breckinridge Long, evaluated the merits of each of the participants. It judged that the German position 'has been . . . and still is, far more liberal than that of the allied governments. Whereas the British seemed for a time to be more inclined than the French to meet German proposals, the respective positions of the British and French now seem to have been reversed.' In London, Kennedy was still 'doing his utmost to bring about some understanding with the British Foreign Office – thus far, unavailingly'. The State Department memorandum concluded that it would be best 'to wait a while and not take any action that would harden the differences between parties'.

It would not be long before the United States would renew its interest in Britain's internment policy, from a position that remained avowedly neutral. Much later in the war, the United States was to display a far more technical and self-interested attitude towards the subject. But, in April 1940, with the State Department recommendation to take no further action, the matter was allowed to rest.

8   A Secret Weapon

April 1940 saw an end to the 'Phoney War'. American journalists had coined the phrase to describe the period when Britain was lulled into believing that there would be no conflict and that the old pre-war life would continue. The great military historian Liddell Hart wrote that the period was better termed the 'winter of illusion'. He added that no illusions were greater than those cherished by the Allied High Command, who had spent their time devising absurd and grandiose offensives against Germany: striking through Germany into the Ruhr, or taking over the Soviet oilfields in the Caucasus to cut off Germany's supplies.

In the end, the spell was broken by an adventure in Scandinavia. It was the first major confrontation between Britain and Germany. The result was a débâcle. And when one illusion is shattered, another often takes its place. In this instance it was that the Allied defeat was brought about not by incompetence, but by a devastating German secret weapon. The instigator of the British operation was Winston Churchill. Ironically, the Norwegian débâcle gave his political fortunes a major boost. It also inspired the first attempts to shift the Home Office from the internment policy it had so boldly staked out at the start of the war.

Churchill had been obsessed with the idea of launching some kind of action in Norway ever since the first days of the war. As First Lord of the Admiralty, he devised a scheme to lay mines in Norway's coastal waters and block the supplies of iron ore which were shipped from Sweden to Germany via Norway's Arctic port of Narvik. It was doubtful whether the scheme had any real strategic value, and it was also open to one overriding objection, which the Foreign Office forcefully pointed out: the plan would mean blatantly violating Norwegian neutrality. To begin with, the War Cabinet accepted this view.

Churchill viewed his defeat as a merely temporary setback, and he pressed for his scheme, as he later wrote, 'by every means and on all occasions'. When the Soviet army invaded Finland in November 1939, he argued that the Allies should respond by carrying out landings the length of the Norwegian coast. In Cabinet, the views of the Foreign Office still held sway, but by way of a sop to Churchill, it was agreed that the Chiefs of Staff might draw up plans for a limited landing at Narvik.

In February 1940 came an incident that rapidly became part of British war mythology. The German supply ship *Altmark* was steaming home with 300 British seamen who had been captured in the south Atlantic by the German battleship *Graf Spee*. Churchill, of course, held strong if not entirely consistent views on the subject and when the *Altmark* sought refuge from British warships in a Norwegian fjord, he ordered the destroyer *Cossack* to go in after her. The *Altmark* was boarded and British sailors greeted the prisoners with the promptly immortalized words, 'The navy's here!'

Hitler had been trying to evaluate British intentions towards Norway and he read the *Altmark* incident – which technically violated Norwegian neutrality – as a sign of an impending invasion. Such a move carried considerable danger for Germany: if Britain occupied Norway, the route to the Baltic, and perhaps Berlin, lay open. Hitler ordered a pre-emptive strike to be prepared. Fearing exactly that, the British in turn drew up their own invasion plans, and in March the Cabinet consented to the full-scale operation Churchill had always sought. It was to be a combined army and navy operation, with the French also taking part. Troops would go ashore at four widely scattered points on the Norwegian coast, from Stavanger in the south to Narvik in the north. The British Home Fleet sailed from Scapa Flow on 7 April. As the combined forces prepared for action, the devastating news came that Germany had struck first.

Soon after dawn on 9 April, German troops landed by sea at Bergen, Trondheim and Narvik – three of the very ports the British had been heading for. By midday the Germans had overcome the minimal Norwegian defences and occupied all three cities. At Oslo they met with slightly sterner opposition. A German cruiser was torpedoed, and parachutists landing at Fornebu airport were held at bay long enough for the Norwegian government and Royal Family to escape. By the evening, however, Oslo had fallen, and within a week Germany held the entire southern half of Norway, as well as all Denmark, which had fallen in one day.

Britain received the news that Germany had struck first with dismay and incredulity. Only on 3 April, Churchill had declared that Germany was simply incapable of landing in Scandinavia. When the Prime Minister, Neville Chamberlain, announced that the German forces had done just that, he could not conceal his own incredulity, repeating the view of naval intelligence that perhaps Narvik had been confused with Larvik, a port 700 miles to the south. By evening that last hope had been dispelled. German forces had indeed taken Narvik, almost 1,000 miles from their home base. The Allies now had to overcome their disbelief and convert an operation anticipating little opposition into a full-scale clash with the enemy. A week behind their original schedule, British forces landed in central Norway to try to take Trondheim from the Germans. With 13,000 British troops facing only 2,000 defenders, the chances looked good. But the British had been poorly trained, lacked vital equipment and were harried by the Luftwaffe. Their best hope of air support lay with a squadron of obsolete biplanes, for which they frantically cleared a runway on a frozen lake. After a night in the open, the planes' motors froze solid and most were destroyed in the first Luftwaffe attack. The British offensive ground to a halt.

The last hope of gains lay at Narvik, where three troopships had spent an uneasy week out at sea. The Narvik venture was bedevilled from the start by the fact that contradictory orders had been issued to the naval commander, Lord Cork and Orrery, and his army counterpart, General Mackesy. The army had forbidden Mackesy to attempt a landing if there were any signs of opposition. On the other hand, Churchill, who briefed Lord Cork in a limousine *en route* to the Commons, had instructed him to capture Narvik as soon as possible and by any means necessary. As he gloomily surveyed possible landing sites, General Mackesy must have felt that the army's caution was justified. His troops were short of vital ammunition and much of their equipment had been loaded in error on to boats which were not taking part in operations in central Norway. He had no artillery or landing craft, and his men would have to land from open boats. Once ashore, they would face snowdrifts three feet deep.

When the first British troops landed on 26 April, they made painful progress. Nor were they encouraged by the fate of three crack battalions of French Alpine troops, who, despite their special training, were fast succumbing to frostbite and snow-blindness and managed to advance just five miles in ten days. The disputes between Lord Cork and General Mackesy were becoming so intractable that they were referred to the War Cabinet for resolution.

Early in May, all forces were withdrawn from elsewhere in Norway to try to boost the Narvik operation. British and French troops finally took the town on 28 May – only to pull out a week later as greater military disasters unfolded in France. The Norwegian campaign had proved an ignominious shambles. The most charitable judgment was that made by the naval historian, Captain Donald Macintyre, when he wrote: 'At moderate cost in casualties, the inefficiencies and defects of the fighting forces were starkly revealed and lessons in the facts of modern warfare thrust home.'

Such a truth was not palatable in 1940. The British press loyally put the best gloss on the débâcle, even though it found itself as upstaged by the German invasion as the War Office. The newspapers of 9 April were full of the triumphal news that the Allies had laid a blockade of mines to hinder Germany's war supplies. By the time they appeared on the streets, they were out of date; the BBC news that morning conveyed something of the grim truth. The newspapers were hard pressed to make up their lost ground. Only the *Daily Telegraph* had a man anywhere near the scene: Hugh Carleton Greene, its chief correspondent, was in Amsterdam, from where he did his valiant best. Fleet Street frantically enlisted the help of foreign newsmen in Scandinavia, mostly Americans, publishing their reports with traditional anonymity: 'By our correspondent', 'By our special correspondent'. One reporter who drove into Norway from Sweden counted thirty-two heavily laden ammunition wagons as he overtook a German column on the road, and it was hard to avoid the impression that a formidable enemy had shown its hand.

From London, it was easier to present events in a more favourable light. Condemnations of the violation of Norway's neutrality were popular – 'this brutal invasion of Norway by the Germans will not go unpunished' was one ringing trade union declaration carried by the press on 15 April. The fact that only Germany's premature arrival had prevented Britain from doing something very similar could now be safely forgotten. Official communiqués reporting actual British successes were naturally given prominence: an Admiralty account of German ships sunk, the one bright spot of the operation, received admiring headlines on 15 April. In general, the British media presented an incoherent picture that made lay appreciation of the turn of events well-nigh impossible. In one of his London broadcasts that month, the esteemed American commentator Ed Murrow declared: 'The handling by press and radio of the news from Norway in the past ten days has undermined the confidence of a considerable section of the British public in the integrity and accuracy of its news sources.'

But then, in mid April, it seemed that a way had been found through the barrier of incomprehension. As if the British press had collectively risen to cry 'Eureka!', a flash of inspiration illuminated the confusion and gloom. An editorial in the *Yorkshire Post* on 16 April was typical: 'There is no doubt that help from a "Fifth Column" in Norway figured in Hitler's invasion plans.' The editorial then amplified its theme:

> Before attacking a country, Hitler always tries to undermine it from within. How does he enlist his sympathizers, ready to work for him when the hour strikes? Partly by a long-continued policy of threats, which compels the chosen country to allow the organization of a Nazi Party, raised around a nucleus of German nationals in its midst. Partly by spreading fears of invasion, which tempt the unscrupulous and the timorous to ensure their good standing with the invaders in advance. Local adventurers and ne'er-do-wells are attracted by the promise of fat jobs when the Nazis arrive.

Within a week, almost every other national newspaper had written in similar terms.

By most accounts, the phrase 'Fifth Column' was coined during the Spanish Civil War. In September 1936, after Franco's forces had lifted the epic siege of Toledo in the centre of the great Spanish plain, they moved on to their next objective: Madrid. Early in October, General Emilio Mola threw down a challenge to the

Republicans who held the city. He boasted that he had four columns of troops ready to march on Madrid, but that was not all.
For already in the city was a *fifth* column prepared to rise and fight
for Franco.

Mola is reported to have made his threat during an interview
with a group of foreign journalists, and also to have broadcast it
by radio, beamed at Madrid. There are conflicting claims to its
origin: the *Daily Telegraph* correspondent, Lord St Oswald, insisted
that he first used it in a dispatch several weeks before Mola; while
it is also supposed to have been used about Russian supporters
inside the fortresses of Ismail, besieged by Suvarov in 1790. Whatever the truth, the phrase was soon in widespread use in the
Republican press, and as the siege of Madrid began, it rapidly
attained the power of a Goya war etching to evoke fears of darkness
and betrayal. The Republicans set up committees to identify and
eliminate the Fifth Column's supposed members. Military men
long since retired, but who were thought loyal to Franco, were
arrested. By night there were constant assassinations of suspected
Franco sympathizers.

British newspapers soon adopted the phrase, *The Times* probably
first, though it wrongly attributed its use to Franco. It received its
highest sanctification in 1939 when Ernest Hemingway, who had
been crashing around Spain in the style of one of his romantic
heroes, wrote a play about life and love in besieged Madrid entitled
The Fifth Column.

One reason for the popularity of the fifth column concept was
that, like the psychologist's ink-blot, it was susceptible to widely
differing interpretations. Thus it made an early appearance in the
Sunday Dispatch on 4 February 1940, as a sub-heading in a report
attacking, among others, the Independent Labour Party and the
Peace Pledge Union. This paragraph is representative:

> The seriousness of the menace in Glasgow, second city of the
> British Empire, can be judged by the following message to the
> *Sunday Dispatch* from Lord Provost Dollan: 'Here there are more
> than 2,000 subversive agents acting on instructions from Mos-
> cow. They disguise themselves as peace societies or genuine
> working-class organizations. It is time they were shown up for
> what they are!

The *Sunday Dispatch*, like the *Daily Mail*, was owned by Lord
Rothermere, who during the 1930s had declared embarrassingly

open support for Hitler, Mussolini and the British fascist, Sir Oswald Mosley. He had welcomed Hitler as a bulwark against bolshevism, excused his campaign against 'Israelites of international attachments', and justified the German absorption of Austria in 1938 with the argument that 'race' was of paramount importance. The declaration of war forced a painful rethink which now expressed itself in xenophobic attacks on aliens in Britain, both those interned and those at liberty.

'Alien Women in Luxury' proclaimed the headline to a report in the *Sunday Dispatch* of 7 January 1940 about internees in Holloway. A recently released prisoner complained:

> The alien women, Germans, Austrians, some of them Jewesses, used to march round the exercise yard singing German songs, accompanied by mouth organs. The day I went into Holloway, I was kept waiting from ten in the morning until nearly ten at night while a big batch of them had their baggage examined before being allowed to take it into the prison.

In an article about the 'enemy alien menace' on 31 March, the *Sunday Dispatch* parroted claims by 'Scotland Yard men' that the Home Office tribunals had adopted a 'kid-glove policy' and reported: 'Servant girls in country districts have supplied valuable information about German girls in their own job who seemed to spend a good deal of time near important military and Air Force Centres.' The following week, on 7 April, the *Dispatch* managed to link two of its *bêtes noires* in the same front-page headline: 'The Great Aliens Scandal – Our Money for Communist Propaganda'. The story complained that communists among the Czech refugees in Britain, who had been granted £2½ million by the British government, were living together and distributing leaflets. This permitted the *Dispatch* the further headline: 'Red Cells Formed by Subsidized Refugees'. One week later, after the German invasion of Norway, the *Dispatch* invoked the Fifth Column to attack all its favourite targets simultaneously.

The impetus came from the newspaper's diplomatic correspondent, one of the band of reporters who retailed gossip, rumours and the occasional facts gleaned from their circuit of embassies and legations in London, interspersed by briefings from Britain's fledgling Ministry of Information. From one of these sources he acquired some snippets about the Norwegian Nazi, Vidkun Quisling, installed by the Germans as their puppet head of government. On 14 April, the *Dispatch* published these on its front page, together with the claim that, 'before the invasion of Norway and Denmark, the Scandinavian local Nazis met in secret in Munich and decided to train local Nazi agents and agitators'. The 200-word report was headed: 'The Fifth Column'. On page 8, the *Dispatch* drew the moral: 'Hitler had a "Fifth Column" in Britain ... made up of Fascists, Communists, peace fanatics and alien refugees in league with Berlin and Moscow.' And it homed in on the Peace Pledge Union, a group of earnest pacifists of minimal effect; in the *Dispatch* they were presented as 'conchies' who constituted 'an underground political force which endangers the very life of the nation'.

Two days later other newspapers took up the theme, though at first with more restraint. The *Yorkshire Post* explored the subject in its editorial and the phrase also appeared in the *Daily Express* and the *Daily Mail*. Both papers had just received dispatches from their chief European correspondents, then in Bucharest: G. Ward Price for the *Mail*, Sefton Delmer for the *Express*.

Each described the preparations Germany was supposedly making for an internal *coup* in Rumania, and each report referred to the Fifth Column. It is temptingly neat to ascribe the inspiration for so doing to Delmer, who had spent much time with Ernest Hemingway in Spain when Hemingway was drafting his play *The Fifth Column*. But the phrase appears only in a cross-head in Delmer's report, and it bears all the marks of a sub-editor's insert in Ward Price's in the *Mail*. On the same day, however, the concept of the Fifth Column received a powerful and apparently factual boost from a long article in the *Daily Telegraph*.

Leland Stowe was one of a small group of American journalists in Oslo when Germany invaded Norway. Stowe was a courageous reporter, a Pulitzer Prize winner who later that month was among the first to report on the reality of the British campaign to capture Trondheim, describing the British troops who had been 'dumped into Norway's deep snows and quagmires of April slush without a single anti-aircraft gun, without one squadron of supporting planes, without a single piece of field artillery', and concluding that it was 'one of the costliest and most inexplicable bungles in military history'.

Stowe's article about the fall of Oslo, which he dispatched from Stockholm to avoid German censorship and which the London

Daily Telegraph published on 16 April, was also long on hyperbole. Stowe claimed that the German invasion succeeded through:

> a gigantic conspiracy which must undoubtedly rank among the most audacious and most perfectly oiled political plots of the past century. . . By bribery and extraordinary infiltration on the part of Nazi agents, and by treason on the part of a few highly-placed Norwegian civilian and defence authorities, the German dictatorship built its Trojan Horse inside Norway.

However, the evidence produced by the usually reliable Stowe for his devastating conclusion was not impressive. He cited just two instances of treachery. The commander of the Norwegian base of Horten had supposedly received false or traitorous orders not to oppose the German invaders; and a minefield guarding the narrows of Oslo fjord had been rendered harmless by being electrically disconnected from its control point. And there are serious doubts about the accuracy of each claim, which we shall consider shortly. But in Britain in 1940, such words fell like sparks on tinder. The *Daily Telegraph* headlined Stowe's report: 'Oslo was betrayed by Nazi plotters within her gates', and referred to 'treachery among Nazi supporters in Norway and highly placed officials'. Although it did not use the phrase that day, by 19 April the newspaper was eagerly referring to the 'recent revelations in the *Daily Telegraph* about the part that Hitler's "Fifth Column" played in the invasion of Norway'. The fire became a conflagration. Stowe's phrase about the German 'Trojan Horse' was widely adopted; *The Times* stated that Norway had been 'honeycombed' with German agents before the invasion; and the word 'Quisling' passed into the British language to mean 'collaborator', 'traitor'.

The most thorough examination after the war of the reality of the Fifth Column was made by the Dutch historian, Dr Louis de Jong. In 1950, de Jong accepted a brief from UNESCO to write an account of the activities of the German Fifth Column to form part of a permanent record of the war crimes of Nazi Germany. De Jong began by accepting the premise behind UNESCO's request, but, as he proceeded, increasingly came to the conclusion that in Western Europe the Fifth Column was almost entirely mythical and that the fall of Norway and Denmark in particular were explicable in straightforward military terms. In capturing the principal Norwegian cities, Germany had the advantage of both speed and surprise to overcome their light defences. German intelligence had been good, but not difficult to acquire. Much came from maps and guides purchased in Berlin, and any vast 'honeycombing' of agents would have been superfluous. As for Quisling, even though he placed himself at the head of a collaborationist government, the Germans hardly took him seriously and certainly had not trusted him enough to inform him of their impending attack. Nor could de Jong find evidence of any act of sabotage by Quisling's supporters. De Jong also considered the specific claims of Leland Stowe. He concluded that no case had been established of Norwegian forces receiving false orders, and that the minefield supposed to have been 'rendered harmless' had never been laid in the first place.

It should be said that Leland Stowe stands by his report today. 'There remains no doubt whatever in my mind that Norway in April 1940 was betrayed from within,' he declares. However, he did shift his position significantly even while the war was in progress, writing that the fall of Norway could have been caused by negligence as well as by treason; and in 1979 he speculated that those issuing false orders may have been not secret Nazis but 'yellow-bellied pacifists'. But Louis de Jong is not the only historian who concluded that the Fifth Column was a myth. A. J. P. Taylor, for example, has written: 'The Fifth Column of supposed traitors was the product of panic-stricken imaginations. It did not exist in reality.'

The spring of 1940 was not, however, the time to conduct inquiries as dispassionate as these. And, just as in Madrid, a scapegoat was at hand, a focus for all the dread evoked by the notion of a Fifth Column. The *Sunday Dispatch* had already pointed the finger. Its Rothermere stablemate, the *Daily Mail*, now joined the accusers. On 19 April an editorial stated: 'Disquiet about Britain's "Fifth Column" is growing. . . The people ask that doubtful enemy aliens should be immediately interned and all other aliens strictly examined. . . The traitors of Norway have shown the perils of the enemy within.' The *Mail* also railed against Rothermere's familiar enemies, stating that 'the people' wanted steps taken against communists and 'peace cranks'.

It was in its claim to speak for 'the people' that the *Mail* was at its most impertinent. It so happened that, in the last week of April, the pioneering social-survey organization, Mass-Observation, conducted an extensive inquiry into attitudes towards the Fifth Column. Mass-Observation reported:

We found that the majority of people hardly realized what the phrase meant. We also found that the level of ordinary people's feelings was much less intense than that expressed in some papers. Detailed interviewing in several areas in London and Western Scotland produced less than one person in a hundred who spontaneously suggested that the refugees ought to be interned *en masse*.

Other newspapers were far more cautious than the *Mail* at this stage. On 23 April, *The Times* recalled that most aliens had come to Britain to seek refuge from Nazi persecution, and had already passed through several stages of scrutiny: 'Our alien problem therefore calls for ceaseless vigilance, but not for the wholesale internment imposed during the last War, nor for the hysterics which the subject sometimes produced in those days.' A day or so later, the *Daily Express* compared the pursuit of aliens with the witch-hunts of seventeenth-century New England, concluding: 'All liberal-minded persons, all who value freedom and liberty in life, should stand against every recrudescence of the witch-hunt, no matter what form it may take.'*

By now politicians were joining in the hunt. Sir Eugene Ramsden, Conservative MP for Bradford, told a meeting in Yorkshire that Britain would not tolerate the creation of a Fifth Column, 'composed of those who support Nazism or who would, if given the opportunity, play a part similar to that which German sympathizers have recently played in Norway'. On 19 April, seventy Tory MPs attended a meeting at the Commons to consider the Fifth Column, and Labour MPs were also becoming concerned. How MPs interpreted the term depended on their position on the political spectrum. Conservatives complained against aliens, communists and pacifists, while Labour members concentrated on Sir Oswald Mosley and other fringe movements of the far right.

It was at this juncture that the Home Secretary, Sir John Anderson, became publicly involved. What view the Home Office took of the growing hysteria can only be guessed at since no files from this period have been released. But a clue can be gleaned

---

* If it seems surprising that the *Daily Express* should have taken such a radical line, it is worth noting that its proprietor, Lord Beaverbrook, who used the editorial column as his mouthpiece, was having an affair with a Jewish woman refugee at the time.

from Anderson's letters to his father, in which he revealed some feeling on the subject. On 2 March he wrote:

> The newspapers are working up feeling about aliens. I shall have to do something about it or we may be stampeded into an unnecessarily oppressive policy. It is very easy in wartime to start a scare.

And, on 26 March:

> There has been a lot of fuss in the papers about aliens, but I have seen no sign of real trouble in Parliament as yet. . . But in wartime people are easily worked up and a spy scare can be started any time as a 'stunt'.

Within a month the 'trouble in Parliament' had started. Anderson met the organizers of the Tory meeting on 19 April, and on 24 April spoke to the party's 1922 Committee. *The Times* said that he satisfied MPs, but the *Mail* judged him 'complacent'. The following day, Anderson answered several questions in the Commons and was evidently content with his performance, for on 26 April he remarked to his father: 'I expect to be able to hold the position unless the war begins to go badly.' Anderson did not know that powerful forces were gathering against the Home Office from whom he was entitled to expect a far more objective view.

9   Backs Against the Wall

On Thursday, 2 May, the Joint Intelligence Committee met at its spacious office in Richmond Terrace, an imposing building whose Georgian façade runs at right-angles from Whitehall opposite the entrance to Downing Street. The Joint Intelligence Committee, or JIC, was the senior body of British military and civilian intelligence, and it now had the task of sitting in judgment on the Norwegian débâcle. The failure its four eminent members had to consider was their own.

The chairman of the committee was William Cavendish-Bentinck, a diplomat in his early forties from distinguished political stock. Among his forbears were Lord William Cavendish-Bentinck, first Governor-General of India, and Lord George Cavendish-Bentinck, private secretary to Canning (Richmond Terrace was once Lord George's home). A former Guards officer with solid experience in British embassies in Europe and South America, he had returned to Whitehall to join the Foreign Office's Egyptian and African department in 1937 and had been appointed the committee's chairman in 1939. He brought to the meetings intelligence submitted by British embassies round the world, and by SIS – the Secret Intelligence Service, alternatively known as MI6. He was a jovial figure whose diplomatic expertise served him well in the rivalry and strife of the British intelligence community. He was the only member of the Joint Intelligence Committee to hold his position throughout the war.

The three other positions on the committee were filled by the heads of intelligence from each arm of the services. In 1940, the Director of Military Intelligence was Paddy Beaumont-Nesbitt, an Ulsterman who had also been a Guards officer in the First World War. He became military attaché at the British Embassy in Paris, and the contacts he developed there unfortunately led him to over-estimate France's military strength. He returned from one trip to Paris to declare that the French had 'five generals as good as Foch' – a judgment that led a colleague to state that it was 'because of Paddy that we didn't see how rotten the French had become'.

The head of RAF intelligence was Archie Boyle, a civilian in his fifties who had been in the post when the war began. During the First World War he had served in the army, winning an MC and bar with the Argyll and Sutherland Highlanders. The Director of Naval Intelligence (DNI) was another former serving officer, Rear-Admiral John Godfrey, who brought to JIC meetings an irredu-cible fear of German infiltration of Eire. His main fault was an intolerance of other opinions and a reluctance to modify his own. When Godfrey sent a deputy to committee meetings, Cavendish-Bentinck, as chairman, sighed audibly with relief.

The JIC had been formed in 1936 in the hope that it would coordinate intelligence whenever Chiefs of Staff were planning joint operations. Its members lacked status then and it was largely ignored. It was beefed up in 1939 through the appointment of Cavendish-Bentinck and the three intelligence chiefs, and given a new and somewhat optimistic brief. It was now supposed to pool and assess intelligence from all overseas sources, advise the Cabinet and Chiefs of Staff of the best course of action, and recommend improvements in British intelligence operations. But it still did not have the standing to perform its new role. The various intelligence bodies guarded their territory jealously and even the intelligence chiefs appeared to mistrust the JIC: they often dispatched their deputies to attend, and it was not until February 1940 that all three coincided at the same meeting. The JIC's early judgments did little to inspire confidence in its abilities. In December 1939, it was asked to forecast Hitler's strategy for the following spring. After much deliberation it outlined various possibilities, but declared that it was unable to decide between them. Hitler's choice, it concluded, 'will depend less upon logical deduction than upon the personal and unpredictable decision of the Führer'.

The particular humiliation of the Allies' operation in Norway was that they had been beaten to the post by Germany. They had planned their invasion blissfully unaware that Germany was preparing much the same course. Their ignorance was not the result of a lack of clues to Germany's intentions but of a persistent misreading of the plethora of signs available. The Norwegian operation provides a classic example of the fatal tendency of intelligence and planning staffs to reject unpalatable truths.

The British, at Churchill's behest, had planned their own action precisely because they feared a similar German move. And there were signs of a build-up of German military activity directed towards Scandinavia from as early as January 1940. Then SIS learned that German forces, including paratroops, were assembling for training in Baltic ports. In March, naval intelligence saw a German spy ship hard at work in Norwegian coastal waters and noticed that German mine-laying in the North Sea had ceased. In the same month, military intelligence learned that Germany had called up Danish-speaking reservists, while the Luftwaffe bombed the Fleet Air Arm base at Hatston in the Orkneys – the closest base to Norway.

Yet all this information was interpreted according to well-entrenched positions and prejudices. Thus the Royal Air Force, who feared a Luftwaffe attack on its bases throughout Britain, read the Hatston raid as merely the prelude for a wider onslaught. Military intelligence had long ago concluded that Germany would need between twenty-five and thirty divisions to invade Scandinavia. Since it could trace only six divisions in the relevant areas, an invasion was out of the question. Naval planners were guided by Churchill's obstinate belief that Germany was simply incapable of landing in Scandinavia. The one body which might have put the pieces together and produced a different picture was the JIC, but it lacked either the power or the conviction to do so.

In the first week of April, as the Allied operation neared readiness, the signs of impending German activity grew too powerful to ignore. German troops were assembling in North Sea ports, the Luftwaffe was making reconnaissance flights, enemy radio traffic around the Baltic was intensifying, fast merchant vessels with anti-aircraft guns and flying crews were gathering at Kiel. Still British intelligence resisted the obvious conclusion. The Royal Navy considered that it all presaged only a possible attempt by the German navy to break out into the Atlantic. On 8 April, military intelligence concluded that the German dispositions did not 'support any probability of a Scandinavian invasion' – the only purpose of the widespread German activity was to go on stand-by in case of *British* action. Even when RAF Coastal Command made the first sighting of German invasion ships steaming towards Norway, the Director of Naval Intelligence, John Godfrey, rejected the evidence of the airmen's eyes. He passed on the suggestion that Germany was about to attack with the comment that 'all these reports are of doubtful value and may well be only a further move in the war of nerves'. Less than a day later, this obstinate and culpable optimism was finally shattered.

It might have been assumed that when the JIC assembled at Richmond Terrace on 2 May it would be in a chastened mood. Even now, however, the illusions persisted. What is remarkable is the extent to which the committee embraced a patently hysterical concept to explain away what had gone wrong. For it declared, in its subsequent two-part report, that both the rapid collapse of Norway and Denmark, and its own total failure to anticipate these events, were the fault of the German Fifth Column.

The JIC considered first the nature of 'German subversive activities in Foreign Countries'. The Germans' method, the committee declared, was 'infiltration under cover of bribery and intimidation', their aim being 'to paralyse opposition by an intensive preparation based on these methods which at the critical moment results in the Home authorities being paralysed and deprived of control'. And the German invasion of Norway, the committee stated, provided 'the *locus classicus* for the result of a successful preparation of the ground'.

However, the JIC was as hard pressed as Leland Stowe had been to provide evidence for this extravagant claim. It limited itself to citing a 'few selected instances' which hardly made its case. Thus, 'telephone exchanges were early in German hands and military communications cut. . . Norwegian munition factories and arsenals were captured by the Germans so early as to pre-suppose an exact knowledge of their location and defences.' Both of these items were well within the ambit of routine intelligence gathering by the German Embassy, which had, after all, remained in business in Oslo until the invasion. Another example was equally weak, pointing merely to disarray among Norway's surprised defenders: '. . . contradictory orders were given to Norwegian forts and arsenals; and also orders which interfered with Norwegian mobilization, thus making it seem that the Germans had a knowledge of Norwegian mobilization procedures.'

In the final instances it provided, the JIC laid itself bare. It claimed that a 'special section' of German intelligence had been given the task, 'utilized to the fullest extent in the invasion of Norway', of spreading 'false reports regarding German intentions and misleading statements as to the objectives for contemplated operations'. In other words, British intelligence had not misread the signs that pointed to a German invasion; it had been deliberately duped. It is scarcely possible to reconcile this claim with the next made by the committee: ' . . . it is of great importance to note that these detailed plans were most carefully concealed until the moment of putting them into force and that there was no premature disclosure of any kind.' Put another way, while the Germans had fooled the British by laying a trail of false and misleading clues, they had managed to prepare for their true objectives in total secrecy.

This part of the committee's report constituted a dismal apology for its own failure, with its sense of bewilderment unconcealed. It was not the limit of the JIC's deliberations, for it now considered the implications for the defence of Britain, in a section headed ' "Fifth Column" activities in the United Kingdom'. If for nothing else, this section is notable for being the first time, so far as we can tell, that the phrase 'Fifth Column' was enshrined in an official document of the British government, just eighteen days after it had resurfaced in the press following the German invasion of Norway. And the committee betrayed the same unreasoning anxiety as the newspapers. 'We cannot rule out the possibility that "Fifth Column" activities in this country, at present dormant, might well play a very active and highly dangerous part at the appropriate moment selected by the enemy.' Then it added, without logic, that 'the absence of sabotage up to date reinforces the view that such activities will only take place as part of a prearranged military plan'. That the absence of sabotage to date might reinforce any other view was apparently rejected.

Where in Britain might the Fifth Column be harboured? The committee had already enumerated the Germans on the Continent who might help to prepare for invasion, including students, businessmen, German women who married foreigners, and the German War Graves Commission, which provided 'cover for an intensive connection with Belgian horticulturists and florists'.

The committee directed its sternest stare at refugees. Germany often planted them abroad 'in order to establish channels of influence (in which money may circulate) in industrial and financial circles. Whether they be refugees or not, there seems little doubt that all residents of German blood or with German marriage ties are regarded by those in control as potential units of influence, whether or not their activities remain dormant until the hoped-for day dawns.' It was desperately flimsy stuff. But here was one transition in the argument which could be made with ease. There were refugees of dubious loyalty abroad; there were refugees in Britain. The committee now drew up a list of 'the main features of "Fifth Column" activity with which we are confronted in this country'. And heading the list was: 'The presence of 73,000 non-interned enemy aliens and 164,000 non-enemy aliens.' QED.

There were other possible havens for the Fifth Column in Britain: the British Union of Fascists ('8,700 subscribing members'); the Communist Party ('well organized with 20,000 pledged subscribing members — the *Daily Worker* circulation is 90,000'); and the IRA ('strength in United Kingdom unknown'). While conceding that direct evidence was difficult to obtain, the committee felt it probable that 'the enemy has an organization drawn from members of the above categories which would act in his support at the appropriate moment'.

The JIC now moved inexorably to its conclusion. 'We fully realize that high political considerations arise in regard to taking firm action against aliens or interfering with the liberty of British subjects. Nevertheless, in our opinion the safety of the State must come first and all evidence shows that action deferred till an emergency arises has been, and will be, too late.' The committee had stopped short of saying so, but the conclusion was clear: all enemy aliens should be interned.

It is, of course, easy to criticize the JIC's lamentable report from a standpoint forty years on. One of those close to the committee's deliberations asks now that Britain's sense of isolation and imminent threat be given due account. The JIC's recommendations were 'rather dramatic', he agrees, but adds: 'There's nothing like being wise after the event — we had our backs up against the wall at the time.' It can also be said that the Norwegian débâcle forced British intelligence, like the rest of the British fighting machine, to confront its own inadequacies. It was not long, for example, before the committee's reports included gradings for the reliability of its sources (A to E) and the strength of their information (1 to 5).

At the end of May, the entire intelligence community was shaken up in a reorganization we shall consider later. And later in the year, in December, the Director of Military Intelligence, Paddy Beaumont-Nesbitt, was transferred to the British Embassy in Washington. The RAF's Archie Boyle left soon afterwards. The intemperate naval intelligence director, John Godfrey, hung on the longest, finally departing after a spectacular inter-service row in the summer of 1942. When his performance was formally reviewed in mid war, his new colleagues on the JIC went so far as to oppose his reappointment. The First Sea Lord, Sir Dudley Pound, took their opposition as a personal slight and insisted on an inquiry. But after evidence from both Cavendish-Bentinck and Sir Stuart Menzies – the mythical head of SIS – Pound was forced to concede that Godfrey's unpopularity was widespread, and tactfully appointed him Commander of the Indian Navy. (His continued irascibility contributed to constant rows and dissent in India, and in 1945 Godfrey was the only naval officer of his rank and seniority to receive no recognition of his war service.)

In May 1940, however, there was nothing to prevent the JIC's report from making due progress through the highest echelons of government. Its first stop was at the committee of the Chiefs of Staff. This committee's members were then Sir Dudley Pound for the navy, Sir Cyril Newall for the air force, and the army's Sir Edmund Ironside: three men whose tenure was to prove as brief as those of the service members of the JIC. The longest *in situ* was Pound, a glutton for work who died from the strain of office in 1943. Newall saw through the Battle of Britain before being relieved at the height of the London blitz in the autumn of 1940, becoming Governor-General of New Zealand. Shortest-lived was Ironside, who left the Chiefs of Staff committee to become Commander-in-Chief of the British Home Forces on 27 May – a post he held for barely one month. And it is clear that the air of unreality which pervaded Britain throughout the winter of 1939–40 was still present when the three military chiefs met in the Cabinet war room during the first week of May to ponder the implications of Germany's attack on Norway and wonder where Hitler might strike next.

On 3 May, they discussed what Britain should do in the event of Germany attacking the Netherlands. They felt that this would be merely a preliminary to an attack on Britain and should be stopped at all costs. As soon as it occurred, the British and French armies should advance into Belgium while the RAF should bomb the Ruhr. On 4 May they turned to the threat of a German attack on France – 'a possibility we cannot ignore'. But they concluded that, with air support, 'there are at present sufficient land forces to maintain the security of French territory against both Germany and Italy'. A day or so later they met again to consider further a potential invasion of Britain. By now they had received the JIC's report on the Fifth Column. And whereas on 4 May they had felt that the main threat to Britain would come from the air, and did not refer to the Fifth Column at all, they now embraced the JIC's assumptions wholesale. Citing the committee's conclusions, they declared: 'Enemy "Fifth Column" activities will be designed to play a dangerous part in any operation which Germany may undertake against this country.' They pointed out the 'extent to which freedom of action is given to enemy aliens in this country'. In proposing a remedy, they were slightly hesitant, recommending only that 'adequate steps' be taken.

While Pound, Newall and Ironside were deliberating, major political and military dramas were being enacted in Britain and abroad. Britain was in the process of acquiring a new Prime Minister. It was Churchill who had been the instigator and loudest advocate of the Norwegian operation, and the most insistent that Germany posed no counter-threat. It was Churchill who now reaped the political reward of the disaster. The great Commons debate which ended Chamberlain's three-year span as Prime Minister began on 7 May; at the end, forty-one Conservatives voted against the government and sixty more abstained. On 9 May, Chamberlain, Halifax and Churchill convened and agreed that Churchill should take over. 'I was conscious of a profound sense of relief,' Churchill wrote later. 'At last I had the authority to give direction over the whole scene.' On 10 May he attended Buckingham Palace to be asked by King George VI to form a new government. At dawn that same day, Germany attacked Holland, Belgium and Luxembourg. German forces moved across the Dutch frontier in the east, while airborne troops attacked Rotterdam and The Hague. Seven Panzer divisions swept into Belgium and Luxembourg and parachutists attacked the giant Belgian fortress of Eben Emael. Luxembourg fell on the first day.

The first Cabinet chaired by Churchill was due to be held at 12.30 the following day, 11 May. The fourth item on the agenda was 'Invasion of Great Britain'. At the Home Office, Sir John Anderson knew that the internment of aliens was bound to be raised.

10 A Precautionary Measure

The date 11 May marks the start of a sustained battle within the British government over internment. It can be divided into three phases. The first was fought in Cabinet and lasted for two and a half weeks, during which internment was discussed nine times. During the second phase, the most murky and sinister in the entire story of internment, the discussion was removed from the forum of the Cabinet, to be conducted out of sight elsewhere. The third phase began when visible disasters struck and the debate was dragged back into the public domain.

The Home Office was fighting on three grounds. The first was the understandable desire of any ministry to defend its territory. The Home Office had initially been afraid of becoming enmeshed in the muddle and chaos that had characterized internment during the First World War. But it found that, to maintain its hold over traditional areas such as aliens and refugee policy, it could no longer hold back from internment, and became more and more involved in its consequences.

The second was Anderson's ingrained determination to see that policy was administered consistently and efficiently, following the pattern of his ten-year spell as the ministry's Permanent Under-Secretary. It is, in fact, possible to interpret the Home Office's behaviour throughout this central period as reflecting concern for that alone. However, it also appears from Anderson's words to his father that he genuinely cared for the content of the policy he was trying to protect. Simply stated, that concern – the third ground on which the Home Office was fighting – was for the freedom of the individual from arbitrary demands by the state.

We have not been helped in our attempt at an interpretation by the infuriating refusal of the Home Office today to shed any light on even this fundamental issue. In vain did we argue that the Home Office had been heaped with undue opprobrium, both at the time and since, and that its record may well have been far more creditable than its critics have allowed. Until its files are released, it is impossible to make any final judgment. But it is important to note that, shortly before the battle commenced, Anderson had been rejoined by Frank Newsam, one of the ministry's towers of strength.

Newsam had been Anderson's private secretary at the Home Office in the heady days of the 1926 General Strike. He progressed to become principal private secretary to successive Home Secretaries from 1927 to 1933. When Anderson returned to the Home Office as a minister in 1938, Newsam helped him in the preparations for air raids and civil defence. It was principally Newsam who devised the system of tribunals in the last days of peace. When the war began, he was seconded to act as Chief of Staff to the Regional Commissioner for the South-East, part of the emergency scheme of government in the event of civil breakdown or invasion.

Newsam was a tall, dominating figure with an intriguingly dark pigmentation, the product of a mixed match among his forebears in Barbados. He was renowned in Whitehall for his unusual inclination to speak his mind. Whitehall also considered him as a liberal, a term not necessarily applied with approval. One senior intelligence man, who complained of the 'cossetting' of aliens, saw Newsam as 'steeped in Home Office tradition'. Newsam would have approved the description. He saw the Home Office as 'the last bulwark of liberal opinion', whose task was 'to maintain, in a world that seems to pay diminishing regard to such a principle, the widest possible liberty consistent with law and order'. He believed that the Home Office should hold 'the necessary balance between too much and too little liberty'. He conceded that, in times of war, the balance might need adjustment: then 'liberty must be curtailed, and novel methods have to be adopted which sometimes run counter to accepted British traditions'. Exactly where the balance should be struck, and who was to control the scales, were issues at the heart of the ensuing struggle.

Newsam returned to the Home Office in the spring of 1940 in the position of assistant under-secretary – number two to Sir Alexander Maxwell, the Permanent Under-Secretary. Maxwell lacked Newsam's presence – as one former colleague put it, he was 'not the kind of person you'd notice on a bus'. But Maxwell, Newsam and Anderson made a powerful triumvirate, doughty opposition for those who wished to alter their arrangements for internment. In its defence, they used every stratagem for obstruction and delay known to Whitehall: setting up committees, calling for reports, seeking to spread responsibilities, making concessions in slow and considered steps. For connoisseurs of the political process, it was a superb performance worthy of greater success than it achieved.

The Home Office's battle coincided with the period when, as Churchill told the world, Britain stood and fought alone. Much the same could be said of the Home Office, which for a time had every major force in the wartime government ranged against it, including the War Office, the Foreign Office, the Chiefs of Staff, the Joint Intelligence Committee and MI5. Not surprisingly, the Home Office succumbed, until alliances forged with former opponents enabled it to assert itself again. The enduring personal tragedy is that those alliances came too late for the victims of the *Arandora Star*.

The Home Office began with a resounding defeat. In the first days of May, the Chiefs of Staff had predicted that a German attack on the Low Countries would be followed by an invasion of Britain. The Chiefs of Staff unveiled their counter-plan, and the British army moved east to link up with the Belgians, cheered valiantly by the British press. On 11 May the page 1 headline of the *Daily Telegraph* declared: 'BEF Moved into Belgium Smoothly as a Machine'.

The Chiefs of Staff turned to the home front. They had already endorsed the JIC's recommendation over the Fifth Column, asking for 'adequate steps' against enemy aliens. They were now strongly placed to see that these steps were taken.

On 10 May Churchill had formed the Home Defence Executive, with a brief to prepare for invasion. It consisted of the Commander-in-Chief of the Home Forces, General Sir Walter M. St G. Kirke, the three Chiefs of Staff, and a solitary Home Office man. Later in the war, Anderson revealed what happened that evening.

The military authorities came to me and represented that, in view of the imminent risk of invasion, it was in their opinion of the utmost importance that every male alien between sixteen and seventy should be removed forthwith from the coastal strip which in their view was the part of the country likely, if invasion took place, to be affected. I listened to the representations of the military authorities and came to the conclusion that it was quite impossible to reject the case put before me.

Anderson was hardly able to resist an appeal from authority in such concentration. He told a Cabinet Committee early the following morning that, at the urgent request of the Secretary of State for War, he proposed 'to issue immediate instructions for the internment of all enemy aliens in areas where German parachute troops are likely to land'. It is clear that, by the time Anderson attended the War Cabinet at 12.30 p.m., he had no options left.

The meeting was the first to be chaired by Winston Churchill as Prime Minister. The fourth item concerned the threat of invasion. Churchill first asked whether the police should not be armed, and Anderson was deputed to pursue the matter with General Ismay, the Cabinet's military deputy secretary.* Then the question of internment was raised. Sir John Dill, Vice-Chief of the Imperial General Staff, summarized the conclusions the Cabinet Committee had already reached. He added:

In the light of the possibility of invasion, it was very desirable that all enemy aliens in counties on the South-East and East [sic] should be interned. No doubt 90 per cent of such aliens were well disposed towards this country, but it was impossible to pick out the small proportion of aliens who probably constituted a dangerous element. In the circumstances, the only course seemed to be that all aliens in these areas should be interned for the present. The number was probably 4,000 or 5,000.

Anderson's reply was brief, and contained only a hint of resistance: 'The Home Secretary, who had been consulted, said that if the course were pressed on military grounds, he would agree to it.' The Cabinet made two concessions to Anderson. He should issue instructions to intern all male enemy aliens between sixteen and sixty, not seventy, in the relevant areas. It was also agreed that

* There was a civil deputy secretary, too, Sir Rupert Howarth. They both served under the Cabinet's permanent secretary, Sir Edward Bridges.

the 'continuance of this measure should be subject to review when the situation seemed less threatening'.

At the Home Office, Newsam drafted a telegram to the chief constables who would be responsible for the arrests. The area concerned appeared to have grown considerably from the 'coastal strip' referred to by Anderson or even the 'counties on the South-East and East' spoken of by Dill. No fewer than thirty-one counties, in whole or in part, were included in the definition, from Hampshire in southern England, to Nairn in north-east Scotland. The telegram instructed the police to start their arrests at 8 a.m. the following day, a Sunday.

Newsam's first draft was a terse document, strictly to the point. Paragraph 2 ordered: 'Any German or Austrian detained in pursuance of this direction should be handed over as soon as possible to the military authorities.' By the time it was transmitted, an important addition had been made. Paragraph 4, notably softer in tone, read: 'Every consideration should be shown by the police to persons detained in pursuance of this direction and the usual facilities should be given to them to make any necessary arrangements before their internment. It must be remembered that the majority are well-disposed to this country and their temporary internment is merely a precautionary measure . . . ' The eleventh and penultimate paragraph was almost an apology:

> The measures described in this telegram are to be regarded as a measure of defence taken as a matter of urgency in an area which must, for the time being, be regarded as a zone of possible military operations. It is intended that the rigour of these measures should be mitigated as soon as circumstances permit.

Several problems now loomed large. The first was that no one knew how many internees there were in the 'coastal counties' – the Home Office could not improve on Dill's estimate of '4,000 to 5,000'. The second was that there was nowhere to put them.

Just which internees were living in the 'coastal counties' was a matter of historical chance. For those desperate to leave Germany, which part of Britain they came to was the least of their worries. One young man who now found himself in the wrong place at the wrong time was Leopold Kohn. Aged sixteen, he had lived with his mother in an apartment in the second district of Vienna. On leaving school, he had worked as an office boy in a Jewish advertising firm, and was there at the time of *Kristallnacht*. His mother had to care for his aged grandmother, but she advised Leopold to go. The Quaker Society of Friends was helping to provide young people with permits to learn skills in Britain, and its Vienna office told Kohn he could train as a butcher, baker or glove-maker. Kohn, who thought he would like to be a pastry-cook, chose baking.

Kohn left Vienna on 13 June 1939, one of a trainload of children – some only infants – who were going to England without their parents. Their route lay through Germany to the Hook of Holland and Harwich. A Quaker met him at the port and took him to his new home, at the village of Bungay in Suffolk. The Society of Friends had offered the local baker three potential trainees and attached their photographs; the baker selected Kohn because he looked very neat in his smart brown lederhosen.

He settled down quickly in Bungay. He enjoyed baking, thought his wages of 10*s* (50p) a week were ample, and was treated well by everyone in the village. Every other weekend he cycled five miles to the next village to see another boy from Vienna. From time to time letters from his mother arrived. He went before a tribunal and was classified as 'C' without fuss. There were few other signs of war.

Bungay's village policeman called for him on 12 May. He told Kohn that he would be away for the night and that he should bring his pyjamas and toothbrush. He was taken to a school at Bury St Edmunds which already held one hundred or so boys and men. It had a concrete floor and there was one blanket between three. When Kohn asked to use the lavatory, he was escorted by a British soldier carrying a fixed bayonet. He handed over his alien's registration certificate; when it came back it was stamped 'Interned'.

Because he was reading mathematics at a world-renowned university that happened to fall within the 'coastal strip', Hermann Bondi was also arrested on 12 May. Bondi, a Jewish doctor's son, left Vienna in the summer of 1937 to take up a place at Trinity College, Cambridge, arriving just before his eighteenth birthday. His parents joined him in Britain in 1938 and lived in London. He received a 'C' at his tribunal in November 1938 and was also classified as a refugee from Nazi oppression. He was one of a large and distinguished coterie of academics and undergraduates who were arrested in Cambridge, including a consignment from the

London School of Economics who had moved to Cambridge at the start of the war. They, too, slept on the concrete floor of the school at Bury St Edmunds.

Edinburgh was also in the 'coastal strip', and Kurt Tebrich had lived there since March 1939. Aged sixteen, he was from Hamburg and, like Hermann Bondi, was the son of a doctor. His parents were liberal Jews.

Tebrich travelled to Britain on a children's train and went to live with an Orthodox Jewish family in Edinburgh. They disapproved when he made non-Jewish friends at school and their strict outlook made him homesick. Thus he was not entirely dismayed at the turn of events of 12 May. He had just heard the latest battle news from Belgium and Holland on the wireless and was trying to concentrate on his homework, when the police arrived. He was thrilled at being arrested and pleased at the prospect of escaping from the Jewish family, even though his foster-mother was in tears. He was taken to the deaf-and-dumb school that already housed Germans and Austrians arrested in 1939.

Sir John Dill had overestimated the male enemy aliens in the coastal counties, for the number arrested was little more than 2,000. It was fortunate for the War Office that the number was no higher. At the start of the war, of course, the War Office had prepared twenty-seven camps to house 18,000 internees. That capacity had since been drastically reduced.

Some camps – Clacton was one – had been closed because they were on the East Coast, considered a likely invasion site; Fontwell Park Race Course had simply been condemned. But the new tribunal system meant that many camps were not being used at all and the War Office eyed them covetously. In January 1940, the Home Office agreed that fourteen camps could be used for other purposes. A remarkably candid briefing to the American Embassy by the Home Office in January 1941 reveals the inevitable consequence: 'When the Cabinet decided that the threat of invasion justified the reinstatement of the original internment policy, no proper arrangements had been planned by the Home or War Office to care immediately for a large number of internees.'

In some desperation, the two ministries searched for fresh accommodation. They lit upon a council housing estate at Huyton, near Liverpool, that was in the final stages of construction. It did not matter that there were piles of rubble everywhere and the contractors' huts were still standing – any deficiencies could be made up by pitching tents in a field near-by. The entire estate was surrounded by a barbed-wire fence eight feet high. The first internees arrived at Huyton on 17 May. Twelve men were allocated to each of the barely completed council houses which contained no furniture at all. In the army manner, they were given a sack each and told to stuff them with straw to make palliasses. The houses did have cold water, but there were no towels, very little toilet paper, and one 2-ounce tablet of soap each per week. As young men, Bondi and Kohn were not too dismayed at the conditions, even though Kohn had to sleep in a tent. It promptly rained, of course, and the field around soon became a sea of mud.

The greatest discomfort was experienced by the distressingly large proportion of sick and elderly internees at Huyton. In his telegram, Newsam had instructed the police to arrest 'all males over the age of 16 and under the age of 60 (excluding the invalid or infirm) . . .' Perhaps Newsam had not emphasized the point enough. An official report to the British Cabinet later related: '. . . a large number of the internees on arrival proved to be suffering from more or less serious complaints, including diabetes, heart trouble, various gastric afflictions, paralysis and blindness. There were even some mental cases and cripples.'

The report was by Lord Snell, a former Labour MP who had been the pre-war Leader of the London County Council. Although dressed in niceties about the staff of Huyton 'doing their best within limited resources', it was a damning indictment of the haste with which internment had been carried out. Snell estimated that 40 per cent of the internees were over fifty, many were over sixty and one third were unfit for internment. A crude hospital had been fashioned out of three of the houses, where most of the patients lay on mattresses on the floor – 'with such attention', Snell records, 'as they could receive from their fellow internees'. There was only one medical officer attached to the camp, although a number of internees with medical qualifications, including British degrees, subsequently helped him in his work. (It must have been a moving moment for the qualified internees who were permitted to assist, as the British Medical Association had adamantly refused to let them practise in Britain.) The difficulties were enormous: 'There was a serious shortage of all medical supplies, in particular of insulin, and the hospital was also short of medical instruments, such as stethoscopes, enemas, and bed-pans. A dentist visited the camp once a week, but was unable in the time to carry out all the work needed.'

Snell also criticized the ban on newspapers, books and wirelesses, and long delays in receiving letters caused by censorship, which led to a feeling of 'complete isolation' and had 'a very bad effect on morale'. The internees were:

> mostly persons who were well-disposed to this country. They felt keenly that they were being treated, not as friends, but as enemy aliens. They had been taken at the shortest notice from their friends and families. The lack of prompt facilities for correspondence with their families and of, at times, news of the progress of the war, caused much mental hardship.

Not all arrested on 12 May went to Huyton. After several nights at the deaf-and-dumb school, Kurt Tebrich was sent 350 miles by train to London. There he was taken to Scotland Yard and fed a lavish English breakfast of bacon, eggs, tomatoes and fried bread. After a morning spent in a cell so crowded that all inside had to stand up, he was sent to Lingfield Race Course. There were well over 1,000 men there, and the majority were German merchant seamen seized by the Royal Navy. In fact it seemed to Tebrich that the camp was run by Germans. One barked at him in a Hamburg accent when he arrived, telling him he would have to obey orders; the British guards seemed gentle by contrast. The most likable sailors were those who were 'International Seamen', a class largely composed of socialists and communists who had left Germany to work on neutral ships. The proportion of Nazis among the German-based seamen was correspondingly high, but a sea captain named Scharf did much by quiet diplomacy to ease tensions between the groups. A young Catholic priest was particularly kind to Tebrich and the other young men at Lingfield, listening patiently as they recounted their problems. Tebrich found his sleeping quarters under Lingfield's grandstand quite comfortable, and did not mind the bucket toilets or the cold showers.

There were now over 5,000 people interned in Britain. Both Lord Snell and the Home Office man who briefed the American Embassy made it quite clear that the government's abrupt U-turn over internment had been the cause of the immense strain on Britain's resources and the consequent chaos and suffering. The onward march of the German army and the fast-deteriorating

position of the Allies now meant that the pressure for wider internment was increasing day by day.

11   The Threat Below Stairs

On 12 May, the German forces who had attacked Holland from east and west linked up across the country. They did so just ahead of the French troops who had been hoping to shore up the Dutch defences. Queen Wilhelmina of Holland and her government fled to London on 13 May. Rotterdam capitulated on being bombed on 14 May. On 15 May Holland formally surrendered.

The news from Belgium was even worse. The parachutists who landed on top of the key fortress of Eben Emael held it long enough for ground reinforcements to arrive. On 14 May, the British and French forces, moving eastwards, linked up with the Belgian army, but their alliance proved short-lived. Further south, General Guderian's tank columns had crossed the Meuse and were pounding along clear roads towards Paris and the Channel. Behind him, massed ranks of German infantry surged through the Ardennes. The British now had to save not Belgium, but themselves. The retreat which ended at Dunkirk began.

Among those who took part in the undignified flight from Holland was Sir Nevile Bland, British Minister to the Dutch government at The Hague. Bland arrived in England in the small hours of 14 May, having crossed the North Sea in a British warship which narrowly survived several air attacks. He met Lord Halifax later that day, and in some agitation described the devastating tactics Germany had used to hasten Holland's downfall. When Halifax asked Bland to write it all down, Bland retired to the

International Sportsman's Club in Upper Grosvenor Street, May-fair, where he penned a 1,000-word account of what he knew. He headed it: 'Fifth Column Menace'.

Bland's report is a remarkable document, running the gamut of the darkest fears which the phrase 'Fifth Column' inspired. It is also notable for giving the concept a new and more fearful dimension, for Bland incorporated with it a dread of another of Germany's most modern weapons: the use of parachute troops. In short, Holland had been simultaneously subverted by invisible traitors within and descended upon by irresistible spectres from the air.

The parachutists who attacked Rotterdam and The Hague were 'all boys of 16 to 18, completely sodden with Hitler's ideas, and with nothing else in their minds but to cause as much death and destruction as they could before being killed themselves. They dropped on the roofs of houses, in open spaces – even in private gardens.' What was more, the enemy troops had arrived in Holland thoroughly briefed about the disposition of the Dutch army, and equipped with a list of officials and Allied sympathizers who were to be 'shot at sight'.

Bland was an old Etonian and a classical scholar. A Dutch diplomat once wrote that he was an Englishman who symbolized 'the image of an era and of a style of life'. There are strong echoes in Bland's report of fears for that era and that style. Who had provided the Germans with their information about the Dutch dispositions, their death list? The culprit, Bland believed, was to be found below stairs. 'The paltriest kitchen maid,' he wrote, 'not only can be, but generally is, a menace to the safety of the country.' His fears soon became a nightmare, worthy of Dante or Blake:

Every German or Austrian servant, however superficially charming and devoted, is a real and grave menace, and we cannot conclude from the experiences of the last war that 'the enemy in our midst' is no less dangerous than it was then. I have not the least doubt that, when the signal is given, as it will scarcely fail to be when Hitler so decides, there will be satellites of the monster *all over the country* who will at once embark on widespread sabotage and attacks on civilians and the military indiscriminately. We cannot afford to take this risk. ALL Germans and Austrians, at least, ought to be interned at once.

As it later emerged, the truth about the fall of Holland was very different from Bland's fevered imaginings. The Germans achieved only mixed results with parachutists, who numbered 4,000 out of a total invasion force of some thirty divisions or 360,000 men. They captured several Dutch bridges across the Rhine, but were much aided by the optimism of Dutch commanders who were expecting French reinforcements to arrive by the same bridges and had omitted to lay explosive charges. At The Hague where Bland was stationed, parachutists largely failed. They landed over a scattered area and suffered many casualties in a fierce Dutch counterattack. This did significantly divert Dutch forces from elsewhere and so contribute to a German victory; but the failure of the parachutists to advance into The Hague enabled Queen Wilhelmina and her government to escape. It is true that Germany had installed agents in The Hague with instructions to help guide the parachute troops to the Dutch seat of government. But they were unable to fulfil this role; and they were certainly not posing as servant girls. It is also true that a list of prominent Dutch citizens and others likely to oppose the occupation was found on the body of a German intelligence officer near The Hague, but Bland's notion that they were to be 'shot at sight' appears to be an invention.

Much else, however, Bland could not have known at the time, and the frightening vision he evoked was shortly to have a powerful impact on the government's thinking. But some British officials were already concerned at the incipient panic over parachutists. On 13 May the *Daily Telegraph* reported that German paratroops had been captured in Holland 'disguised as peasants or clergymen, or wearing Dutch uniforms'. (The Dutch historian Louis de Jong was later able to find only very limited examples of the use of disguise, as when a small group of German soldiers wearing Dutch-style cardboard helmets tried to capture a bridge; they were soon spotted and the attack failed.) On the same day, the *Daily Express* described how some British villages and districts were organizing 'parachute patrols'. This alarmed the Air Ministry for on several occasions already Allied airmen had parachuted to safety over Britain or France, only to be attacked by civilians on landing.

The Home Office took up the Air Ministry's cause and drafted precautionary instructions to civilians. One of these ordered: 'No civilian must fire on any parachutist or airman until he has landed, and not then, until he is certain that the airman or parachutist is an enemy.' The instructions were never published. (Discussions on

the subject eventually led to the formation of the Local Defence
Volunteers – the Home Guard, or 'Dad's Army'.)

The panic afflicted every party to the conflict. On 12 May, the
French Prime Minister, Paul Reynaud, claimed that German parachutists had been disguised as civilians or Allied soldiers, and
warned that they would be shot as spies. On 13 May, the German
Foreign Ministry denounced Reynaud's claim as a lie:

> M. Reynaud is no soldier, and he seems therefore not to know
> that parachute battalions are regular units of the German armed
> forces established in peacetime and trained for their particular
> task. . . Their uniform is generally known . . . and cannot be
> confused either with civilian clothing or with any uniform of a
> foreign army. Should M. Reynaud nevertheless be seeking an
> excuse to vent his hatred on the gallant parachutists, immediate
> retaliation will be taken by the German armed forces against
> this unprecedented violation of international law.

The revenge Germany threatened was scarcely in keeping with
international law either: for every German parachutist shot as a
spy, *ten* Allied prisoners would be executed. The problem for the
German Foreign Ministry was how to communicate its threat. As
it had done during the attempts to repatriate civilians, it handed
its statement to the American Embassy in Berlin, and asked for it
to be forwarded to the British, French, Belgian and Dutch governments. In Washington the intemperate language on all sides so
alarmed the State Department that it decided that it should not
'mix in this bitter controversy between the belligerents', and
declined to pass the warning on. It was only later that the British
received a copy of the German note via the Swiss government.

It was thus almost without challenge that the Bland report was
given prompt distribution in Whitehall. It was typed out in the
early hours of 15 May – the colleague supervising this operation
noting that it was 'damned good stuff' – and a copy was waiting
for Lord Halifax when he arrived at his desk in the morning. Sir
Alexander Cadogan sent another to Anderson at the Home Office.

Halifax took his copy to the Cabinet meeting at 11 a.m., and as
is natural when Ministers present their officials' work, enthusiastically endorsed its contents. Halifax said that Bland had described
'the elaborate organization for cooperation between German parachutists and Fifth Column elements in the Netherlands', and asked

that his report be 'brought to the attention of those responsible for Britain's defences'.

Several of those responsible for Britain's defences were present at the meeting. One was the Chief of Air Staff, Sir Cyril Newall, whose contribution to the discussion reflected the RAF's concern about its airmen being attacked. He told the Cabinet that there had been several reports of parachute descents on Britain the previous night. Some had been inspired by lightning striking barrage balloons, and none had been substantiated. 'These rumours were indicative of the nervous state of the public,' Newall felt. Churchill was in no doubt what should be done. He wanted 'a very large round-up of enemy aliens and suspect persons', adding that it was 'much better that these persons should be behind barbed wire'.

All eyes must have been on Anderson. He warned that the question of aliens and the Fifth Column raised 'a number of very difficult problems', and he proposed that a committee be set up to study them. It was a classic Whitehall defensive ploy, and it succeeded. A three-man committee was formed, comprising Anderson and two Labour men, Clement Attlee and Arthur Greenwood, whom Churchill had brought into the Cabinet in the interests of national unity. Churchill impatiently asked the committee to present its report 'in a few days' time'.

The most intriguing aspect of Anderson's performance lay in what he did not say. On 12 May, the day of the arrests in the coastal counties, the Home Office had drafted provisional instructions to the police to intern Category 'B' aliens throughout Britain. Anderson did not reveal this to his Cabinet colleagues then or on 15 May. But when he emerged from the Cabinet meeting, he told his officials to instruct the police to start arrests the following day.

The most positive interpretation of Anderson's move is that he ordered the move, and kept silent about it, to hold in reserve a concession to inevitable demands for mass internment. At all events, the new orders brought a further 3,000 men into the net. Among them was a forty-three-year-old Jewish journalist named Richard Broh.

Like Franz Eichenberg, Broh had fought bravely for Germany in the First World War, surviving two years of mud and snow on the Eastern Front before being invalided home in 1917. He was found a desk job as controller of medals in the German War Office, and in 1918 his war record helped him win election to the Soldiers and Burghers Council – a local government assembly – of Berlin. He also became active in trade union affairs.

Broh became a journalist in 1926, specializing in economic affairs and writing for a range of papers and magazines that included the official journal of the German socialist party (SPD). In 1933, his war record gave him a degree of immunity from the ravages of the Nazi police. It lasted until 1935, when Josef Goebbels, Minister of Propaganda, was affronted to discover that the Reich Press Chamber – the state-controlled journalists' association – still contained twelve Jews, Broh among them. He ordered them to be expelled.

The twelve journalists decided on a bold and provocative response. They would fight Goebbels through the Peoples' Courts which were still supposedly free from party control. They exploited every legal loophole and dragged the case into 1936. Their chances seemed to improve when Germany staged the Olympic Games and the Nazis wanted to show their fairest face. But by June 1937, their last delaying tactic was exhausted, and the court confirmed their expulsion from the Press Chamber.

The Nazis were now determined to crush those who had dared to challenge them. Only Richard Broh managed to escape. A publisher gave him a letter promising employment as a British correspondent, and Broh and his wife caught the next plane from Berlin to Croydon airport. The other eleven journalists were arrested and sent to concentration camps. Broh and his wife lived in a flat in Streatham, and he continued to write for German newspapers. They moulded his material as best they could and published it without a byline.

When the tribunals were announced in September 1939, Broh assumed that he would receive a 'C' and be dubbed a refugee from Nazi oppression. But he grew apprehensive when the weeks passed without a summons to appear. He called at Brixton Police Station several times to ask for a hearing, and eventually a date was fixed. Then he was told that the hearing would have to be postponed as all his papers had been lost. Broh appealed to the Council for German Jewry, but they seemed unable to help. His fears were realized on 16 May 1940, when the head of Brixton CID called and told him that he appeared on the list of Category 'B' aliens. 'I'm very sorry,' he told Broh, 'but I have my orders.' Broh was sent to Kempton Park Race Course, where he met another journalist who had just been interned by the British for the fourth time in his life: Karl Wehner.

After his release from Seaton, Wehner assumed that MI5 had cleared him once and for all. None the less he and his wife Johanna were called before a tribunal and were mortified to be placed in Category 'B'. Wehner was arrested in Highgate on 16 May. It was clear to both him and Broh that the army had been all but over-whelmed. They were billeted in the offices of the Tote organization, while others slept in the stables or in tents. They were given thin mattresses and two blankets each; one room which contained 100 men had no furniture at all. They soon found that the men guard-ing them were somewhat confused about who they were. As Weh-ner was queueing for lunch in the canteen, he saw an officer brandish a revolver at a sixteen-year-old youth.

'Are you Jewish?' the officer asked.

'Yes,' the boy replied.

'Are there many Jews here?'

'About 80 per cent.'

'Damn!' the officer exclaimed. 'I knew we'd got the wrong lot.'

On 15 May, the Joint Intelligence Committee met to consider the Fifth Column again. It had more knowledge of German methods, but its deliberations that day provide a further illustration of the tendency of intelligence bodies to select information pointing towards courses of action they already favour.

Like Sir Nevile Bland, the JIC had a German document to ponder. It had been taken from an officer of the German 22nd Airborne Division captured by the Dutch, and summarized its plans for landing near The Hague. It scarcely bore out the picture of the Germans as super-efficient: the division was comprised of two infantry regiments and an artillery regiment, but the artillery regiment had arrived without any guns. It also revealed that the Germans had acquired their latest intelligence without undue sub-terfuge. Two days before the invasion, the German military attaché at The Hague had inspected Holland's defences on the simple pretext of making a tour of the Dutch tulip fields.

The British army had also supplied a surprisingly cool appraisal of Germany's use of parachute troops, in the latest of its series 'Periodical Notes on the German Army' (sternly marked: 'Not to be Taken into the Front Line'). Carefully sifting available evidence and statistics, it analysed the role of German parachutists since the war began. They had succeeded in Poland in September 1939 because Poland contained one million Germans with legitimate grievances who had willingly supported them. In Norway, there was no such German minority and only limited use of parachutists had been made. Many who did go into action had jumped from insufficient height and had been injured or killed. Others lacked supplies or reinforcements and were soon captured. The army report judged that parachute and airborne troops could only operate successfully where the German air force had clear superiority, where other troops could reinforce them, and where they could be provided with transport and supplies. In the case of Britain, the report concluded, none of these factors was likely to apply.

The JIC was disinclined to accept such conclusions, which did not accord with its well-entrenched prejudices. It gave at least as much weight to a report by Admiral Godfrey, who was preoccupied by Ireland again. This was entitled: 'Fifth Column Activities in Eire' and was based on a letter received through the ordinary post. Godfrey claimed the source was reliable, although even he conceded that the letter was rather 'cryptic'. It related that the Irish Nazi leader Becker was becoming increasingly bold in his speeches, boasting that Eire could be controlled by 2,000 Germans. It also passed on rumours that an 'unknown Austrian' had landed in Eire from a boat – Godfrey supposed this must mean a U-boat – and that the Galway Golf Club had enrolled several new Austrian members. Godfrey's report had already been widely circulated, with one copy marked for Churchill himself.

In preparing its own summary of the invasion of Holland, the JIC combined realism with further promulgation of Fifth Column myths. It recorded that some German paratroops had to be pushed from their planes; it also contended that the parachutists had made widespread use of bogus uniforms. In its conclusions, it swept all qualifications aside. It made twenty recommendations, some covering relatively minor matters: military uniforms should not be sold to civilians, for example. Others were more drastic: the police should be armed, and Britain should have a military government if the invasion seemed near. The most sweeping conclusion was also its first: the 'limited internment' that had already been ordered was 'inadequate'; it was now 'essential that all enemy aliens, both male and female between the ages of 16 and 70 should be interned'. William Cavendish-Bentinck, the JIC's chairman, sent the report to Sir Alexander Cadogan on 17 May.

Both the committee's offering and that of Sir Nevile Bland were restrained in comparison with a further report then being prepared in a government outpost on the Victoria Embankment named Electra House. It contained a department with somewhat mysterious functions headed by Sir Campbell Stuart whom Chamberlain had appointed 'Director of Propaganda in Enemy Countries' in 1938. At first sight, Stuart was well qualified for his position: a former employee of the Otis Lift Company in Canada, he had written anti-German propaganda in the First World War and had been on the board of *The Times* ever since. Some in the Foreign Office regarded him as a grotesque figure: he was a blatant homosexual with a penchant for buttoned boots, and had achieved a certain notoriety through his attempt to enlist the services of Noël Coward for the nation in September 1939. Stuart had asked Coward to set up a British Bureau of Propaganda in Paris on the outbreak of war. When war came, Coward cancelled his two plays then in rehearsal – *This Happy Breed* and *Present Laughter* – and installed himself in Paris's Ritz Hotel. He found that no one was expecting him and that the Germans were already dropping lurid anti-British cartoons by the ton on France. When he discovered that Stuart had responded by bombarding Germany with six million copies of speeches by Chamberlain and Halifax, Coward sent an acid memorandum: 'If it is the policy of His Majesty's Government to bore the Germans to death, I don't believe that we have quite enough time.' A disillusioned Coward finally left Paris in March 1940.

Later, Stuart's department was absorbed into the Special Operations Executive, and Stuart became Chairman of the Imperial Communications Advisory Committee, with the weighty task of taking care of the General Post Office's submarine telegraph cables. In May 1940 he still had some power, and his officials hurried to interview members of the Dutch government as they arrived in London. Their report provides an extreme example of how information can be distorted to make a particular argument. It will also be interesting to compare it with the result achieved by others who interviewed the Dutch government officials, but who sought to substantiate an entirely different case.

Stuart's memorandum was entitled: 'Operations in Holland' and began with the ludicrous claim that German parachutists had killed between 35,000 and 40,000 Dutch troops. The parachutists had 'manifold disguises', including German, Dutch, Belgian,

French and British military uniforms, and those of the Dutch police. Moreover, they were 'dressed as ordinary civilians on bicycles, peasants, priests, clergymen and schoolboys. Some boys were dressed as girls, while real girls were dressed as nurses, servants and so on.' All were armed with modern automatic weapons and hand grenades – the 'peasant girls' naturally hid these in their baskets. 'They also gave poisoned cigarettes and chocolates to passing troops and civilians.'

Like Sir Nevile Bland, the Stuart report made the fatal elision between paratroops and fifth columnists – who, like parachutists, were to be found everywhere, and in many guises. These included German refugees, Germans who had taken Dutch nationality, German women married to Dutchmen, and Dutch shopkeepers who went to Germany to purchase their supplies. 'The Germans have a gift of making anybody with whom they get into contact into a spy,' the report inelegantly claimed. It included a specific warning, supposedly passed on by the Dutch government: be very careful with refugees.

In truth, the report marked the point where intelligence became fantasy, and fantasy propaganda. Both it and Sir Nevile Bland's report found their way to the Ministry of Information, to be used as the basis for articles offered to the British media. The Ministry of Information was still struggling to be taken seriously. Set up at the start of the war, it was already under its third minister and its third director-general, and was suffering from the irreverent delight which greeted the revelation that it had 999 employees. The ministry was tardy to take up the 'Fifth Column' theme, its own early efforts merely recycling items that had already appeared in the press. Nor did it discern, as it used the new material, the trap it was helping to lay. Lord Haw Haw was soon gleefully broadcasting spoof instructions to fifth columnists from Berlin, and German generals have subsequently related their amusement as the Fifth Column scare spread.

On 30 May, Bland magnified the effect with a talk broadcast by the BBC in which he expanded on his report:

It is not the German or Austrian who is found out who is the danger. It is the one, whether man or woman, who is too clever to be found out. That was apparent in Holland – where, as I have already said, many of the obvious fifth columnists were interned at the outbreak of war – but where there still remained a dreadful number at large to carry out the instructions they had from Germany.

I have had German friends in the past, and I hope that I may live to have a German friend or two again one day; and I hate to have to say this to you but I find it my duty to say it, and say it I will: be careful at this moment how you put complete trust in any person of German or Austrian connections. If you know people of this kind who are still at large, keep your eye on them; they may be perfectly all right – but they may not, and today we can't afford to take risks. . .

Bland's written report was also transmitted word for word to British Embassies around the world, with personal instructions from Lord Halifax: 'You may use the material in conversation as you think suitable to impress the authorities in the country where you reside with the danger from this form of German activity. In this connection you will no doubt find the passage regarding the lists of individuals detailed for murder particularly impressive.'

That both reports were used for blatant propaganda purposes, where truth no longer mattered, did not prevent them from receiving influential and apparently straight-faced circulation in Whitehall. Bland's account, as we have seen, went straight to Cabinet on 15 May; and on 17 May Stuart sent his to Gladwyn Jebb, who had, as Cadogan's private secretary, the additional and sensitive role of liaising between all the intelligence bodies inside and outside the Foreign Office. Jebb promptly passed Stuart's report to Cavendish-Bentinck, marking it: 'Please return to me to show to MI5.' Cavendish-Bentinck meanwhile had been working hard to rally support for the JIC's own latest document, which had called for the internment of all enemy aliens. He had sent it to Cadogan on 17 May with the advice that the recommendations would shortly be placed before the Chiefs of Staff. He also pointed out that the JIC had discussed the paper with the Home Office, War Office, MI5, and SIS; and he expressed the hope that Lord Halifax would support the recommendation in Cabinet. Cadogan placed the JIC report in a file containing the Bland and Stuart reports and other Fifth Column material.

The file was perused soon afterwards by Lord Vansittart, who had been Permanent Under-Secretary at the Foreign Office until replaced by Cadogan in 1938, when he had been awarded the consolatory post of Chief Diplomatic Adviser to the government.

Vansittart's influence was on the wane, but that did not prevent
him from adding his observations. He endorsed Stuart's fantasy,
drawing 'special attention' to his strictures on refugees. And he
pointed out that the JIC had called for the internment of all aliens,
'both male and female'. Vansittart complained that the Home
Office had 'only interned the males. This is just silly. The females
are often quite as dangerous; sometimes more dangerous. Experience in Holland showed that.' Vansittart clearly knew how to
obtain public support for his views. On 23 May, a *Times* leader
echoed his sentiments, although with more style, invoking Rudyard
Kipling to proclaim, 'The female of the species is often more deadly
than the male.'

Sir John Anderson had been busy too. On 16 May he had been
received by King George VI at Buckingham Palace. The king had
already received reports on events in Holland from Sir Nevile
Bland and from Queen Wilhelmina's husband, Prince Bernhard,
and he told Anderson that he shared their views. At the same time,
Anderson and his officials – Newsam was certainly one – had been
working on the report the Cabinet had requested, which was completed on 17 May. It was entitled: 'Invasion of Great Britain;
Possible Co-operation by a "Fifth Column" ', and its particular
fascination is that it incorporated information acquired by the
Home Office staff from members of the exiled Dutch government,
including the Minister of Justice. Stuart's department had interviewed the same officials, and he, like Bland and the JIC, claimed
to have proof of the dire threat posed by refugees. Yet Anderson's
officials found their Dutch informants 'very emphatic' that any
help given to the German invaders had been solely from 'Nazi
German residents in Holland. . . They had no evidence that such
assistance had been given by the refugee element in the German
resident population.'

Anderson was at pains to point out the enormous difference
between Holland and Britain. Holland had a common frontier
with Germany, with free communications and access until the
moment of the invasion. Britain had exercised strict control over
the entry of all aliens for twenty-five years, and in the nine months
since the war began there had been no traffic between Britain and
Germany at all. All Nazis in Britain in September 1939 had either
fled or been interned; the great majority of the 73,000 Germans
and Austrians in Britain were refugees from Nazi oppression and
bitterly opposed the German régime.

Anderson's aim, of course, was to oppose mass internment, and he showed that the Home Office was not above using emotive language to plead its case. 'If thousands of women, including pregnant women and young children, were subjected to the conditions of barrack-room life in some sort of internment camp, there would soon be a public outcry against this treatment.' The report was also notable for its revelations about the activities of MI5 and MI6, which Karl Wehner had already experienced. 'Widespread investigations by the Intelligence Service have not revealed any evidence of any plans for obtaining, in the event of invasion, assistance from Germans and Austrians in this country.' Anderson pointed out that he had nevertheless ordered the internment of all male Germans and Austrians between sixteen and sixty from Hampshire to Nairn. 'If there *was* any prearranged plan by which invaders were to be helped, such a plan will have been disorganized completely by the measures already taken.'

The battle was resumed at the Cabinet meeting in the early evening of 18 May. Halifax took along the 'Fifth Column' file prepared for him by Cadogan. Anderson presented the Home Office report in the names of himself, Attlee and Greenwood. In the long discussion that ensued, Anderson at last revealed that he had now interned Category 'B' men and announced that he proposed to intern Category 'B' women too. Churchill growled that he felt the Cabinet wanted to 'stiffen up' measures against enemy aliens and asked Anderson, Attlee and Greenwood to present another report in a week's time. In so far as nothing more was required, the result was satisfactory to the Home Office: as if it had secured a draw in a soccer match. But Anderson's opponents were preparing hard for the replay.

As Cavendish-Bentinck had advised Cadogan, the JIC's report calling for mass internment was due to go before the Chiefs of Staff for their approval. When they met to consider it, the Chiefs of Staff modified several of the JIC's more controversial recommendations. Over arming the police, for example, they added the rider that this should be 'for their own protection'; and they were not in favour of a military government, only that military control should apply once an invasion had started, and then strictly 'in the area of operations'. But on internment, they agreed whole-heartedly with the JIC, endorsing their demand that all male and female enemy aliens between sixteen and seventy should be rounded up, and adding the emphasis that this should apply to 'every part of the country'.

Anderson was now under greater pressure still. While at work on the latest report on internment, he was called to a meeting of ministers and Chiefs of Staff on 20 May and asked whether arms should be withdrawn from the civilian population and handed over to the army. Anderson said he did not think it would be worth the trouble. At the same time, he was considering whether the police should be armed, as the JIC and Chiefs of Staff sought. Sir Nevile Bland had recommended this step, too, arguing specifically that it was better for innocent people to be killed than for parachutists to escape; Churchill also thought the police should be armed. Anderson consulted the Metropolitan Police Commissioner, Sir Philip Game, and found that even at this time of crisis in the nation's history, the police remained committed to their traditional policy of not carrying arms.

In the draft of his response on internment, Anderson prepared to fight another rearguard action. He pointed out that Category 'B' aliens were already being arrested, and that wider measures were 'to be considered further'. But as Anderson rehearsed the arguments against mass internment, news came that appeared to justify every fear his opponents had expressed about the Fifth Column. An official of the American Embassy in London and a young British woman of foreign ancestry had been arrested on charges of passing military secrets to Germany. And their suspected accomplice was a British Member of Parliament.

12 Britain Betrayed

Neville Chamberlain broke the story of treachery to the Cabinet on 22 May. Churchill had flown to Paris that morning with Sir John Dill, now Chief of the Imperial General Staff, to confer with the beleaguered French government, and had deputed Chamberlain to deal with the matter in his place. Chamberlain said Churchill had received a document, 'the general effect of which was that Captain Maule Ramsay, MP, who was the principal organizer of an organization known as the Right Club, had been engaged in treasonable practices in connection with an employee (a United States citizen, by name Tyler Kent) at the United States Embassy'.

Anderson told the Cabinet that he, too, had a report on the affair. He explained that Tyler Kent was a code and cypher clerk at the American Embassy, who had been 'in relations with' a woman named Anna Wolkoff. Both of them knew Ramsay; Ramsay knew Sir Oswald Mosley. With the American Ambassador's consent, the police had searched Kent's rooms and found 'a large mass of incriminating documents', including a list of the members of the Right Club.

Chamberlain drove the point home. The Right Club had been carrying on 'pro-German activities and secret subversive work, with the object of disorganizing the Home Front and hindering the prosecution of the war'. Chamberlain added that Wolkoff was known to have 'means of communicating with persons in Germany'.

The information was considered so sensitive that it was not included in the Cabinet minutes, merely being outlined there as 'evidence which showed that the leader of a certain organization had been concerned in subversive activity'. A more detailed account was confined to a Confidential Annex marked 'most secret' of which copies were sent to Anderson and Churchill. The tale that Chamberlain and Anderson had outlined was bad enough. Other details to which they were privy made it appear even more damning.

Anna Wolkoff was born in Russia in 1902 and had emigrated to Britain with her parents before the Revolution. Naturalized British in 1935, she remained virulently anti-Russian and anti-Jewish, and had flyposted notices in London opposing the war. (One Right Club specimen protested: 'This is a Jews' war.') It was she who had introduced Captain Ramsay to Tyler Kent. Among the documents found at Kent's home were top-secret telegrams between Churchill and Roosevelt on the conduct of the war. Kent had shown them to Wolkoff and Ramsay; Wolkoff had been caught trying to communicate with Lord Haw Haw, the propagandist who made anti-British broadcasts from Berlin.

Wolkoff and Kent were eventually charged under the Official Secrets Act and tried *in camera* at the Old Bailey. Both were found guilty; Wolkoff received ten years, Kent seven. Ramsay was arrested and spent three years in prison. The judge who sentenced Wolkoff and Kent said that 'at a time when this country is fighting for her very life and existence . . . it is difficult to imagine a more serious offence'. A post-war account spoke of the pair's 'shameless betrayal of Britain'.

The truth is far more complex. An examination of the Kent/ Wolkoff affair leads to the unpalatable conclusion that it was part of a political conspiracy at the heart of power in Britain. The conspirators needed to defeat Anderson and the Home Office, and the method chosen was to open up a massive second front against them. From defending the liberal treatment of enemy aliens, Anderson found himself fighting over nothing less than the liberty of the subject in Britain, and the rights of habeas corpus founded on Magna Carta. Anderson found an unlikely ally in General Kell, the veteran head of MI5. Their defeat left power concentrated, for a time, in a few unaccountable hands. In a battle of such dimensions, Kent and Wolkoff were no more than insignificant pawns.

The battleground chosen by Anderson's opponents was the far right of British politics. Anderson had already alluded to its most impressive figure, Sir Oswald Mosley, the former Cabinet minister under Ramsay MacDonald who had left the Labour Party in 1930, launching the British Union of Fascists (BUF) in 1932. Mosley had been an enlightened economist who believed he knew how to lead Britain out of depression. Having failed to secure himself a firm extra-parliamentary base among British working people, he resorted to marches and rallies at venues that guaranteed confrontations with his opponents, culminating in the battle of Cable Street in London's East End, in October 1936. His flirtation with violence, his use of uniforms, his open admiration for Hitler and Mussolini attracted Jew-haters and thugs who were in acute contrast with his own privileged background. Even though 20,000 BUF supporters flocked to a rally at Earl's Court in July 1939, the party's dismal showing at local and by-elections confirmed Mosley's political failure. At the beginning of the war, MI5 estimated that the BUF had 8,700 subscribing members spread among 188 branches. Colin Cross, the leading historian of the movement, later calculated that its membership had averaged 5,000 with a peak of 7,000.

A long way behind the BUF in size and impact came two other organizations: the Right Club and The Link. The Right Club, with 300 members was – as Anderson had told the Cabinet – the anti-Jewish society founded by Captain Ramsay, Conservative MP for Peebles since 1931. Ramsay, who had served with honour in the First World War, believed that a conspiracy of Bolsheviks, Jews, and Freemasons was threatening to dominate the world. Similar pathological views were held by Admiral Sir Barry Domvile, who had founded The Link in July 1937. Domvile coined the term 'Judmas' to represent the unholy alliance of Jews and Masons, who were, he believed, working together to establish their 'dream of world domination'. It was somewhat remarkable therefore that he had been Britain's Director of Naval Intelligence from 1927 to 1930.

The Link and the Right Club had scant political importance; and socially they were less significant than the Anglo-German Fellowship, founded in 1935, which attracted a disparate group of German sympathizers with a variety of motivations. There were writers like Henry Williamson and Edmund Blunden who had seen the horrors of the trenches in the First World War and considered that only friendship with Germany could prevent them taking place again. There were businessmen with interests in Germany which, they believed, the fellowship would promote. There were members of the British aristocracy who felt more kinship with their European cousins than with the working people of Britain. Most of the fellowship saw Britain and Germany as twin bulwarks against the tide of international communism. Many were attracted by the stage-effects of Nazism: the marches, rallies, songs and uniforms. Some venerated Hitler or became infatuated with him, like Unity Mitford, sister-in-law of Mosley. Hitler enjoyed their attentions, which accorded with his view that Britain and Germany were true European allies. Members of the fellowship would return to Britain to write adoringly of their encounters with him, like the Marchioness of Londonderry, who found Hitler a 'born leader' who possessed an 'extraordinary simplicity and the characteristics of dignity and humility', and was fond of children.

The fellowship held gala dinners attended by the German Ambassador, and once by the British Foreign Secretary, Lord Halifax. Such glittering occasions have come to be seen as the most acute symbol of the amorality of the doomed British policy of appeasement, its refusal to admit to the Nazis' persecution of political opponents and Jews. The members of the fellowship had agreed with the less disreputable premises of that policy – that the Treaty of Versailles, for example, had imposed unworkable and dangerous humiliations on Germany. But when appeasement was abandoned after the failure of Munich, and Britain went to war over Poland, they were stranded, appearing in retrospect like social and political anachronisms, relics of a lost age.

The British left naturally hated them all, from Mosley to the fading aristocrats who attended the fellowship dinners, and described them as the British Quislings, Hitler's potential *Gauleiters*. When the war began even Rothermere, who had broken with Mosley several years before, lumped them with the communists and pacifists into the Fifth Column. But Mosley always protested that he was, above all, a patriot who would not betray his country. In so doing, he touched upon an important argument, concerning the difference between subversion and collaboration. To assist a German invasion through spying and sabotage was clearly treason. What happened after the invaders had arrived was another matter: how far one cooperated with an army of occupation in the hope of mitigating its effect was a topic discussed in corners of the Commons by MPs of all persuasions.

Anderson had alluded to precisely this distinction in the papers resisting mass internment which he presented to Cabinet on 18 May, buttressed with other arguments why action against Mosley and the far right would be unwise.

> Although the policy of the British Union of Fascists is to oppose the war and to condemn the Government, there is no evidence that they would be likely to assist the enemy. Their public propaganda strikes a patriotic note. . . In my view it would be a mistake to strike at this organization at this stage by interning the leaders. Apart from the fact that there is no evidence on which such action would be justified, it is to be borne in mind that premature action would leave the organization itself in being and other leaders could be appointed to take the place of those who had been apprehended. In my view we should hold our hand. . .

In his repeated emphasis on the need for *evidence* before he could arrest British subjects, Anderson was, of course, touching on the foundations of liberty in Britain. The internment of enemy aliens had been carried out under the 'Royal Prerogative', which gave war-time governments such powers as they required, irrespective of what specific Alien legislation might have to say. But locking up British subjects was quite another matter, and considerable controversy had already been roused by various attempts to frame laws that would permit the government to override individual rights in the interests of the state.

During the Abyssinian crisis in 1935, the Committee of Imperial Defence had set up a secret committee chaired by Sir Claud Schuster, a civil servant who had been permanent secretary to the Lord Chancellor since 1915, and was also a noted mountaineer. (He was later president of the august Alpine Club.) Schuster was asked to devise emergency legislation that would be required if war came. The committee's deliberations ranged from the questions of air-raid compensation to whether rare birds should be de-protected so that their eggs could be eaten in times of food shortage. The most fraught question concerned those held to be 'disaffected persons' of British nationality. During the First World War, the government had powers to intern only 'persons of hostile origin or associations'.

When it interned British subjects under this clause, lengthy law-suits had ensued, culminating in a rather cloudy judgment from the House of Lords. Schuster, who presented his report on a proposed Emergency Powers (Defence) Bill early in 1937, told the Committee of Imperial Defence that the position should be clarified.

Schuster wrote: 'In a future war . . . there is a serious danger that attempts to impede the war effort might be made by persons actuated not by sympathy with the enemy, but by "internation-alist" affiliations or by disinterested opposition to the war.' Schus-ter proposed a clause enabling the government to intern anyone 'whose detention appears to the Secretary of State to be expedient in the interests of the public safety or the Defence of the Realm'.

The CID considered Schuster's report on 1 July 1937. As we have noted, the Home Secretary, Sir Samuel Hoare, observed that 'the growth of Communistic international organizations might involve us in some dangers from our own people in time of war . . . most of the people working on behalf of the Comintern in this country [are] British nationals.' The CID approved of Schuster's clause, but clearly felt some embarrassment at its draconian nature: the timing of such legislation would be a delicate matter. Hoare neatly summed up the dilemma: 'His main fear was that if legislation were introduced in peace, the Defence Regulations would be watered down in Parliamentary debate. It would be difficult to get Parliament to agree in peace to measures which they would unhesitatingly pass in time of war.' The CID concluded that the best course would be to prepare the legislation, but not to tell Parliament until the eve of war. For the same reason, it decided not to show the vital clause to the Cabinet until, as one committee member put it, 'the emergency arose'. The clause was first circu-lated to the police during the Munich crisis in September 1938, the Home Office describing it as 'a draft Regulation which it is proposed to make in the event of invasion'. It did not surface publicly for almost another year.

On 24 August 1939, Sir Samuel Hoare presented the Emergency Powers (Defence) Bill in the Commons. Even then, the precise details were not revealed for, as Hoare warned, the government was seeking 'very wide, very drastic, and very comprehensive pow-ers', adding: 'We do not intend to introduce regulations that would affect the liberty of the subject . . . until the country is actually involved in hostilities.' The government did not reveal its hand until 1 September, the day Germany invaded Poland. And it issued its Defence Regulations, not through Parliament, but by an Order in Council which did not need parliamentary assent.

Schuster's original wording had been only slightly modified: the Home Secretary could make a detention order 'if satisfied with respect to any particular person that with a view to preventing him acting in a manner prejudicial to the public safety or the Defence of the Realm, it is necessary to do so'. The regulation was numbered 18B.

The police liked 18B. Sir Norman Kendal, assistant commissioner at Scotland Yard in charge of the Criminal Investigation Department and Special Branch, noted on 3 October: 'We have got the strongest possible Restriction Order and it is to be hoped that it will have some effect.' By the end of November, forty-six British subjects had been detained (twenty-one were released after only a short time). But the government found that it had misjudged the readiness of Parliament to confer such sweeping powers on the executive, even in war. There were vehement protests, and after consulting MPs of all parties, the Home Office modified Regulation 18B considerably. The Home Secretary could now detain either those of 'hostile origin or associations' – the wording relied upon during the First World War – or those concerned 'in acts prejudicial to the public safety or the Defence of the Realm'. Thus, whereas before he could detain people to *prevent* them from acting against public safety or the Defence of the Realm, he could now do so only if they were *already acting* in such a manner.

During the Cabinet discussion on 18 May, Anderson evidently emphasized this basic distinction once again. 'The Home Secretary explained at length the difficulty of taking any effective action in the absence of evidence which indicated that the organization as such was engaged in disloyal activities.' It was almost as if Anderson was issuing a challenge. It is therefore startling to discover that the first overt action against Kent and Wolkoff was also taken on 18 May, when officers from Scotland Yard – almost certainly from Special Branch and MI5 – called on the American Ambassador Joseph Kennedy to tell him that one of his officials was involved in treason. Within hours, Kennedy had obtained permission from Washington to waive Kent's diplomatic immunity. On 20 May, police raided Kent's bed-sitter in Gloucester Place and arrested him, and Wolkoff was arrested too. Two days later, on 22

May, Chamberlain told the Cabinet that evidence of treasonable activities by members of the British right had been obtained.

Anderson valiantly repeated his view that Mosley was not a traitor. He used his well-tried concessionary tactic of suggesting that only twenty-five to thirty arrests were needed to 'cripple' the British Union of Fascists, and pointed out that, if the Cabinet wanted them carried out, it would have to change the law.

Chamberlain took the discussion by the scruff of the neck. He told reporters that Churchill had said, 'If any doubt existed, the persons in question should be detained without delay.' The minutes record that 'this view met with general approval'. Within hours a new regulation had been drafted, as Clause 18B(1A). It left little to chance. Members of hostile organizations could now be arrested if they were 'likely to endanger' public safety, public order, the prosecution of the war or the defence of the realm. The new regulation was published that night and announced in the Commons the following morning. The first arrests took place immediately. Special Branch officers and uniformed police found Sir Oswald Mosley at his flat in Dolphin Square. Others raided the BUF's headquarters in Great Smith Street and arrested Neil Francis-Hawkins, the party's director-general, and Alexander Raven Thomson, editor of its newspaper *Action*. Fifty-nine people, including ten women, were picked up in two days; the men were taken to Brixton Prison, the women to Holloway. Among them was Captain Ramsay, who was arrested under 18B as it previously stood.

It was stunningly convenient of Kent and Wolkoff to have committed their act of treason at that moment. It was indeed difficult 'to imagine a more serious offence' at such a time, as Mr Justice Tucker remarked on sentencing them to long prison terms at the Old Bailey. The *Daily Telegraph* crime reporter, Stanley Firmin, saw no reason to disagree when he wrote of their 'shameless betrayal' in a heroic account of MI5's wartime role, published in 1946. Since then, material has become available from which a more considered evaluation can be made. In 1954, Sir William Jowitt, the Solicitor-General who prosecuted Kent and Wolkoff, published an account of the trials. In 1963, the transcript of the secret Old Bailey trial was released to the Library of Yale University. And in 1964, a biography of Joseph Kennedy was published in which the author, Richard Whalen, quoted copiously from his own correspondence with Kent. From these sources it is possible to demonstrate that Kent and Wolkoff were far from being the outright traitors they were painted, and that, to obtain the crucial evidence against them, MI5 set them up. This in itself did not form part of the political conspiracy. But their arrests did. MI5 had obtained the evidence needed for convictions early in April. It did not move against them for almost six weeks. Consideration of what happened in between shows that the timing of their arrests, so opportune to Anderson's opponents, can scarcely have been mere coincidence.

Tyler Kent was born in China in 1911. His father had been posted there as a member of the American Consular Service, and Kent emulated him by joining the Diplomatic Service in 1934. He spent the next five years as a code and cypher clerk in the US Embassy in Moscow. While there, he started to remove copies of secret embassy documents and take them home, the habit which led to his conviction as a traitor. But it is clear from Kent's own account that he considered himself to be, in modern jargon, a whistle-blower. He was an isolationist who believed that his country should avoid involvement with Europe. He considered that Roosevelt's foreign policy ran counter to this, and that his European diplomats were 'actively taking part in the formation of hostile coalitions in Europe . . . which they had no mandate to do'. He believed that the American people were 'being told half-truths' and intended to leak the cables he collected to the US Senate or the press. But before he could summon the courage to do so, he was transferred to the London Embassy and instead destroyed the documents. He arrived in London in October 1939, and soon had his earlier views confirmed, first from the copies of European cables received by London, later by a series of communications that he considered more damaging still.

Early in the war, Churchill established a direct channel to President Roosevelt, signing himself 'Naval Person' to reflect his position as First Lord of the Admiralty. Churchill later asserted that Chamberlain knew of his actions, but he composed and dispatched most of the cables without reference to his colleagues, while, in the US Embassy, Kennedy often read them only after they had been transmitted. Their contents supported Kent in his belief that the United States was being drawn into the 'catastrophe' of war. He started to extract copies of the embassy's cables again, taking them to his London apartment where he methodically sorted and classified them. He felt that his duty again lay in revealing them 'to the American people', although once again he was not precisely sure how to do so.

Early in 1940, he met Anna Wolkoff. The 'anti-Semitic tendencies' to which he admitted were amply encouraged by her own venomous anti-Jewish feelings. They had a common interest in Russia, too. It is not clear just what Chamberlain meant when he said, perhaps coyly, that they had been 'in relations'. At all events, Kent found Wolkoff witty and vivacious; she visited his apartment frequently, and he sometimes lent her his car. Eventually Kent showed her his collection of embassy documents.

Wolkoff was already friendly with Captain Ramsay, founder and organizer of the Right Club, and she soon took Kent to meet him at his home in Onslow Square. Kent found Ramsay 'misinformed' on the war and offered to 'enlighten' him through the embassy cables. When Ramsay called, he was naturally most interested in Churchill's messages to Roosevelt, sent outside the normal diplomatic channels, and considered asking a question about them in Parliament.

Soon afterwards, Wolkoff borrowed several of the Churchill cables from Kent and made photographic copies of them, giving Kent the photographic plates afterwards. That action of Wolkoff's remains the most mysterious part of the story, for Ramsay later denied any knowledge of it. Kent said that Wolkoff would not tell him why she had done it, and the photographer said that he did not know what had happened to the prints he had made. At the trials of Kent and Wolkoff, the prosecution offered no explanation either, and its case rested on all that had occurred before.

MI5 knew about these activities at a very early stage. It had penetrated the Right Club long before, and several of the club's ostensible members were in fact MI5 agents. None of the three people in question were at all discreet: Ramsay was wondering whether to ask a parliamentary question about Churchill's irregular channel of communication with Roosevelt, while Wolkoff talked freely of her activities. She was friendly with a junior attaché at the Italian Embassy in London, and boasted to one of MI5's clandestine Right Club members that she could use the Italian diplomatic bag to smuggle material out of Britain.

MI5 was clearly entitled to its suspicions over Kent and Wolkoff. But when it considered exactly what evidence it needed to arrest them and put them on trial, it ran into a large stumbling block. For, as the government's law officers advised, any prosecution of Kent and Wolkoff was bound to be a tricky affair. There was, first, the problem that Kent was a foreigner with diplomatic protection, which would have to be waived. The second problem was far more complex, and resulted from difficulties in the wording of the Official Secrets Act.

The 1911 Act covered the acquisition or communication of secret documents. But a defendant could be convicted only if the document could be useful to an enemy, and if it was communicated for a purpose 'prejudicial to the state'. The experience of prosecuting suspected traitors in the First World War showed that it was sometimes hard to satisfy both these conditions, and a new Official Secrets Act was passed in 1920 to make convictions easier to obtain. It did so by introducing the species 'Foreign Agent'. A defendant could now be convicted if he had 'communicated or attempted to communicate with a foreign agent'. And a foreign agent did not necessarily have to be foreign, only to have committed an act that was 'prejudicial to the safety or interests of the State'.

Sir William Jowitt wrote frankly of these problems in his account of the case. He argued in court that Kent had communicated documents to Wolkoff by showing them to her. The argument succeeded. But, as Jowitt bluntly put it, to convict him and Wolkoff it was necessary to demonstrate that Wolkoff, who 'received' the documents, was a foreign agent. It is clear from his account, although not so bluntly admitted that, in order to establish this, Wolkoff was set up.

The venue was the Russian Tea Rooms which were run by Wolkoff's parents and patronized by Russian émigrés who reckoned that they served the best caviar in London. Wolkoff received a message to go there on 9 April. She arrived at 11 a.m., and was introduced by a young naval officer she knew to a friend of his. The friend's identity was never revealed in court, and Jowitt referred to him as 'X'. He was almost certainly an MI5 agent – Captain Ramsay evidently suspected as much, for he told Wolkoff later that the man had several aliases and was not to be trusted. The mystery man reminded Wolkoff of her boast that she could send documents out of Britain via the Italian diplomatic bag and produced an envelope which he asked her to send abroad on his behalf. It was addressed to 'Herr W. B. Joyce, Rundfunkhaus,

Berlin' – Lord Haw Haw. The man told her it contained 'good anti-Jewish stuff', and she took it from him. Wolkoff's boast proved an empty one. But she knew a woman in the Right Club who claimed to have access to the Rumanian diplomatic bag. On 10 April, Wolkoff asked her to help. The woman was another MI5 agent who later gave evidence against Wolkoff in court, identified only as 'Miss A'. She told Wolkoff she would dispatch the letter to Lord Haw Haw. She delivered it to MI5 that night.

MI5 decided to entice Wolkoff further. The next morning, Miss A telephoned her and arranged that Wolkoff should add her own message to the Haw Haw letter. Miss A invited Wolkoff to her flat, and even obligingly lent her a typewriter. Her message was a brief, amateurish affair, ending with the words: 'It is now very important that we hear more about the Jews and Free Masons.' Miss A sealed the letter and took it back to MI5. In its agent's presence – indeed, on the agent's typewriter – Wolkoff had written a letter to the notorious Lord Haw Haw. The evidence against her was bolstered soon afterwards, when Wolkoff proudly told a second member of the Right Club what she had done. That woman appeared in court as 'Miss B', for she was another agent of MI5. Thus, by mid April, MI5 had obtained enough evidence to convict Kent and Wolkoff of treason. They were now left at large.

It was quite understandable that MI5 did not move against Kent and Wolkoff at once, but rather waited to see if they led to bigger fish. They were watched constantly. Miss B even accompanied Wolkoff when she delivered a letter to the junior Italian attaché; it proved to contain an innocuous US press release. But, as Jowitt was later forced to admit, Wolkoff made no attempt in the following six weeks to pass documents to the Italian attaché or commit any other harmful act. It is because they clearly presented no real danger that the timing of their arrests assumes such significance. We believe that the course of events was as follows.

As we have seen, the attack on the Low Countries heralded a period when the leaders of the British government felt that extraordinary actions and powers were needed to meet the peril they believed the nation faced. Irritating opposition to that process came from the Home Office, backed by General Kell, who was still arguing that any internal threat had been disposed of in September 1939. His argument was supported by the inconvenient fact that the two latest suspects, Wolkoff and Kent, posed no danger at all.

Despite any impression given by the climactic Commons debate of 8 and 9 May, which led to the resignation of Chamberlain and his replacement by Churchill, the two men were directing the nation in tandem. Churchill liked to handle foreign and military matters, and left domestic affairs to Chamberlain. And Chamberlain had a direct line to the British security services in the shadowy figure of Sir Joseph Ball.

Ball was no stranger to intrigue. He had been a member of MI5 during the First World War and was appointed the Conservative Party's director of publicity soon afterwards. In that role he discreetly carried out the embarrassing task of making one of the final payoffs in the affair of the Zinoviev letter, one of the truly great 'dirty tricks' of modern political history. An ex-MI5 man named Donald im Thurn had helped the Conservatives to extract the maximum political capital from the affair and secure victory in the 1924 General Election, and in 1928 Ball was deputed to pay im Thurn the £5,000 he was owed. Three years later, Ball became the Tory Party's first director of research. As such, he served as an intelligence scout and courier for Chamberlain, providing information about currents of thought within the Conservative Party, as well as acting as a link with overseas governments when Chamberlain wished to bypass the Foreign Office. When the war began he moved into the strange world where propaganda and intelligence were blurred, becoming 'Head of Films' at the propaganda department, MI7.

Ball maintained good contacts with MI5. He was a close friend of Kell's deputy, a fifty-year-old brigadier named Allen Harker, who had joined MI5 from the Indian Army and was a devotee of all forms of field sports. Harker shared the interest with Ball, and they belonged to two of the same clubs, the Army and Navy and the Flyfishers. Harker did not view the Fifth Column in the same sanguine light as Kell. He saw Britain as a fortress which contained 'large numbers of persons of doubtful loyalty' who must be dealt with urgently. 'It is clearly essential,' Harker wrote, 'that every person within the fortress must be either harnessed to the national effort or put under proper control.'

It is logical to suppose that, from Harker, Ball learned of Kent and Wolkoff, primed for arrest at the most opportune time. Kell was hoping to use them to catch bigger prey; they were now turned against him. When Anderson once again stonewalled demands for sweeping action against both aliens and British subjects, the arrests were activated, either by Harker himself, or by a direct order to

Kell. Through Ball, Chamberlain and Churchill received their own personal report on the affair. Anderson was briefed by Kell and thus managed to avoid appearing totally nonplussed when Chamberlain broke the story on 22 May. But his position was totally undermined, and he was powerless to prevent the amendment to Regulation 18B and the arrests on the following day.

There is evidence that, even now, the Home Office fought back. On 23 May it took out a deportation order against Kent, hoping to remove him from the country. But he was too valuable for that. The case against Kent depended on that against Wolkoff, and vice versa. And convictions against both were necessary to justify the wave of detentions under 18B that followed their arrest.

After the first flurry of activity in London, when Mosley and other prominent figures were taken, there was a slight lull. Early in June, the scope for action was considerably widened when every police force in Britain was told it could use the new powers. In a letter to chief constables, Sir Alexander Maxwell attempted to circumscribe their activities as far as he could. He explained that the Home Office policy was to detain 'the active members who may be engaged in specially mischievous activities'. He asked the police to assign their 'detective officers with the best available experience' to the work, and warned that the powers should be applied only in 'specially selected cases. . . Apart from other considerations, the difficulties of finding accommodation must be borne in mind.'

The police went to work with enthusiasm. Among those detained were Lady Diana Mosley, Sir Oswald's wife; Sir Barry Domvile, founder of The Link; Captain Franz von Rintelen, a German spy in the First World War who had emigrated to Britain and applied for British nationality; the former British heavyweight boxing champion Joe Beckett, and his wife; two brothers of William Joyce (Lord Haw Haw); a Dorset landowner named Captain George Henry Lane Fox Pitt-Rivers, who had said that evacuated children should not be billeted in rural homes; a former king's messenger named Major James Hamilton Davidson-Houston; half a dozen policemen; and the borough surveyor of Guildford. After Dorset police arrested a prominent local pacifist, the Home Office sent chief constables a second letter, warning them not to detain people merely 'because they are Communists or Pacifists, or members of the Peace Pledge Union, or Conscientious Objectors', and to take care not to 'cause resentment among trade unionists or workers engaged in occupations of national importance'.

By the end of August, the number detained reached a peak of 1,428, and, on reviewing the figures soon afterwards, Sir Norman Kendal observed: 'It looks to me as if the country forces were overdoing it.' Thereafter releases began and the number fell.

A month later, Kent and Wolkoff finally appeared at the Old Bailey. They were tried separately, with brown paper pasted over the windows in the courtroom doors to block unofficial eyes. The press contained only the barest notification of the verdicts and their sentences. They had performed well in the roles assigned to them in May, enabling the Home Office to be overridden and the first stage in the concentration of power inside the government to be achieved.

While Chamberlain pondered the next step, Anderson withdrew to consider his next move. In the Home Office that day, his officials revised the paper on internment under preparation by inserting references to the decisions just taken. It was due to be presented to the cabinet on 24 May. But encouraged by Anderson's recent defeat, the Chiefs of Staff went on to the offensive once more.

13   A Special Body

On 23 May, the news from France was as bad as it could be. The British and French had started their retreat from Belgium on 16 May. Churchill predicted that the German advance would soon run out of steam, but Guderian's tank columns raced westward without pause and reached the English channel at the mouth of the Somme on 20 May. There they turned north and headed for the Channel ports of Boulogne and Dover. Heavy German reinforcements surged after Guderian, brushing aside counter-attacks by the French and by the British, who made a brave assault at Arras. The trap around the British Expeditionary Force was closing fast. Churchill returned from his French excursion on 22 May blaming the generals for the catastrophe and nurturing dreams of a counter-offensive that would turn 'defeat into victory'. But the eyes of Lord Gort, the BEF's commander, were already on Dunkirk. The only realistic objective now was to save the British army from annihilation.

It was against this sombre background that the War Office turned to Chamberlain for help in achieving its aims in Britain. Chamberlain had just shown his hand in the debate over regulation 18B. As Lord President of the Council, he chaired a small informal committee of ministers which, on the evening of 23 May, received – in Chamberlain's words – 'a request made by the War Office for the internment of all enemy aliens and the imposition of severe restrictions upon neutral aliens'. Chamberlain reported this request to the Cabinet when it met on 24 May.

There was a timely intervention from the Rothermere press, plumbing new depths of hatred that morning. In the *Daily Mail*, G. Ward Price recalled his visit to Rumania. 'As the head of a Balkan State said to me last month: "In Britain you have to realize that every German is an Agent. All of them have both the duty and the means to communicate information to Berlin." ' Ward Price had no doubt about what had to be done. 'The rounding-up of enemy agents must be taken out of the fumbling hands of local tribunals. All refugees from Austria, Germany and Czechoslovakia, men and women alike, should be drafted without delay to a remote part of the country and kept under strict supervision.' The headline matched Ward Price's fervour. 'Act! Act! Act! – Do It Now!'

The Cabinet met at 11.30, with Churchill, safely returned from France, restored to the chair. Chamberlain reported the request he had received the previous evening from the War Office, whose pre-emptive strike succeeded to the extent that Anderson's latest defensive memorandum was not presented. But in the ensuing argument, Anderson showed that he was still quick on his feet. He said that 'an attempt to intern all enemy aliens forthwith would cause a breakdown of the machinery'. He also turned the argument back against the War Office. Earlier, Chamberlain had said that he was 'disturbed' by reports about conditions in some camps: 'Freedom of movement, inter-communications with persons outside, and the use of wireless sets were permitted.' Anderson made prompt and cynical use of Chamberlain's criticism.

> He shared to the full the Lord President's views as to the need for immediately tightening up the conditions necessary for the internment of aliens. . . It was essential that the Military authorities should recognize that arrangements made for prisoner of war camps were totally unsuitable for detaining internees and suspects. Very special precautions were necessary for the latter, as experience in Ireland and India had proved. . .

The speech pushed Anthony Eden, Secretary of State for War, on to the defensive. Eden told the Cabinet that there would be 'a full investigation as soon as possible', but admitted that General Kell, head of MI5, had complained that he was 'insufficiently provided with funds to undertake the necessary security measures for watching internees'. The outcome was a victory for Anderson.

The Cabinet resolved that internment should be extended only to German and Austrian women in Category 'B'. It also imposed irksome restrictions on other aliens: they were banned from owning cars or bicycles, and must stay at home from 10 p.m. to 8 a.m., apart from those who worked at night. But the bulk of enemy aliens, the 60,000 in Category 'C', remained free.

Churchill, who shared the War Office view, seemed impatient at being thwarted. Anderson was opposing him on a second matter, the arming of police, which Anderson said could not be carried out 'for some time to come'. Churchill said that his view on internment had 'greatly hardened . . . the German technique in the occupation of the Low Countries had shown the weaknesses to which we were exposed'. Then Churchill took an unexpected tack. He added that 'he was strongly in favour of removing all internees out of the United Kingdom'. No one at the Cabinet meeting responded to this chilling aside.

At the Home Office, Maxwell and Newsam were clearly confident of the outcome of the meeting. The Cabinet was still deliberating when Maxwell sent a letter to the chief constables of Britain, instructing them to prepare to arrest all German and Austrian women in Category 'B' the following Monday, 27 May.

Maxwell amplified his instructions in a memorandum. 'Arrests', he ordered, 'should be carried out as a rule in the early morning.' The only women to be spared were those who were invalid, infirm or in advanced pregnancy, or mothers with children who were dangerously ill. Other mothers were to be told they could take children under sixteen with them, and it was expected that most would do so. The police were also to search the women's homes and tell MI5 of 'any information suggesting the existence of plans for assisting the enemy'.

The police making the arrests were to be assisted by policewomen, police matrons or 'any other suitable women that may be available'. The Home Office had enlisted the aid of the doughty ladies of the Women's Voluntary Service, and a letter from WVS headquarters asked its regional organizers to supply women of 'sound character and integrity'.

The arrested women were allowed to take one suitcase each and anything else they could carry, such as rugs; they should be advised to take as much warm clothing as possible. Maxwell added: 'Women should be given reasonable time to pack their requirements for the journey, and they should be informed that it might be two or more days before they reach their destination.' Maxwell warned that it had not yet been decided 'whether, or if so when, this scheme is to be put into operation, and the existence of the scheme should for the present be kept secret'. Confirmation of the instructions followed soon afterwards, and on 27 May the arrests began.

Since visiting her husband at Seaton at Christmas 1939, Irmgard Fehle and her sons, Gus, by then seven, and Rolf, five, had not been having an easy time. Without Bruno's salary, there was no income at all, so she cashed the family's insurance policy, worth just over £200, and drew on her small savings in the bank. She soon found she could no longer afford the rent on the semi-detached in Hillside Gardens. On a friend's advice, she sought help from the London German Hospital which was still functioning in Hackney. A sympathetic almoner offered Mrs Fehle board and accommodation in return for assistance at the hospital's convalescent home near Hitchin, in Hertfordshire. As she and her husband had decided, Mrs Fehle had tried to arrange to travel to Holland, and found some encouragement from the Home Office, still committed to its policy of repatriation. The German invasion of the Low Countries on 10 May put paid to that scheme.

Gus and Rolf Fehle went to school as usual on 27 May. They had started the morning lessons when the headmaster came into the classroom with a policeman, and told them that the policeman had come to take them home. There they found their mother in tears, packing a suitcase. When the police drove them away, Gus's main regret was at leaving his bicycle behind. They were taken to Cambridge, where they spent the night in the dining hall of a university college, with mattresses laid out on the floor. In the morning they were put on a train that made a circuitous journey to Liverpool. There they were taken to a bleak and cold sailors' hostel near the docks, crowded with women and children in the same predicament. Mrs Fehle slept in a deck-chair and the two boys lay on the floor.

The next day, 29 May, was Rolf's birthday, which they celebrated with soup and tea poured from enormous enamel jugs. Then they were escorted through the docks by soldiers armed with bayonets, while onlookers pelted them with rubbish. As they climbed a gangplank on to a small steamship, another woman told

Mrs Fehle where they were going. The name meant nothing to her – the Isle of Man.

After its part in the defence of Great Britain during the First World War, the Isle of Man had settled back into its comfortably ambiguous relationship with the mainland. Formally, it was ruled by the Lieutenant-Governor, appointed by the British Crown; it continued to pass its own laws and levy taxes through the 900-year-old parliament of the Tynwald, whose decrees were still proclaimed from Tynwald Hill each Midsummer's Day. The island saw its independence symbolized by the rugged cliffs of its western shores, bastions against the winter storms that swept in from the Irish Sea. But it could never afford to sever its links with Britain, for every summer steamboats brought tens of thousands of holiday-makers from Liverpool to stay in the hotels and boarding-houses of its sheltered east coast. When war returned in 1939, the relationship was disturbed once again. The Home Office tightened the strings linking the island to Britain, and on 2 September an amendment to the new Defence Regulations extended them to the Isle of Man.

The island had not been included in the list of camps drawn up by the War Office in August 1939. It came as a shock to the boarding-house keepers of the northern town of Ramsey to read a letter dated 12 May from B. E. Sergeaunt, secretary to the island government. Sergeaunt told them that the Lieutenant-Governor, acting on instructions from the British War Office, required them to leave their premises within six days, leaving behind 'all furniture, bedding, linen, cutlery, crockery and utensils'. Soon afterwards, villagers in Onchan, just north of the main town of Douglas, were given the same orders.

Alec Clague, the young town clerk of Port Erin at the rocky southern tip of the island, received his instructions from the Lieutenant-Governor's office a day or so later. Emanating from the Home Office, they were milder in tone; Clague learned that the Home Office intended to set up a camp at Port Erin for women and children for whom it – not the War Office – would be responsible. Clague toured Port Erin's hotels and guest houses, asking proprietors if they would take in internees. The prospects for the summer tourist trade were looking distinctly gloomy, and most willingly agreed. Clague told them they would be paid 3s (15p) a day for each internee; they would provide the food, which the internees would cook for themselves.

As camp commander, the Home Office had sent to the island Dame Joanna Cruickshank, a formidable disciplinarian who had served as a nursing sister with officer rank in the First World War, and had since risen to the top of the nursing world, becoming matron-in-charge of the British Red Cross Society in 1938. She and Clague supervised the construction of a barbed-wire fence round Port Erin, with a road-block at the entrance. The people of Port Erin had to present their identity cards to pass through. The first women arrived on 29 May, a ferry of the Isle of Man Steam Packet Company docking in Douglas at 8.30 a.m. after an over-night crossing from Liverpool. Three trains and a fleet of buses were ready to transport them to Port Erin, where the last of the barbed wire was being nailed into place. Port Erin's stationmaster did not know they were coming until he received a phone call telling him that a train bearing several hundred internee women and their children had just left Douglas.

Irmgard Fehle and her two sons were among them. At Port Erin they were shown to the immaculate and spacious hotel that was to be their new home. Gus and Rolf soon spoiled that. Finding their way to the hotel dining room, they emptied a pepper pot into their hands to make themselves sneeze and were in the midst of convulsions when the landlady came in. In the morning, Alec Clague agreed that the Fehle family should be transferred to a boarding house of lesser pretensions.

Renate Scholem arrived on the Isle of Man a week or so later, thoroughly bewildered by this latest twist in her life. Her mother was in Hampstead; her father was in the concentration camp of Oranienburg. Aged seventeen, it was six years since she had left Germany in somewhat traumatic circumstances.

Her father, Werner Scholem, had been a prominent left-wing activist during the Weimar Republic. He was Jewish, and one of the founders of a breakaway socialist party, the USPD, having been sent to prison during the First World War for saying that German troops, like their Russian comrades, should down their arms and come home. He was among the revolutionaries who formed the Spartakus League and tried to foment an uprising in Berlin. He edited the Communist Party paper, *Die Rote Kapelle*, sat in the Reichstag, and in 1925 went to Moscow with his wife to meet Stalin. Soon afterwards, he withdrew from active politics and put most of his energies into becoming a lawyer.

For much of her early life, Renate was brought up in Hanover by her mother's parents, who were not Jewish and gave her a conventional German working-class upbringing. In March 1933, Renate returned to Berlin to stay with her parents again. Despite his quiescent years, her father remained high on the Nazis' list of enemies. Barely a week after the burning of the Reichstag, a gang of men in brown shirts burst into her Berlin apartment and took her parents away. Renate went back to her grandparents in Hanover.

Renate's mother was released from prison after a year, and escaped to Czechoslovakia. Renate went to visit her father, who told her: 'I wish I'd become an actor instead of a politician.' It was the last time she ever saw him. In August 1934, she went to live with her mother and her older sister in Muswell Hill, North London. At first she attended a Roman Catholic convent school, but then attended a Jewish bible class as well. There she won a prize which was awarded to her by Naomi Bentwich, the sister of Norman Bentwich, one of the leading figures of the Jewish refugee and welfare movement. Naomi Bentwich had started a school for young children in her spacious house, Carmel Court, in Kent.

Soon Renate went to live at Carmel Court, attending a girls' day-school at Ramsgate. At Carmel Court she read the *New Statesman* and the latest offerings from the Left Book Club, and shared the family's vegetarian diet. She wrote to her mother in London, and from time to time rode up by train from Kent to visit her. Life at Carmel Court struck Renate as rather frugal, but very secure. She came to feel that she was a guest at a timeless, artistic Edwardian house party.

In 1936, Renate's comfortable existence received a jolt. Her mother disappeared. Renate eventually learned that she had gone to fight in Spain. Renate's greatest concern was for her father, by then in Buchenwald. Her mother had been sending him 5 marks a month to buy food, but Naomi Bentwich helped Renate to send the money instead. When Renate's mother returned from Spain, she announced that Europe was doomed and the family must all emigrate to South America. She took her two daughters to see the Ecuador consul, who promised them visas if he could sleep with Renate's sister for one night. The idea of emigrating was aban-

doned. Renate returned to Carmel Court, the day-school in Ramsgate and the Edwardian house party.

It came to an end in 1939. When the war began, Naomi Bentwich went to live in Devon. Renate stayed in Kent, intending to
stay at school until she had taken her exams, lodging with a local
family. She opened the door on the morning of 27 May to find a
policeman and policewoman standing on the doorstep. They told
her to pack a suitcase and go with them to the police station.
Renate asked if she could telephone her mother, but the policeman
refused her request. Renate, then seventeen, had never been before
a tribunal (her mother had received a 'C'). But Ramsgate, on the
coast of Kent, was in a sensitive area, and the local police had
evidently made some attempt to check on her. They told Renate
that they had asked her headmistress to accept responsibility for
her, but she had declined, they said, 'in the light of the evidence'.

'What evidence?' Renate asked.

A detective told her that she had been reading left-wing books.
Renate said they belonged to Naomi Bentwich. He asked why she
was living in Ramsgate; Renate explained that she wanted to take
her exams. Why had she been seen on Ramsgate sea-front with a
man in RAF uniform? Renate explained that he was the brother
of her sister's husband (she had married at the start of the war).
It was all to no avail.

Renate spent the night in a cell. In the morning, still wearing
her green school uniform, she set off by car for London with a
detective in plain clothes and a policewoman. Their route lay
through Rochester, where the detective's mother lived. They called
for a cup of tea, but the detective asked Renate not to say who she
was – he explained that his mother was worried in case the Germans invaded, but he always told her that everything would be all
right. By the time they arrived in the London suburbs, night was
falling, and the detective asked Renate if she knew the way to
Holloway.

It was dark when they eventually found the prison, one of the
largest and most forbidding of all those the Victorians built. Its
enormous studded front gate appeared to Renate like a dungeon,
and when she stepped inside, she could see two arms reaching out
from a barred window high above.

It was clear that the wardresses to whom she was consigned had
spent a long and tiring day. One barked at her to 'strip off' and
take a bath. Undressing next to her was an old woman bedecked

with jewellery who was almost dwarfed by the cabin-trunk she had brought with her. After her bath, a doctor examined her and she was given back her school uniform to wear. Then she was led to a cell, furnished with a straw palliasse laid on a wooden rack, and with a bucket for a lavatory. Graffiti covered the walls, and there was a barred window too high for Renate to reach. She lay down on the palliasse and wept.

In the morning, Renate found she was in cell B12, on the second landing of one of Holloway's enormous cell blocks, built in the shape of a church aisle with netting across each landing to prevent suicides. She was introduced to the degrading slopping-out routine, joining the queue of prisoners waiting to empty their buckets. She soon made friends with a German girl of twenty in the neighbouring cell. But she was tongue-tied when some of the Jewish women spoke to her in German. Having been brought up first as an Aryan, then as a potential member of the British upper classes, she found herself in turmoil. She suspected, too, that they were laughing at her school uniform. At first she felt more at ease with the internees with British backgrounds, like the English women who had married Germans and had been visiting their families when war broke out; the East End woman whose German husband had never bothered to be naturalized; the German nun who had been in an English closed convent for twenty years. A teacher named Minna Specht, who had been at Carmel Court, helped Renate to come to terms with her predicament. When Renate first arrived in Holloway, she asked Minna what had gone wrong. 'Don't worry,' Minna told her. 'The British aren't Fascists, it will all be cleared up.' Then Minna came to her aid after an incident that proved a turning-point for Renate. After a knife had gone missing from the canteen, Renate helped the prison wardresses to search for it. Some of the other internees called her a collaborator and a spy, and threatened to ostracize her. Minna talked to Renate about their reactions, and afterwards Renate decided, as she said later, 'to become a German, a prisoner and an enemy alien. I had no more problems after that.'

There were 3,600 women in category 'B', of whom over half had been classified as refugees from Nazi oppression. Like Renate, many spent some time in British prisons before room could be found for them on the Isle of Man. The village of Port St Mary, a mile or so from Port Erin on the island's south-west promontory, was also surrounded by barricades and became part of the Home

Office Women's Camp. Port St Mary was crowded when Renate arrived, and she had to share a bed with another girl. Minna Specht had already advised her about lesbianism, saying that it was not immoral, but if Renate's first sexual experiences were with women, it would make it difficult with men later. 'If you haven't had it, you won't miss it,' she said. Renate heeded her words and at night placed a bolster down the middle of the bed. That apart, Renate felt she was fortunate to have come to such a beautiful place, with its marble beaches, rampant fuchsia bushes, and the fields that were full of sheep.

A group of 823 men was sent to the Isle of Man in the same week as the first women, and others soon followed. As the local government hastily reorganized the island as a virtual prison-camp, the pressures on London for more sweeping measures of internment were mounting. At the same time, Chamberlain was preparing the next step in the concentration of the government's power. It was heralded by the sacking of General Kell.

Kell was sixty-six. He remained proud of his achievement in the First World War and believed that his round-up had helped to keep the nation safe at the start of the Second. He had carried it out with a professional staff of only fifty men, and was determined to meet the wartime needs of the service by recruiting a number of gifted amateurs to its ranks. His professionals enjoyed working with them, and so did he. But two things made him vulnerable. There was his age, and his health: Kell suffered from increasingly acute attacks of asthma.

Until now, Kell's downfall has been ascribed to one or more of three events. The first was the loss of the *Royal Oak*, torpedoed by a U-boat in Scapa Flow with the loss of 833 lives. It was supposed that a spy must have provided Germany with information about Scapa Flow's defences and the movements of the *Royal Oak,* but MI5 could not find the culprit. The second was the explosion that destroyed a gunpowder factory and killed three workmen at Waltham Abbey, Essex. It was an uncanny echo of the explosions that sank four British ships in harbour during the First World War, widely ascribed then to a solitary subversive genius, but almost certainly caused by the spontaneous combustion of coal dust. Once again, MI5 could not produce a culprit. The third incident was the destruction of Kell's cherished files by an incendiary bomb that landed on MI5's makeshift headquarters in the London prison of Wormwood Scrubs.

The problem with each theory lies in the timing. The bomb that destroyed Kell's files fell in November 1940, six months after he had departed. The Waltham Abbey explosion was in January 1940, four months before Kell left; the *Royal Oak* was sunk in October 1939, four months before that. If timing is the crucial factor, then the irresistible conclusion is that Kell was overthrown by the same conspiracy which brought about the arrests of Kent and Wolkoff. For it is possible to fix Kell's departure with some precision. He was still in office on 24 May, as Eden's reference to him in Cabinet that day shows. Three days later he had gone, for a Foreign Office file contains a letter written that day to Gladwyn Jebb by Kell's successor. He was Sir Joseph Ball's fellow clubman and MI5 contact, Brigadier Allen Harker.

27 May was a day of cataclysmic military events. The Belgian army surrendered, the French First Army was trapped, and the evacuation from Dunkirk had just begun. That day the Chiefs of Staff presented to the Cabinet a paper entitled 'British Strategy in a Certain Eventuality'. The eventuality was the collapse of France, the loss of most of the British Expeditionary Force, and the threat of invasion: and the Chiefs of Staff predicted that invasion would be heralded by prolonged air bombardment and 'internal attack by the Fifth Column'. They warned that 'Alien refugees' were 'a most dangerous source of subversive activity', and recommended once again that they should all be interned. 'The most ruthless action should be taken to eliminate any chances of Fifth Column activities.'

When the paper was discussed, the only Cabinet member to speak on the Fifth Column was Chamberlain. He said that a special branch of the Home Defence Executive should be set up to deal with 'the whole question of the control of aliens', and asked for the authority to consider 'what measures were necessary to this end, and to give effect to them'. Without discussion, the Cabinet agreed.

The new body was to be called the Home Defence (Security) Executive. Its chairman was Viscount Swinton of Masham. Churchill said later that he had made the appointment himself; if so, it was an intriguing choice. In his previous incarnation as Sir Philip Cunliffe-Lister, Swinton had been Chamberlain's Air Minister before the war, winning Churchill's opprobrium for the RAF's supposed unpreparedness.* Churchill now had no hesitation in giving Swinton a pivotal position in Britain's defences.

Once well-described as a Tory grandee, Swinton had been President of the Board of Trade under Baldwin, and had served in the National Government of MacDonald. For twenty years he was one of the most important men in the Conservative Party, renowned for his ability to sniff out rebellion and hold the back benches together. He also headed an interlocking network of business enterprises in Britain and overseas. Churchill clearly held that his long experience in the allied worlds of commerce and Conservative politics suited him to his new post.

The Home Defence (Security) Executive met at Kinnaird House in Pall Mall. It eventually attracted the curiosity of MPs who were anxious to learn more about this mysterious and apparently powerful body. They knew it as the Swinton Committee and pressed Churchill for more information. Churchill stonewalled all such questions. 'Committees of this kind are not fitted for public discussion, least of all in times of war,' he said on 15 August. The Home Defence (Security) Executive remains an officially closed book to this day. Although its files are listed among the papers in the Public Record Office, they are variously marked: 'Closed for 50 years,' 'Not yet open to public access,' 'Retained by department'. Needless to say, the Home Office has declined to show us any papers pertaining to this phase; and even the usually forthcoming Foreign Office has withheld two files relating to it.[†]

One document has escaped the weeding. It is to be found in a Foreign Office file concerning the treatment of non-enemy aliens, and consists of an extract from the minutes of the Home Defence (Security) Executive for 22 July, when MI5's proposals for the 'vigorous enforcement' of controls within Britain were discussed. (Such extracts were customarily distributed to those affected with the preamble: 'I do not know whether you are aware of the existence of the Home Defence (Security) Executive. . .') The meeting was held at the committee's offices in Kinnaird House at the Trafalgar Square end of Pall Mall. At the head of the extract is a

* After the war, Churchill wrote that he had meant nothing personal in his attacks on Swinton.
[†] In a letter dated 30 November 1978, the Foreign Office archivist told us, incredibly, that they had been destroyed.

list of the members present that day. Viscount Swinton was in the chair. The others were as follows:

Brigadier A. Harker CBE: the new head of MI5.

Colonel R. C. Reynolds, MC: a staff officer from the War Office, winner of the Military Cross in the First World War.

Major-General Sir Alan Hunter, KCVO, CB, CMG: aged fifty-nine, a serving officer in 1914–18, retired from the War Office in 1938, brought out of retirement in 1940 to become director of the Prisoners of War Department at the War Office.

Lieutenant-Colonel Valentine Vivian, CBE: a former Guards officer in his late fifties who had served in both the Boer and First World Wars, and was later assistant military attaché at the British Embassy in Paris. In the current *Who's Who*, he listed his position as 'one of HM's bodyguard of the Hon. Corps of Gentleman-at-arms'. This elegant sobriquet provided cover for his true position as a senior member of the Secret Intelligence Service, or MI6. An alumnus of SIS, though hardly an unbiased one*, described him then as 'long past his best – if indeed he ever had one'.

Mr A. N. Rucker, CBE: principal private secretary to Neville Chamberlain since 1939.

Mr A. S. Hutchinson, CVC: an assistant secretary at the Home Office who had been Anderson's private secretary 1937–39.

Mr A. M. Wall: general secretary of the London Society of Compositors.

The MPs who badgered Churchill about the committee believed that they had discovered the names of several of its members, and asked Churchill how much they were paid. Churchill would not be drawn. Nor did he tell the MPs their information was wrong. Two of the names cited by MPs were not members, as is clear from the minutes of the 22 July meeting where they appear in a list of those 'also present'. One of these was a Mr W. C. Crocker, a solicitor. Others 'also present' that day, but not mentioned by MPs, were three members of MI5: Captain Guy Liddell and two civilians named Curry and Turner; and, from the Home Office, Frank Newsam and E. N. Cooper, an official who had helped to prepare for internment before the war. One other man named by

* Kim Philby.

MPs was there too. Although merely 'also present' on 22 July, he became the committee's deputy chairman soon afterwards. His name was Sir Joseph Ball.

After the war, Swinton included a few details of the Home Defence (Security) Executive in his memoirs, *I Remember*. His account is more revealing for what it omits. He named only two of his committee's members: one was Alfred Wall, clearly the token Labour representative. The other was Isaac Foot, whom Swinton describes as 'a lifelong Liberal and a passionate defender of freedom'. Swinton implied that Foot belonged to the committee from its inception, claiming that Foot agreed that, as Britain awaited invasion after Dunkirk, 'drastic measures were necessary' and that 'the safety of the State was the supreme law'.

Swinton was being less than honest about Isaac Foot. He did not join the committee until the late summer, after the MPs questioning Churchill had protested that it contained no Liberal member. Foot, a Liberal who had been Minister of Mines in Ramsay MacDonald's National Government, and was the father of today's distinguished Foot generation, was selected. By then the committee's work was becoming broader, to cover such topics as the security and welfare of British merchant seamen in the United States, where it helped to organize hospitality and entertainment in their ports of call. Such benevolent areas were not its concern in May 1940.

It may seem strange that when, on 27 May, Chamberlain obtained Cabinet sanction to set up the new organization with virtually untrammelled powers, Anderson made no comment. It is likely that he knew what Chamberlain was about to propose. He would also have known that, in future, the debate over internment was to be conducted elsewhere; and he can equally have surmised that the single assistant secretary from the Home Office would be easily outgunned by the War Office and Secret Service members.

As there was no discussion in Cabinet of the next move to affect Germans and Austrians in Britain, we can safely assume it was instigated by the Swinton Committee. It was promulgated in a letter from the Home Office to chief constables on 31 May. The letter itself was notably different in style from those the Home Office had previously issued. The discursive missives favoured by Maxwell, with their careful ancillary instructions to bodies like the WVS, had been replaced by a terse single sheet. It informed chief

Four of Britain's internees. Renée Goddard (above left) – formerly Renate Scholem – was aged seventeen when she was interned in May 1940. Clive Teddern (above) – formerly Kurt Tebrich – was interned at the age of sixteen. Later he joined the British Army, landed in Normandy, and fought through to Germany. Henry Teltscher (below left) was deported to Australia and decided to stay there. Karl Wehner (below) was interned in Britain four times in two world wars.

Three internees who survived the sinking of the *Arandora Star*. Bruno Fehle (left), from Germany, wrote a report on the sinking, never before published. Serafino Pini (above), born in Italy, owned two West End restaurants. Gerhard Mitchell (below) – formerly Gerhard Miedzwinski – came from Vienna, and now lives in Sydney, close to the Harbour Bridge.

Five more from the *Arandora Star*.
Uwe Radok (above left) was one of
three brothers being deported to
Canada. Erwin Frenkel (below) was a
rabbi's son from Vienna, and was
photographed in Melbourne, where
he now lives. Peter Jacobsohn (top
right) fled from Berlin with his
mother in February 1933. Frank
Eaton (middle) – formerly Franz
Eichenberg – emigrated from
Australia to Portland, Oregon, where
this spring photograph was taken.
Nobby Fulford (bottom) was a
steward in the *Arandora Star*'s crew.

Winston Churchill (above left) wanted mass internment, and demanded deportation for internees. The deposed Neville Chamberlain (above right) loyally carried out Churchill's wishes. Sir John Anderson (below left), much vilified as Home Secretary, did his best to oppose mass internment. Eventually Anderson struck an alliance with Lord Halifax (below right), Foreign Secretary, to reverse Britain's internment policy.

Sir Nevile Bland, seen arriving (top) in London from Holland on 14 May 1940, was Britain's Ambassador at The Hague until Germany invaded. He told Cabinet that 'the paltriest kitchen maid' could be an agent of the German Fifth Column.

William Cavendish-Bentinck (left) was chairman of the Joint Intelligence Committee which blamed the Fifth Column for Britain's failure to predict the German attack on Norway. Lord Swinton, chairman of the secret Home Defence (Security) Executive (above), pressed for deportations to go ahead.

Three who conspired against Britain – or were they victims of another conspiracy? Captain Maule Ramsay M.P., seen (left) at the Eton-Harrow cricket match at Lords in 1937, was founder of the anti-Jewish 'Right Club'. Anna Wolkoff (above), born in Russia but naturalized British, belonged to the Right Club. Tyler Kent (below), a cypher clerk at the United States Embassy in London, showed Ramsay and Wolkoff secret diplomatic cables. Wolkoff and Kent were imprisoned, Ramsay detained under Regulation 18B. But they were also pawns in a larger political game.

Hotels, boarding houses, and private homes on the Isle of Man were commandeered and fenced in with barbed wire (above) to serve as internment camps. Husbands and wives were interned separately at first, although they were permitted monthly meetings at Collinson's Café, Port Erin (above right, pictured today). Occasional excursions outside the camps (left) were always under military escort. No British camps were as cold as those in Canada where deportees spent the winter of 1940-1941. The photographs (right) were taken illicitly by a Canadian army guard.

The *Arandora Star* spent the 1930s taking the sybaritic rich in search of the sun; (top) she visits Venice during a Mediterranean cruise. The Blue Star Line boasted that she was the 'world's most delightful cruising liner' and offered lavish public rooms (middle) and modern cabins (bottom).

While carrying German, Australian and Italian deportees to Canada in July 1940, the *Arandora Star* was torpedoed and sunk by U-boat ace Gunther Prien (right), commander of the U-47. Prien had made his name by sinking the British battleship *Royal Oak* in Scapa Flow in October 1939; he is seen (below) returning in triumph to Germany.

At all Hotels and Spirit Stores Vol. V. No. 145 (*New Series*) Telephone: M2406 SYD

ENEMY PRISONERS HERE FROM ABROAD

Non-S

PRISON TRAIN on a Sydney wharf, waiting to take aboard German and Italian internees and prisoners of war who arrived in the ship alongside.

SOME OF the men brought to Sydney in the prison ship, looking out of the train which carried them to an undisclosed destination.

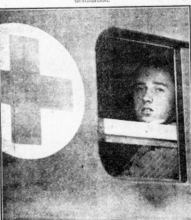

PRISON SHIP arrival looking out of the window of an ambulance which took him from the wharf.
☛ *Exciting Prison Ship Voyage*—Page 2, Columns 4, 5, and 6. Other pictures, Page 3.

CAROL OF RUMANIA ABDICATES

Daily Telegraph Service and A.A.P.

LONDON, Friday.
King Carol of Rumania has abdicated and his arrest has been reported.

Earlier reports stated that King Carol had left Bukarest for Switzerland.
Dozens of other arrests include that of the former Prime Minister (M. Tatarescu).
Carol previously abdicated in 1925, but returned to the throne in 1930.
His earlier abdication was due to opposition to his mistress, Madame Lupescu, with whom he lived in France in exile.

Michael King

His 18-year-old son, Crown Prince Michael again becomes King.
The Prime Minister (General Antonescu) has taken the title of "Leader of the State."
Carol abdicated at 6 a.m. today after nightlong demonstrations against him, King Michael took the oath at 10.25 a.m.
Rumanian secret police have arrested two of King Carol's most intimate friends, Victor Iamandi (former Minister of Justice) and Nicola Omalaxa, Rumanian manufacturer.
King Michael is the nominee of the Nazi-controlled Rumanian Iron Guard.
Berlin reports say King Carol's abdication has "surprised Nazi circles."
King Michael has issued a decree investing the Prime Minister (General Antonescu) with full dictatorial powers.
General Antonescu arrived at the palace at 9 o'clock last night.

Australians May

The *Dunera* berths in Sydney (above) after her nightmare two-month voyage from Liverpool with 2,550 deportees in the summer of 1940. As the Sydney *Daily Telegraph* of 7 September 1940 shows (right) the internees were transferred to trains waiting on the quayside, and then taken to a camp at Hay, celebrated as one of the hottest places in Australia. When the truth about the voyage emerged, the British government sent Major Julian Layton (left) to Australia to offer compensation and invite the internees back to Britain. Meanwhile the internees at Hay minted their own currency (far left).

The release of internees began in earnest in the autumn of 1940. As a *Picture Post* photograph (above) of a group of Italians clearing bomb-damage shows, many ex-internees were only too willing to help the British war-effort. Most of the internees were freed by the end of 1942; those remaining were eventually repatriated. The first returned to Germany on a Red Cross ship in October 1943 (below), in exchange for British prisoners of war and internees held in Germany.

constables that they could now intern any German and Austrian men or women of Category 'C', 'where there are grounds for doubting the reliability of an individual'. The instructions effectively sanctioned MI5 to nominate its own arrests, to be carried out by its partners in Special Branch. It also allowed local forces to follow their own initiative, and prejudices, in doing the same. The elaborate system of internment in controlled phases, devised and protected so long by the Home Office, lay in ruins; power now rested with a tiny body of men whose very existence was secret, whose members were not responsible to Parliament or even to Cabinet, among whom MI5 and the War Office were in clear ascendancy.

The external situation was more grave than ever. Most of the British army had escaped from Dunkirk, but France was close to defeat and the German army was ranged along the Channel coast, apparently poised to invade. On 8 June the last act in the humiliation in Norway was played, when the remaining British troops were withdrawn from Narvik. On 10 June, Benito Mussolini could no longer resist the temptation to share the spoils of Germany's triumphs and declared war on Britain. The fate of the 19,000 Italians in Britain was placed abruptly in MI5's hands.

14 'Collar the Lot!'

It was the British appetite that benefited most from the Italian presence in Britain between the wars. At one end of the social scale were the fashionable restaurateurs whose names were affectionately dropped by the denizens of Mayfair: Zavattoni, banqueting manager at the Savoy; Bianchi, head chef at the Café Royal; Zangiacomi, general manager of the Ritz Hotel for thirty years. At the other, were the ice-cream factories in the London suburbs, who supplied local shops and sent hand-carts round the streets with names like 'Bertorellis' inscribed in spidery writing on a painted background. In between was a range of eating places to cater to all pockets and tastes, particularly in Soho, and in the Seven Dials district on the other side of Charing Cross Road, known as 'La Piccola Italia' – Little Italy.

The Italian community had established itself in Britain before the First World War, when up to half a million people emigrated from Italy each year, a large proportion seeking escape from the poverty of Italy's mountain regions. One such family were the Pinis, who left the village of Sarzana, between the mountains and the sea close to La Spezia, in 1890. They settled at Seven Dials, returning to Italy for a while when Signora Pini lost her first baby in childbirth. After their son Serafino was born in 1902, they came back to Seven Dials and had three more sons and a daughter. They ran a popular local restaurant and later opened a second establishment in the more prosperous environment of St James's

Street, off Piccadilly. As the family's eldest son, Serafino Pini took a major hand in its management.

When Benito Mussolini came to power in 1922, the first flush of his economic policies reduced emigration from Italy. The name and the symbol of his party was the *fascio* – the bundle of sticks borne before the magistrate to denote his authority in Roman times – and in 1926 Mussolini established the fascist state, with himself as *duce*, or leader. At first, the Fascio was an élitist group, but soon its membership was widened, becoming compulsory for virtually all who wished to work in the new corporate state. Among those who had to join were government officials, teachers in schools and universities, nurses, journalists, charity workers, employees in public and municipal undertakings and all who worked for large firms. Even those not compelled to belong, such as doctors and lawyers, found themselves at a severe disadvantage if they did not do so. Membership became a passport to work and 13 million people out of Italy's 43 million were eventually recorded as having joined.

Joining the Fascio was less of an obligation for Italians living abroad. But it did make dealings with the Italian Embassy much easier; and the Fascio became a social club where expatriates could express their nostalgia for their former home. The London Fascio met in a small, ornate hall in Charing Cross Road. Like many restaurateurs, the Pinis attended its dinners and dances and joined in the toasts to 'Musso'. Not all Italians in Britain shared this benign acceptance of Mussolini and his régime. They included refugees from the fascists' persecution of their political opponents, heralded by the murder in 1924 of the Socialist deputy Giacomo Matteotti, as he was about to expose graft and corruption in the fascist party. Several relatives of Claudio Treves, a founder of the Italian Socialist Party, came to Britain, where they helped to form the Italian League for the Rights of Man to continue the struggle from exile. Their ranks were increased in 1939 when Mussolini passed race laws to ingratiate himself with Hitler, and several hundred Italian Jews fled to Britain.

By now, the British government knew that if war came, Italy could be among its enemies. In 1936, Britain and France had conceded Abyssinia to Mussolini to assuage his demands for an African colony. But Mussolini's main aim was to score over France, Italy's long-standing rival, and he believed Hitler could help. He visited Germany in 1937 and Italy's anti-Jewish laws soon followed. When the British Home Office and War Office drew up their first plans for internment in 1938, Italians were included with Germans and Austrians as likely candidates. That view was strengthened when Germany and Italy made a formal alliance in May 1939, but when Italy did not join the war in September, the instructions to intern selected Italian suspects were deleted.

The question did not arise again in Cabinet until late May 1940, when it was clear that Mussolini was moving irrevocably towards war. But a curious episode in April shows that MI5 had stayed on the alert. It began on 24 April, when F. V. Cochis, the Italian general manager of Claridge's Hotel, was peremptorily sacked.

Cochis had worked for Claridge's for twenty-one years and lived with his wife in rooms in the hotel. A letter from Mr Walter Hore, secretary of the Savoy Hotel Company which owned Claridge's, instructed him to leave the hotel at once, with one month's salary in lieu of notice. Cochis was astonished and aggrieved. After failing to obtain an explanation from Hore, he saw Mr Rupert d'Oyly Carte, chairman of the Savoy Hotel Company. According to Cochis, d'Oyly Carte said that the company had nothing against him personally. 'But the company had decided to make a change and that owing to the serious anti-British attitude taken by the Italian press and the outspoken speeches made by Italians in Italy, it was impossible for me to retain my position as General Manager at Claridge's.'

This explanation did not satisfy Cochis: the newspaper articles expressing the greatest xenophobia at that time were not Italian, but British. The most virulent example was published in the *Daily Mirror*, with the byline John Boswell, on 27 April.

There are more than twenty thousand Italians in Great Britain.
London alone shelters more than eleven thousand of them.
The London Italian is an indigestible unit of population.
He settles here more or less temporarily, working until he has enough money to buy himself a little land in Calabria, or Campagnia or Tuscany.
He often avoids employing British labour.
It is much cheaper to bring a few relations into England from the old home town.
And so the boats unloaded all kinds of brown-eyed Francescas and Marias, beetle-browed Ginos, Titos and Marios. . .

Now every Italian colony in Great Britain and America is a seething cauldron of smoking Italian politics.

Black fascism. Hot as Hell.

Even the peaceful, law-abiding proprietor of the back-street coffee shop bounces into a fine patriotic frenzy at the sound of Mussolini's name. . .

We are nicely honeycombed with little cells of potential betrayal.

A storm is brewing in the Mediterranean.

And we, in our droning, silly tolerance are helping it to gather force.

Cochis persisted in his complaints, and on 3 May saw Sir George Reeves Smith, the company's managing director. Now Cochis came nearer the truth. Reeves Smith told him that he had inquired at Scotland Yard and found that Cochis was near the top of a 'Black List' of Italians – he was a fascist, had given £25 to the Fascio Club in London, and was also 'a link of information for the Italian government'. For good measure, Reeves Smith added that Scotland Yard had said that Cochis would be interned immediately if Britain and Italy went to war. At this point Cochis, who freely admitted that he had contributed to the London Fascio, but adamantly denied any role as a 'link of information', abandoned his protests.

It seems certain that Cochis was dismissed *after* Reeves Smith had made informal inquiries about him at Scotland Yard, and there was evidently some sensitivity on the point inside British intelligence. Cochis had carried his protestations to the Foreign Office, and when his file reached Gladwyn Jebb, the Foreign Office security and intelligence coordinator, Jebb suggested that the 'line' to be given to the Italian Embassy was that 'in view of the publicly expressed opinions of the Italian Government, it is surprising that the services of any Italians are retained by any respectable firm'. Certainly, it can be inferred, no word of any 'Black List' should be breathed.

It was logical for MI5 to maintain a list of suspect Italians, just as it had for Germans and Austrians. But whereas it had been able to monitor Germans and Austrians as they entered the country, scant documentation existed on the Italian community in Britain, many of whom – like the Pinis – had put down their roots in the nineteenth century. MI5 had managed to obtain the names of the

1,500 members of the British Fascio: a useful starting point, though hardly a definitive guide to Italian loyalties. The Cochis incident suggested that there was some attempt to make gradations among them, and, early in May, Halifax and Anderson agreed that, if war came, 'professing Fascisti' should be arrested – a term which could be taken to refer to more than nominal members. In one of his papers opposing mass internment, on the other hand, Anderson proposed that the 1,500 members of the Fascio should be interned on the outbreak of war, to be followed at some later stage by all Italian men between sixteen and sixty who had been in Britain less than ten years. The Cabinet patently did not favour moderation, for on 18 May it extended the time limit to twenty years. And the ranks of the hawks were strengthened by the arrival, a week later, of Brigadier Harker at the head of MI5.

Harker was quick to make his views on the Italians known. He telephoned Gladwyn Jebb with a warning which he confirmed by letter on 27 May. Invoking the spectre of the Mafia, Harker wrote: 'We have reason to suppose that the first act of war on the part of Italy might be an attempt to use the Italian Fascist Organization for attacks on key individuals and key points in this country by the employment of gangster methods. We are therefore anxious that our arrangements should be made so as to forestall such attempts if possible.' These arrangements would entail arresting 'all known suspects as soon as instructions to this effect are issued by the Home Office'. Harker appealed to the Foreign Office for its support. The next day, Cadogan wrote to Maxwell about some Italian engineers who worked for an electrical supply company in Lincolnshire. Cadogan said that MI5 believed the Italians were planning to sabotage 'key points' of Britain's power supplies.

> It is not for me to advise on questions of security [Cadogan wrote]. But I cannot refrain from saying that the position being what it is, and the chances of Italy coming into the war being what they are, the danger of continuing to employ Italians in these companies for a day longer seems to me to be tremendous . . . In the circumstances I can hardly believe that any technical difficulties or legal points will be allowed to hold up immediate action by the proper authorities.

Such clarity of vision was soon muddied by the Cabinet's faint hope that it could still keep Italy out of the war. The British Ambassador in Rome, Sir Percy Loraine, remained on good terms

with the Italian Foreign Minister, Count Galeazzo Ciano, Mussolini's son-in-law. The British government had offered Italy a
substantial prize to remain neutral: victor's status at a peace conference when the war was over. But, on 28 May, Ciano told
Loraine that war between their two countries was 'a certainty'.
Halifax reported their conversation to the Cabinet on 29 May.

When it considered the Italians in Britain, the Cabinet's conclusions were shot through with ambiguities. Anxious even now to
placate Ciano, it instructed Loraine to tell him that Britain would
deport all Italians in Britain, so long as the British in Italy were
allowed home. At the same time it was contemplating internment,
but could not decide how sweeping this should be: it felt that 'large
numbers' should be interned, but the measures should stop short
of 'wholesale internment'. Furthermore, Harker's perceptions
seemed to be carrying weight, for the 'professing Fascisti' were
now regarded as 'desperate characters who would not hesitate to
commit acts of sabotage'. They numbered 1,000, and 'action could
be taken against them at short notice'.

The confusion persisted at meetings on 30 and 31 May. Anderson reported that all preparations had been made to round up the
Italian 'desperate characters'; it was also agreed that a vessel
would be made available to return the 1,500 'desperate characters'
to Italy (no one seemed to notice that the number had crept up
from 1,000 again). In Rome, meanwhile, Sir Percy Loraine interpreted his instructions to mean that he was to arrange a mutual
exchange of diplomatic personnel and other government officials,
for which he concluded an agreement with Ciano on 4 June.

As war with Italy drew nearer, the different understandings
could be summarized as follows:

1. One thousand, or 1,500, 'desperate characters' to be arrested
   at once and interned, or deported.
2. Other Italian males between eighteen and sixty to be interned
   at some later date.
3. British and Italian diplomats and officials to be exchanged.

Resolution of these contradictions was to be swift and dramatic.

In Rome, Mussolini was pondering events in northern Europe
with increasing anxiety. Despite his prediction to Loraine, Ciano
told Mussolini that Italy should remain neutral, and Italy's generals had warned that they were not ready to fight. But Italy had

shared in the fruits of victory in 1918 and, with the fall of France imminent, Mussolini was sure that the opportunity was about to arise again. On 10 June, French and German troops north of Paris joined for the final engagement, and Mussolini announced from his Rome balcony that Italy was at war.

In London, Churchill responded immediately. Displaying no regard for the elaborate arrangements the Cabinet had agonized over, he issued the terse instruction: 'Collar the lot!'

The police went into action at once, arresting several hundred Italians in London that night. Among them was Serafino Pini, taken from his home in Seven Dials. The police searched his cupboards and drawers for subversive material, but found only a handful of street betting-slips (then illegal). As he was led away, a constable told his wife Lisa, 'Don't worry, your husband will be all right.' Pini was taken to the Oratory School in Brompton Road, which Eichenberg, Frenkel and Fehle had passed through on their way to Seaton the previous year. In all, 1,687 Italians were taken there by 14 June.

It was soon obvious that many of those held there were far from 'professing Fascisti', and some of the officers arresting or guarding them were very puzzled men. But the most pressing problem for the police and MI5 was the agreement for the exchange of diplomats and government officials. On 10 June the Italian ambassador, Giuseppe Bastianini, handed over a list of 730 Italians who were to sail on the *Monarch of Bermuda*, which awaited them in Glasgow. But the speed of the first arrests was proving a severe handicap. Diplomatic staff in London had been seized in their homes and, as MI5 had cut the embassy phones, it was hard to tell what was happening elsewhere. Several days passed before the Italian consuls in Liverpool and Cardiff were found languishing in police cells.

Bastianini appealed to the Foreign Office to intervene. But when the Foreign Office tried to trace some of the Italians on the diplomatic list, it found that the War Office was 'either unable or unwilling to say where they were or to whom orders for their release should be addressed'. Eventually forty-nine Italians were retrieved from the Oratory School. The Foreign Office also discovered that MI5 was refusing to release Italians who belonged to the London Fascio. After an arcane debate on what membership of the Fascio really signified, MI5 cleared all but forty on the ambassador's list. Some of the forty were young men who might

join the Italian forces; others had 'special knowledge' of benefit to
Italy. As Ciano and Loraine had agreed that the exchange was
subject to the 'interests of national security', the Italian ambassador had to acquiesce. On the other side of the coin were the
Italians on the list who refused to go. 'Many were outspoken on
the matter,' the Foreign Office observed, and they insisted on being
interned instead. In the end, 629 out of the 730 nominated by the
Italian ambassador joined the *Monarch of Bermuda*, which sailed
from Glasgow in time to reach Lisbon by 26 June. There it
exchanged its passengers for the British party which had left Italy
in the SS *Conte Rosso*.

The problem of who should sail on the *Monarch of Bermuda* soon
paled before the question of who was actually being interned. To
the bewilderment of some of the police handling the affair, those
arrested naturally included a large number of restaurant proprietors, café owners, chefs and waiters who formed the core of the
Italian community in Britain. Inspector William Rogers of Special
Branch was on duty at Lingfield Race Course on 11 June when
the first of the Italian internees were brought in. As they were
supposedly the most desperate characters of all, Rogers was astonished when they greeted the Germans in the camp with jeers and
insults – 'I am quite satisfied that the hostility of the Italians
towards the Germans was sincere,' Rogers wrote. He was puzzled
that most of the internees were 'connected with the catering trade
and had been established in this country for some years. They
have little or no desire to return to Italy and are anti-Nazi in
sentiment.'

Police officers in other forces shared Roger's dismay. In Manchester, a young detective in Special Branch was sent to arrest
Ernani Landucci, who had been a waiter at a Manchester hotel
for the best part of thirty years, and had a British-born daughter.
The detective constable later described how, far from seeming an
enemy agent, Landucci 'looked like a simple, decent, but very
frightened Italian waiter'. When told he was under arrest, Landucci burst into tears. He explained that he belonged to the
Manchester branch of the Fascio solely because he owned a small
patch of land in southern Italy on which he had to pay taxes of 2s
6d (12½p) each year to the Italian consul. Before being taken
away, Landucci opened a bottle of wine, handed glasses to his
wife, daughter and the detective constable, and drank the toast,
'Bugger the Fascio!' The account survives because the policeman

involved was Robert Mark, later to become Chief Commissioner of the Metropolitan Police, who, in his autobiography, described the incident as one of the most formative of his career.

It was soon discovered that not only innocuous fascists were being interned, but also determined anti-fascists. They included the two sons of the Italian socialist leader Claudio Treves: Paolo Treves, a distinguished linguistic expert who had been a translator and announcer in the BBC Italian service since the beginning of the war; and his brother Piero, who was a research student at St John's College, Cambridge. Their cousin, Uberto Limentani, who also worked for the BBC, was a third member of the family to be interned. Dr A. F. Magri, chairman of the Italian League for the Rights of Man, and the league's secretary, D. Anzani, were arrested too. It was particularly ironic that they should have been included for they had headed a list of Italians sympathetic to Britain which British intelligence had asked for from the International Secretary of the Labour Party, William Gillies. What was more, Anzani had lived in Britain for thirty-one years and had not been back to Italy in that time. He and Magri visited Gillies at the Labour Party offices in Smith Square on 11 June to ask how they could help in Britain's war effort. The police, who had already raided Anzani's home once that morning, arrested them an hour later.

Greater anomalies still were enacted.

Gaetano Antonio Pacitto, a naturalized British subject, was arrested in Hull on 10 June; Clement Fiorini, who had lived in Britain for forty years, was taken from his home in Rusholme, Manchester, on 11 June. Another victim was Alberto Loria, an Italian Jew who had come to Britain in 1911, had a British wife, two British-born daughters, had fought with the Italian army on the side of the Allies in the First World War, and had been awarded the OBE for his work with the British Ministry of Munitions. And one man was arrested because he came from a Jewish family in Constantinople and was accounted Italian because his family had acquired 'Italian protection' at some point in the dispersal of the Turkish Empire after the First World War. It did not matter that his father had since renounced this dubious privilege, or that he had tried to enlist in the British army in 1939.

Some 4,000 Italians were arrested in the two weeks that followed Italy's declaration of war, and a further 300 British subjects of Italian descent – including Serafino Pini's sister and three brothers

– were detained under Regulation 18B. Although it was fewer than some had predicted, even that number was to add an almost impossible burden to those responsible for accommodation, as the immediate fate of several hundred Italian internees shows. Within a week of their arrests, they were sent to a camp which was described by François Lafitte as 'by far the worst of which we have any knowledge'.

The camp was a derelict cotton factory at Bury in Lancashire, known as Warth Mills. It was not on the list of original War Office camps, and it is clear from the accounts of Serafino Pini and others that it had been pressed into service at a moment's notice. Cotton waste littered the entrance and the floor was slippery with oil and grease. The mill was lit only through the glass roof; as many of its panes were broken or missing, it also let in the rain, which collected in large puddles below. There were eighteen cold-water taps for each 500 men and the lavatories were filthy; after several Italian doctors led a protest to the camp commander, Major Braybrook, lime was supplied in an attempt to make them more hygienic. The food was sparse: the evening meal consisted of a lump of bread, a small piece of cheese and a cup of tea. There were few mattresses at first, and most internees slept on boards covered by two or three blankets, some of which proved verminous. At night they could hear rats scuttling among the remnants of the mill machinery. The entire building was surrounded by two fences of barbed wire, with armed guards patrolling in between.

The internees' description was largely confirmed by Monsieur R. A. Haccius, the delegate to Britain of the Geneva-based International Committee of the Red Cross. The Red Cross was performing its traditional neutral role of trying to secure the best conditions for the captives of war, and was visiting prisoners and internees in Britain, France and Germany. Haccius, who had been given offices by the British government in St James's Palace, visited Warth Mills on 12 July. In his report he singled out the mill's dilapidated condition, the absence of lighting, and the poor hygiene, which included the small number of taps, the absence of hot water and the dirty lavatories. He also criticized the camp's inadequate sick-bay, with only thirty beds for the 250 internees who required special treatment.

Haccius presented his report to the Foreign Office, which had by now equipped itself to deal with the Red Cross. Sir George Warner was a former British minister at Berne who had been brought out of retirement at the age of sixty to head the Foreign Office's new Prisoners of War Section (not to be confused with the War Office department of the same name). Warner passed the report to the War Office with the spare observation that Warth Mills had been found to be 'below the general standard'. That Warner permitted himself even that comment was a sign of increasing concern over internment in some echelons of the Foreign Office.

At the head of the Foreign Office, the tall, lugubrious figure of Lord Halifax had remained quiet during most of the internment debate. Having loyally praised Sir Nevile Bland's report on the Fifth Column, he had been characteristically content to go wherever the Cabinet consensus led. Besides, his senior officials were making much of the running.

Cavendish-Bentinck, in the chair of the JIC, had been one of the loudest voices calling for internment. Cadogan had succumbed to the stridency of MI5, endorsing their demands and noting in his celebrated diary his observation to the Italian ambassador on 11 June that 'Britain was not going to take any chances this time'. And MI5 had found a listener in Gladwyn Jebb.

On lower levels, officials tended to see aliens as Home Office territory and were reluctant to trespass upon it. The General Department contained a Refugee Section (which later did become a fully fledged department) whose head was a cautious former diplomat named Thomas Snow. Beneath him was a determined and articulate official named Richard Latham who, even from the lowly rank of temporary clerk, was to have considerable impact later on the struggle over MI5. Latham, the son of Australia's Attorney-General, had come to Britain as a Rhodes scholar with a place at Magdalen College, Oxford. He had first become involved in the plight of European refugees in a dramatic fashion in March 1939. On behalf of the 'British Committee for Refugees from Czechoslovakia', he travelled to Oldenzaal on the Dutch–German border and told Dutch immigration officials to let Czech refugees cross as they would all be accepted into Britain. In some consternation, the British passport officer at The Hague telephoned the Foreign Office at 1 a.m. to say that Latham 'had a list of 2,000 persons and was proposing to add to it'. He phoned again twelve hours later, and reported that the Dutch 'were seriously perturbed lest Mr Latham's presence should lead to a rush of refugees to the Dutch frontier . . . the Dutch might find themselves confronted with a mob of 25,000 and might have to mobilize troops in order to control them.' Sir Nevile Bland himself had to attend the Dutch Foreign Ministry the following morning, 'in order to explain Mr Latham's position. . . '.

Despite Latham's apparent predilection for direct action, he was accepted by the Foreign Office in a temporary position when the war began. He had been awarded the supreme academic accolade of a fellowship at All Souls' College, but did not take it up as his only ambition was to fly for the RAF, joining the Foreign Office meanwhile. When it was announced on 11 May that, as a corollary to internment in the 'coastal counties', there would be severe restrictions on all non-enemy aliens there, Latham helped to field the complaints from Foreign embassies and legations. The Foreign Office asked the Home Office to be lenient to the French, who were, after all, Britain's allies. The Home Office at first merely passed on such requests to the police with its own recommendations, and when three elderly French professors at Cambridge were deprived of their bicycles, Frank Newsam himself reported that the bicycles had been restored. But, in early June, the Home Office agreed that French citizens throughout Britain should be free of all restrictions. Despite this victory, Latham was soon complaining about a lack of warning and consultation by the Home Office, and wrote scathingly of the 'panic alien restrictions'.

Other officials became bold, too. Sir George Warner let slip the occasional criticism, as we have seen. And when the Foreign Office saw for itself the chaos over Italian repatriation, it lost all inhibitions; even William Cavendish-Bentinck, one of the architects of internment, was affected by the mounting anger. On reading an MI5 bulletin which proposed interning a further 6,000 Italians, he wrote the admittedly two-edged statement:

> It seems strange to me to intern Italians such as the restaurant keepers, 'Luigi' and 'Quaglino' who have a stake in this country, even though they may be members of the local Fascio, which is, in fact, nothing more than the equivalent of the British Society in a South American capital, and to allow liberty to Germans in this country who have no stake in this country and on whom pressure can be brought by threats that their relations in Germany will suffer.

Although it was expressing its anger more forcefully, the Foreign Office remained on the side-lines, lacking power to influence policy or even information about its course. This was made only too clear when Harold Farquhar, another overseas diplomat recently recalled to Whitehall, attended a meeting at the War Office on 17 June about 'Refugees and Prisoners of War'. He found that he was the only Foreign Office man present. The Home Office had five representatives, and there were eight army officers, including Captain Stevens of MI5 (the same Stevens who had interrogated Karl Wehner in 1939). Farquhar had gone expecting the meeting to discuss what he later termed the 'Italian imbroglio'. He was horrified to discover that arrangements were being made to deport 4,500 Germans and 1,500 Italians to Canada.

15 *Fait Accompli*

That the Foreign Office man responsible for internees did not know plans for their deportation were well advanced may be seen, of course, as a damning reflection on his ministry's efficiency. It points more significantly to the close secrecy with which the plans were being laid, and the care taken to exclude their potential opponents for as long as possible. Even the Cabinet was kept in the dark during the vital negotiations with Canada. After Churchill's brief utterance on 24 May, which no one appeared to take seriously, there was no further mention of the scheme in Cabinet until 11 June. Then Chamberlain announced that Canada had agreed to accept 7,000 men and the Cabinet was presented with a *fait accompli*.

Those two Cabinet meetings encompass a period when absolute power over internees was transferred to Lord Swinton and the Home Defence (Security) Executive, and the Home Office was rendered its most impotent. But embarrassment alone may not explain why the Home Office has once again declined to release any documents pertaining to this phase; the refusal must also stem from what they would disclose of the activities of the Swinton Committee. It is fortunately possible to construct a framework of events from files of the Foreign and Dominions Office in the Public Record Office, and those of the Canadian and Australian governments in Ottawa and Canberra.

They reveal a disreputable story.

We have already seen that it was probably Anderson's stone-walling at the Cabinet meeting of 24 May that provoked Churchill to declare himself 'strongly in favour of removing all internees out of the United Kingdom'. Three days later, Chamberlain secured approval to set up the Home Defence (Security) Executive. He also resolved to see that Churchill's new wish was gratified. Although he was already suffering from the bowel cancer which was to kill him by the end of the year, he performed his task with ruthless dedication. And while Chamberlain formally accepted responsibility for deportation, sufficient clues have surfaced to show that the Swinton Committee was also determined that it should be carried out.

The first known event in the saga occurred on 30 May, when Viscount Caldecote, Secretary of State for the Dominions, dispatched a note to Vincent Massey, High Commissioner for the Canadian Government in London. Caldecote, a sixty-four-year-old barrister and former Attorney-General, had been appointed to his post in succession to Anthony Eden just two weeks earlier; when he was Prime Minister, Chamberlain had liked to deal directly with the Dominions, and would undoubtedly have kept a firm grip on Caldecote's transactions. Caldecote's note asked Massey if his government could accept some of Britain's internees. Its tone was restrained: there were 9,000 Germans and Austrians interned already; the number was growing; and their custody raised 'serious questions of security'. Could Canada help? How many could she take?

The Canadian Cabinet met to consider the British request on 5 June. The subject was introduced by William Mackenzie King, Canada's Prime Minister since 1935. He told his colleagues that Britain had asked Canada to accept 'a large number of enemy aliens'. The Cabinet was less than enthusiastic. One minister said that Canada had enough problems with her own aliens, especially in Saskatchewan; another said that the fear of Fifth Column activities were already having 'an unsettling effect'. The Cabinet conceded that Britain was more vulnerable to such activities than Canada, and helpfully suggested alternative locations such as Newfoundland or the West Indies; or perhaps Canada's own bleak northern regions. The Cabinet asked Canada's Director of Internment Operations, General Edouard Panet, to report on the possibility of accepting 'limited numbers' of internees. At the same time it sent Britain a somewhat gloomy response. Canada could not agree to the proposals immediately: there were 'considerable difficulties' in the way; and a survey was needed of the facilities 'possibly available'.

Canada's response must have dismayed Chamberlain, who was being assailed with demands from on high to carry the scheme through. On 3 June, Churchill had dictated a note to the Cabinet secretary, Sir Edward Bridges. It evinced a feeble grasp of the details of the scheme, but the message was clear enough:

> Has anything been done about shipping twenty thousand internees to Newfoundland or St Helena? Is this one of the matters the Lord President has in hand? If so, would you please ask him about it. I should like to get them on the high seas as soon as possible, but I suppose considerable arrangements have to be made at the other end. Is it all going forward?

Viscount Swinton spoke to Chamberlain on the same day, reiterating the view that it would be dangerous to keep alien internees and war prisoners in the United Kingdom. Such pressure was clearly reflected in the hyperbole of Caldecote's renewed request to Massey on 7 June:

> The total number of German internees in this country is now over 12,000, of whom 2,500 are definitely pro-Nazi in sympathy and allegiance and therefore a source of danger in the event, for example, of parachute landings or invasion of the country. . . In the circumstances, the United Kingdom Government sincerely hopes that the Canadian Government may be pressed to come to the assistance of the United Kingdom by agreeing to receive at the earliest possible moment, at least the internees whose removal from this country it is desired to secure on the ground that their continued presence in this country is bound to be a source of the most serious risk. Any expenditure on account of the transport and maintenance of these persons in Canada will be borne by the United Kingdom Government.

Massey duly passed the request to Ottawa.

By now, General Panet had consulted the Departments of Justice and Internal Affairs, and the Royal Canadian Mounted Police, and he gave the Canadian Cabinet a more positive report. Accommodation was available, as were retired army veterans who could act as guards. It was true that, for Canada, the internees were 'potentially dangerous people', but Panet felt that Britain faced the greater peril of German parachutists landing in the British internment camps, overpowering the guards and arming the prisoners. On 8 June, the Canadian government sent a new message to Massey in London, asking how many and what sort of men Britain wanted to send, and advising that prisoners of war would present 'less difficulty' than internees.

On 10 June, Massey told Caldecote that Canada needed 'particulars as to the numbers and categories of prisoners whom it is particularly desired to send to Canada'. His request for information was interpreted as further hesitation, and a high-powered delegation was hastily assembled. It included representatives from the Dominions, War, and Cabinet Offices, with the Home Office conspicuously absent. They met Charles Ritchie, Second Secretary at the Canadian High Commission, on the same day, and explained that Britain had 'the most urgent need' to dispose of more than 6,000 internees and prisoners of war. They comprised 2,633 German internees in Category 'A', including those arrested at the start of the war, those detained by tribunals, merchant seamen, and 350 'Nazi leaders' who were to be segregated from the rest; 1,823 German prisoners of war; and – as war with Italy was expected by the hour – 1,500 members of the Italian Fascist Party. Massey cabled the details to Ottawa in time for the day's Cabinet, which accepted that the prisoners were a 'pressing military problem' for Britain and agreed to take 4,000 internees and 3,000 prisoners of war. At eleven the next morning, an undoubtedly relieved Chamberlain announced Canada's decision to the British Cabinet. The 4,000 internees, Chamberlain added, would consist of 2,500 Germans and 1,500 Italians who were the 'most dangerous characters of all'.

When Chamberlain made his announcement, Lord Halifax, Foreign Secretary, remained silent. He had referred to Italians earlier in the meeting, expressing the hope that the scheme for the 'reciprocal deportation' would be enacted. He was still apparently hoping that the complex plans devised by the Cabinet at the end of May would be carried through, adding: 'It was to our advantage to get rid of as many Italians as possible. Italy would have to feed them, and they could probably form centres of disaffection in Italy, since many of them had no desire to return to that country.' The possibility that Italians might have no desire to go to Canada either evidently did not occur to him. Nor did he comment three days later, when Sir John Dill, Chief of the Imperial General Staff, told the Cabinet that ships earmarked to take twelve battalions to India would first be used to transport internees to Canada.

It seems that Halifax hardly realized the implications of Dill's words; or, at least, that he did not communicate the information to his officials most directly concerned. They, in turn, might have received their first intimation of the deportation plans from a meeting on 13 June of the Home Office's Aliens Advisory Committee (successor to the Committee of Imperial Defence Sub-committee on the Control of Aliens in Wartime). Chaired by Frank Newsam, its subject was: 'The desirability and feasibility of repatriating Italians to Italy.' The War Office and MI5 representatives strongly pressed that Italians should be 'removed at the earliest possible moment', but Harold Farquhar, present from the Foreign Office, cannot have noticed when Canada was mentioned as an alternative to Italy. As it was, Farquhar learned the full truth at the War Office four days later.

Farquhar wrote afterwards that he had been asked at the meeting if he knew of any legal reasons why internees should not be shipped to Canada; he supposed that, since the Geneva Convention permitted prisoners to be transferred within one country, this sanction could legitimately be extended to all parts of the British Empire. The War Office minute writer put a wider gloss on his contribution, recording that 'the Foreign Office stated that they had no objection to Italians being sent to Canada'. Farquhar complained at the Foreign Office that he had received no forewarning of the meeting, and his protest was taken up by Sir George Warner, head of the Prisoners of War Section, who added that he was afraid that Germany might retaliate by sending British prisoners or internees to 'very bad quarters in Poland'. When Snow of the Refugee Section complained that he did not know what was going on either, Warner asked the Dominions Office to send him copies of the relevant correspondence. But the Foreign Office was being left far behind in the pace of events.

The Home Office also seemed to be no more than a passive spectator, resigned to the dominant role taken by the War Office. The five Home Office men Farquhar had observed made almost no contribution to the meeting at the War Office on 17 June. Its chairman, Colonel Robertson, came from the Prisoners of War Department, which was headed by Major-General Sir Alan Hunter, a member of the Swinton Committee. Robertson steered

the meeting where he wished, and the Home Office made no
objection to the contribution from Captain Stevens of MI5.

> MI5 agreed to send at once . . . a list of 1,500 Italians whose
> removal they desired. If possible, the names of 350 'bad hats'
> would be specially marked on the list. MI5 would also send a
> second list of 500 to make up a total [sic] in case the first 1,500
> are not available.

The War Office announced that three ships were ready to sail,
with a capacity of between 7,000 and 7,500, and that the date of
embarkation was probably 24 June.

Even on its own ground, the Home Office merely attended
mechanically to the details of the operation. On 18 June it convened the Aliens Advisory Committee to decide 'what steps should
be taken to give effect to the policy of interning an additional
number of male Germans and Austrians' – of whom 25,300
remained 'at large'. Major N. Coates, also from the War Office
Prisoners of War Department, announced that when all the Italians had been arrested, there would still be accommodation for
another 10,000 internees. 'In addition, when the batch of internees
have left for Canada, there will be room, after June 24th, for an
additional 6,000 persons.'

In the Dominions Office, Caldecote was continuing the search
for countries who would come to Britain's aid. On 14 June, he sent
telegrams to the governments of Australia, South Africa and Newfoundland. They were couched in the same terms as the final
appeal to Canada, with the additional argument that Canada had
already consented to help. Australia responded with alacrity,
cabling its agreement on 16 June and concluding 'we will await
your further advice as to details'. Newfoundland agreed to take
1,000 internees soon afterwards. Only South Africa said no. On 16
June, the South African Prime Minister, Jan Smuts, admitted he
was 'in real difficulty' through having already interned 2,000 Germans as well as a number of South Africa's own citizens (they
included a future Prime Minister in John Vorster). Smuts suggested St Helena and the Falkland Islands, and resisted further
blandishments from Caldecote a week later.

By now, any weighing of the merits of deportation had been
abandoned. It had been superseded by a mere juggling of numbers,
as if a train timetable was being arranged, not the disposition of
human beings. When bureaucrats reach that stage, secrecy is their

great ally, for it saves them from having to consider the human dimension of their policies, and prevents others from reminding them of it too. They were about to lose that protection.

The government had managed to stall several speculative questions in the Commons about the possibility of sending war prisoners to Canada, but on 16 June the *New York Times* repeated the suggestion, and a *Daily Mail* reporter put the story to the Foreign Office. His question brought consternation: 'an ill-judged announcement could do great harm', one official noted, adding: '. . . steps are being taken to stop the press from mentioning or commenting on the idea.' On 19 June, the story broke: the source was the Prime Minister of Canada.

For several weeks, families throughout Canada had been enthusiastically preparing to receive 100,000 child evacuees from Britain. At the last minute, the British Cabinet had second thoughts about the scheme, sharing Churchill's feeling that a break-up of family life would be a disastrous blow to home morale. Persistent questioning in Ottawa finally goaded Mackenzie King into revealing that the British government had given priority to internees and prisoners of war. 'The reasons they give are that the interned aliens in Britain might be in a position to help German parachutists in the event of a descent on the British Isles, which they are expecting hourly,' Mackenzie King explained.

The revelation caused near panic at the Foreign Office. Sir George Warner drafted a note for the Swiss Legation – Germany's protecting power in Britain – and sent copies to the War Office, Home Office and Dominions Office for their approval. 'The matter is somewhat urgent,' he observed, 'as it appears that some P/W are being sent off at once and not on the 24th as we were led to believe.' His alarm was justified.

On 20 June, A. N. Rucker of the Swinton Committee wrote to the Dominions Office, pressing for the 'the Australian possibilities to be examined at once by the War Office and the Ministry of Shipping'. At the Cabinet on 21 June, the Minister of Shipping, Ronald Cross, announced that the first liner was due to leave for Canada that night.

The 21 June is one of the most eventful dates in the history of internment: it was not only the announcement by Cross which made it so. On that day, the Home Office capitulated almost unconditionally to demands for mass internment. Its officials were already following lamely where the War Office led, and Anderson showed no trace of his former defiance when he told Cabinet that:

> Enemy aliens were being locked up as fast as accommodation could be provided and . . . the accommodation vacated by internees would be filled at once. . . Reliable aliens were being combed out from those who had already been interned, but this would only result in the release of a limited number.

On the same day, Alexander Maxwell sent new letters to chief constables: 'His Majesty's Government have decided to adopt a policy of interning, subject to certain exceptions, the male Germans and Austrians now at large in this country.' As there were 25,000 and accommodation for all was 'not immediately available', internment would be carried out in three stages. The first would take in all Germans and Austrians who did not have refugee status, apart from those who had been in Britain for more than twenty years; and all Germans and Austrians who were unemployed, no matter how long they had lived in Britain. The second stage would take all other Germans and Austrians outside London; the third, those living in London. Chief constables were to start drawing up lists at once, and the first stage of arrests would start on 25 June.

There was no announcement of this move to Cabinet, where the sole reservation about the course of internment was voiced by Lord Halifax. He was probably reflecting the growing anxieties of his officials when he suggested a 'quick comb-out' of aliens willing to fight for Britain. There was no response. All other discussion was on a technical level, although there was a hint of a possible snag. After Cross had announced that the first ship for Canada would sail that evening, Caldecote admitted that Canada had asked that 'no more requests of any nature should be made . . . for the time being, as they had their hands full'.

The item is notable in one further respect. When he minuted this part of the discussion, the Cabinet secretary, Sir Edward Bridges, used, for the first time, the heading: 'Deportation of Internees'. It was, presumably, an accurate reflection of the Cabinet's state of mind. It was also a disturbing echo of the nineteenth-century British habit of dispatching to the colonies undesirables of every kind, from common criminals to the Tolpuddle Martyrs: 'transportation' was the term then in vogue. Even the Tolpuddle Martyrs were paid one dubious courtesy which the twentieth-century deportees did not receive: they were at least told where they were being sent.

On 20 June, Kurt Tebrich, the sixteen-year-old boy who had been so glad to escape from his foster-parents in Edinburgh, was told that he would be leaving the internment camp at Lingfield Race Course the following day. In the morning, he gathered together his belongings and marched with the camp's other inmates to Lingfield Railway Station. There they boarded a train which set off to the north; as nameplates had been removed from the stations they passed through as an invasion precaution, no one could tell precisely where they were heading. They asked the British guards escorting them, but they had no idea either. That evening the train came to a halt outside a large city which someone recognized as Liverpool, and the rumour now spread that they were being sent to the Isle of Man. After a long delay, the train pulled into a station and they were marched to the Liverpool docks. At the quayside was a large passenger ship painted grey. She was the Canadian Pacific *Duchess of York*, a 20,000-ton passenger liner that had sailed regularly on the North Atlantic run before the war. Tebrich wondered why so large a vessel was needed to take them to the Isle of Man: others suggested it was merely that more passengers could be carried.

The *Duchess of York* was crowded to almost twice her capacity. The 500 military prisoners on board were given the best passenger cabins, a measure of the War Office's anxiety to secure the best reciprocal conditions for British prisoners of war in Germany. Of the civilian internees on board 1,700 were German merchant seamen who had been placed automatically in Category 'A'. The remaining 400 were Category 'B' and 'C' civilians, Tebrich and a handful of young men from Lingfield among them; sheer administrative muddle had put them on the first ship to Canada. And by the time Tebrich arrived, there was no sleeping accommodation left at all. He and a group of other young men were guided to the dining-room, and told to sleep where they could. Some commandeered the dining tables; Tebrich, with not even a blanket to cover him, simply lay down on the floor.

He awoke in the morning to find the *Duchess of York* steaming steadily westwards. There was land to port which a German seaman said was Northern Ireland. He told Tebrich that the Isle of Man lay far behind, and they could only be bound for Canada.

At 10 a.m. that day, soon after Tebrich made his discovery that he was going to Canada, another Cabinet meeting was held in London. Caldecote announced that Australia had agreed to take as many internees as Britain cared to send, which was not strictly true, and that Newfoundland would accept 1,000. The Cabinet took note. At the Foreign Office, Warner sent his note about the deportation plans to the Swiss Legation, with a copy to the Brazilian Embassy, who acted as Italy's protective power. He also asked the War Office to send him minutes of all their meetings in future. For a moment it seemed that some order had been restored to the proceedings. But when the Cabinet reassembled the following day, it was to hear some melodramatic news. The First Lord of the Admiralty, Albert Alexander, told his colleagues:

> The *Duchess of York,* which was taking some 6,000 German internees and prisoners of war to Canada, had signalled that she had had one man killed and two wounded and feared a further rising.

Sir Edward Bridges headed the item: 'Mutiny of Enemy Aliens en route to Canada'. At that moment it must have seemed that the worst fears about enemy aliens had been realized. Those on board the *Duchess of York* tell a very different story.

The *Duchess of York* was carrying 2,100 internees and 500 German prisoners of war, a total of 2,600, not 6,000 as Alexander had told the Cabinet. After the evening meal of 22 June, a number of internees and military prisoners were on deck, some smoking cigarettes, others escaping from their cramped and stuffy quarters. Around 7.15 p.m., a British officer appeared and ordered the prisoners and internees below. Among them was Kurt Tebrich. He says:

> As I recall it there were people sitting on deck and the sun was shining. An officer came on deck and ordered everyone below. People started moving slowly and I have the impression they weren't carrying out the order quickly enough. I heard a shot and I turned round and saw a man lying there. I was about thirty-five yards away at the time.

Another account was compiled by a German army officer, Colonel Georg Friemel, from statements from seven other prisoners of war who witnessed the incident. According to Friemel, the crowd on deck was already going below when the British officer ordered one of the sentries to level his gun. The prisoners divided into two groups, 'the greater part crowding into the stern'. The British officer ordered the sentry to prepare to fire. Although some German officers tried to calm the crowd, 'a slight panic arose'. The British officer then 'placed himself behind the sentry and showed him one of the men. The soldier, evidently excited when ordered to shoot, tried to lift the muzzle of his rifle to fire over the heads of the crowd.' But the British officer pressed down the barrel of the sentry's gun towards the crowd. He then, Friemel continued,

> energetically repeated several times his order to fire ('Shoot him!'). About 7.30 a shot was fired. A panic arose. . . Machine-guns were placed in direction of the deck [sic]. Two sentries drove the people down the staircase with their bayonets. One of the casualties was taken away. Several officers and internees were hurt. Casualties were: one dead and ten wounded. The shot was fired at a distance of about 15 metres.

The man killed was a German merchant seaman named Karl Marquart. Friemel's statement, which he had made to the International Red Cross, was forwarded to the British government in August. The British officer was eventually court-martialled. But on 23 June 1940, there was nothing to contradict the version of events presented to Cabinet by the First Lord of the Admiralty. It did not matter that neither the man who was shot nor the principal witnesses were civilian internees. There could be no more dramatic confirmation of the danger to Britain from the enemy within.

16   The Liverpool Train

The first stage in the mass arrests of Category 'C' internees began promptly on 24 June. The second and third stages were activated in the following two weeks, and would bring the total number interned since the war began – including merchant seamen – to 27,200. It was perilously close to the figure of 29,000 reached in the First World War, so ringingly denounced by Viscount Cobham from the War Office in October 1939, and *eighteen times* the maximum Cobham had predicted.

Cobham had departed from his post as Parliamentary Under-Secretary of State for War in May 1940, and was able to concentrate once again on the finances of the MCC, and to care for his 6,000 acres of land, and his paintings by Reynolds and Van Dyck, at the Cobhams' Worcestershire seat of Hagley Hall. It was less easy for Sir John Anderson to forget his earlier pronouncements, in particular the time he abandoned his customary caution to endorse the distinction between Germans who were 'properly under suspicion' and those who were the victims of Britain's enemy. In mockery of Anderson's words, these same victims were now pouring into internment camps throughout Britain. They included some of the most talented and courageous people to escape from Germany.

One of the most intent observers of internment was François Lafitte, who had just started work on his book *The Internment of Aliens*. He had an intriguing background. His father was American, his mother French, but they had separated and he acquired as a stepfather the pioneering sexologist Havelock Ellis. Lafitte absorbed a determined radicalism from Ellis and his mother, and for a time belonged to the British Communist Party, taking part in the renowned battle with the British Union of Fascists in Cable Street. He spent some time in Vienna before the war and helped many socialists and Jews to make their way to England. He and his wife opened their house in Herne Hill, south London, to refugees, and became especially aware of the barriers encountered by the professionally qualified, like the dentists and psychiatrists who had brought their dinner jackets to England and wore them when they worked as waiters in West End restaurants.

Lafitte worked as researcher for the International Miners' Federation for a year, and then joined Political and Educational Planning (PEP), a private ginger group which produced reformist papers on contemporary social issues and advocated Keynsian policies of economic expansion as an antidote to unemployment. PEP also had close links with MPs and others active in the refugee movement. Lafitte was called up in May 1940, but to his dismay was discovered to have a heart condition. He returned to PEP to find it immersed in the plight of the refugees. At the end of June, PEP assigned Lafitte to write a book on internment. He completed his task by September 1940 and corrected his proofs by candlelight in the Anderson shelter in his garden in Herne Hill. PEP deducted Penguin's fee of £50 from his salary. *The Internment of Aliens* was published as a Penguin Special in November 1940, and almost all 50,000 copies – at 6*d* (2½p) a time – were sold. We have already pronounced it the best work on internment in forty years. And, in the absence of Home Office files, no better compilation exists of the extraordinary array of distinguished men who were interned in the spring and early summer of 1940. We have drawn heavily on Lafitte's book in assembling the following list.

Dr Franz Borkenau, Austrian: a distinguished historian and sociologist, whose book *The Totalitarian Enemy* was fiercely anti-Nazi.
Max Braun, German: leader of the Social Democratic Party of the Saarland, the disputed territory on the border of France; fled to Paris after the Nazi annexation in 1935, escaped to England when France fell in 1940.
Siegfried Charoux, Austrian: a sculptor with works in the Vienna State Gallery – which the Nazis removed.

Heinrich Fraenkel, German: a well-known campaigning journalist, author of *The German People versus Hitler*, who was recruited by the British Ministry of Information and continued to write anti-Nazi propaganda from internment on the Isle of Man.

Dr Martin Freud, Austrian: son of Sigmund Freud and Fellow of the Royal Society.

Richard Friedenthal, German: novelist, and editor of the mass-circulation *Knaur's Encyclopaedia*, first published in 1933.

Hans Gottfurcht, German: leader of the German Trades Unionists in London.

Sebastian Haffner, German: lawyer and journalist, author of *Germany, Jekyll and Hyde*.

John Heartfield, German: the pioneer of photo-montage whose anti-Nazi works were already world-famous; born Helmut Herzfelde, he had adopted an English name during the First World War to demonstrate his hatred of Prussian militarism, and on escaping to Britain in 1938, contributed anti-Nazi graphics to *Picture Post* and other publications.

Heinz Heckroth, German: eminent stage-designer and painter, whose work was banned by the Nazis.

Gerhard Hintze, German: well-known left-wing actor who had spent several years in concentration camps.

Kurt Joos, German: a ballet master and Germany's leading choreographer.

Dr Ernst Kitzinger, German: an outstanding young art historian who worked for the British Museum on arriving in London, and helped to evacuate the museum's art treasures.

Dr G. V. Lachmann, German: a leading aerodynamicist who had worked for the British company, Handley Page, since 1930.

Sigurd Leeder, German: choreographer and dancing master.

Dr Ludwig Münz, Austrian: art historian, and specialist in educating blind children.

Robert Neumann, Austrian: anti-Nazi writer who founded the Austrian PEN Club in Britain in 1938.

Dr Otto Neurath, Austrian: renowned statistician who emigrated to Holland in 1934. When Holland fell, he and his fiancée escaped to sea in a rowing boat and were picked up by a British destroyer. When they landed in England they were interned.

Rudolf Olden, German: distinguished journalist and lawyer who defended the Nobel Prize-winner Carl von Ossietzky; editor of

Berliner Tageblatt, one of the last papers to succumb to nazifica-
tion; author of biographies of Hindenburg and Hitler.

Hans Oppenheim, German: conductor and musician.

Franz Osborne, German: concert pianist.

Franz Pixner, Austrian: sculptor, and veteran of the Spanish Civil
War, where he was seriously injured by a landmine.

Eugen Prager, Austrian: publisher who worked with the British
Ministry of Information.

Professor E. Pringsheim, German: authority on Roman Law, who
was teaching at Oxford.

Otto Lehmann Rüssbuldt, German: socialist, pacifist, colleague of
Carl von Ossietzky, and general secretary of the International
League for the Rights of Man; sixty-seven years old when
interned.

Kurt Schwitters, German: celebrated Dadaist painter, who had
sought refuge from the Nazis in Norway, only to be captured by
British troops in April 1940, shipped to England, and interned.

Peter Stadlen, Austrian: concert pianist.

Fred Uhlman, German: anti-Nazi barrister from Stuttgart, also a
successful painter.

Professor Egon Wellesz, Austrian: composer of songs and operas,
and an authority on Byzantine music, elected an honorary Fellow of Lincoln College, Oxford, in 1939.

Men of such distinction should not be seen as an unrepresen-
tative élite among internees. They were the tip of an eminent
iceberg, with much of the submerged portion formed from the well-
educated and professional classes: those, in short, who had been
best equipped to leave Germany and Austria in the first place.
Evidence for this is to be found in a survey that one group of
internees conducted among themselves in July. They were the
inmates of Onchan, one of the first camps to be set up on the Isle
of Man. It held 1,491 internees.

The inhabitants of Onchan learned that they included 121 artists
and literary workers, 113 scientists and teachers, 68 lawyers, 67
graduate engineers, 38 physicians, 22 graduate chemical engineers,
19 clergymen and 12 dentists. At the other end of the social scale
were 103 agricultural workers. The survey also found that 1,230
(82 per cent) of the internees were Jewish; 148 had married British-
born women; and they had 332 British-born children between
them. No fewer than 1,080 had applied to join the British army,

Pioneer Corps, or some other government service; 145 had close relatives in the army or working for the government. They had employed a total of 6,499 British workers. And 660 intended to emigrate to the United States or elsewhere – although how many wanted to do so as a result of being interned is not made clear.

By now there were internment camps the length of Britain. Some were substantial edifices, such as castles, country houses and schools; others were clearly temporary affairs, like the camp at Prees Heath in Shropshire, which consisted of army tents erected in a field. Camps had spread throughout the Isle of Man: to Ramsey, Onchan and Port Erin had been added others at Peel, Port St Mary, and the capital town of Douglas.

The camp instructions that had applied in September 1939 were still in force, and were interpreted with varying degrees of strictness. Soon the internees imposed their own order and customs on camp life, a theme which we shall develop later. For now it is necessary to return to the events of the last week of June. The coming flood of new internees had boosted the government's drive to deport as many of them as possible. That drive had acquired an unstoppable momentum.

As deportations proceeded, the Foreign Office found that the only subject it was consulted over was the weather. It had managed to persuade others to take the question of retaliation against British prisoners seriously, and the topic was discussed by the Home Defence (Security) Executive on 25 June. The sole outcome for the Foreign Office was a request for advice on the danger of reprisals 'if we send internees to tropical, semi-tropical or sub-arctic climates'. Sir George Warner asked the Foreign Office Southern Department if Italians were likely to object to Jamaica or Mauritius. 'I should have thought not, provided that living conditions are made tolerable,' was the reply; 'cold climates are the ones to avoid.' Warner told Swinton's secretary that Jamaica was unsuitable for Germans but not for Italians.

The Foreign Office was still chasing the remnants of the repatriation scheme and a memorandum recounting the whole weary saga reached Cadogan on 25 June. Cadogan's reaction was not entirely consistent with the hawkish attitude he had displayed in his diary; he feared that, 'by now, owing to their treatment, the 1,500 "degenerate characters" will, in fact, have become so'. He recommended that the Foreign Office should meet Anderson and

MI5 for the purposes of 'straightening out' the question. On 26 June, Halifax agreed, in somewhat unfortunate terminology, that the question should be 'liquidated' as soon as possible. But Ronald Cross, Minister of Shipping, mercifully put the scheme to the sword the same day. He told Halifax that Britain had not seized any Italian ship that might be suitable; 'and in any case I should be very sorry to part with any of these prizes as we want every ship we can lay our hands on'. He also doubted whether the Italian government would accept deportees 'unless they get more than equivalent compensation in the return of shipping'. Cross concluded: 'I suggest that the idea should be dropped.' It was.

The Foreign Office must have been feeling in a delicate condition when, on 28 June, it received a devastating new protest against the deportations. Passed on by the American Ambassador in London, Joseph Kennedy, it emanated from no less a person than Cordell Hull, the American Secretary of State.

On 27 June, Hull had sent Kennedy a thunderous cable. He had learned of Britain's plan to deport German internees and prisoners of war to Canada, and wished Kennedy to point out that Germany could well:

> resort to reprisals against British nationals in Germany which might have far-reaching and distressing consequences for many British nationals, and might well prejudice this Government's ability to protect the British interests entrusted to its care. It is, of course, possible that the British Government has no intention of putting such a plan into execution. However, if such a move is in prospect, the Department hopes that serious thought will be given to the foregoing considerations.

Hull sent Kennedy a second cable that day, relaying a message he had received from the American Embassy in Rome. If Britain deported Italians, the Ambassador warned:

> It is absolutely certain that the Italian Government will retaliate in some manner against more than 1,000 British subjects believed remaining in Italy. Consequently I should appreciate it if the Department could verify British intentions in this regard and obtain full details and explanations for communication to Italian Government. This Embassy is already greatly handicapped in its efforts to protect British subjects because of reports

reaching the Italian Government of mistreatment of Italian subjects in England.

Kennedy drafted a note based on Hull's telegrams, which was delivered to the Foreign Office by Theodore Achilles, the Embassy's Third Secretary, the next day. Sir George Warner had to reveal that some Germans had already been sent to Canada, and his difficulties are clear from his subsequent note. 'The decision to transfer German P/W and internees to Canada was taken before the P/W Department knew anything about it. . . I presume that whatever the Germans will do to our P/W, HMG will adhere to their policy.' Kennedy cabled Achilles' version of the conversation to Hull:

The Foreign Office today confirms that the Government's intentions in this matter are quite definite and that the first group of Germans has already sailed. . . It emphasizes that its action is entirely in accordance with the letter and spirit of the 1929 [Geneva] convention, that the prisoners and internees are merely being moved 'outside the area of hostilities' and that the action is in no sense punitive. It holds that any reprisals by the German or Italian Governments . . . would be entirely unjustified and would cause the British Government to consider retaliatory measures.

Despite its defiant response, Kennedy's protest plunged the Foreign Office into deep anxiety. Its desperate desire to engage US sympathies had dominated the tortuous negotiations over the earlier American proposals for an exchange of internees, which had none the less left the State Department disposed towards Germany. Now Kennedy had made criticisms which the Foreign Office privately shared. A weighty response by Halifax was obviously called for. It took twelve days to compose. When finally delivered it pointed out that Canada had a good climate and an 'abundance of food', and that the camps there were open to inspection. Halifax asked the American Embassy in Berlin:

to give such information and explanations to the German Government as may convince them that the transfer of German prisoners of war and internees to Canada is in no way prejudicial to them but rather the contrary, and that there is, therefore, no ground for any retaliatory action against British prisoners of war or British internees in Germany.

Despite Halifax's specific request, the State Department never passed on the British assurances to the German government. For the British government had fallen victim to a cynical ploy: the protest against deportation had originated within the State Department itself. As an internal memorandum by the State Department's 'Special Division' revealed on 18 July: 'No indication has been received from Berlin at any time that the German Government has the slightest objection to the transfer or that it contemplates any reprisals.' Only later did the Foreign Office learn that, although the cable from Rome was genuine, Hull's dire warning about the 'far-reaching and distressing consequences' for British subjects in Germany had been composed solely on the initiative of Breckinridge Long, his Assistant Secretary of State. Long had read of Mackenzie King's premature announcement in the *New York Times* on 20 June, and – according to the Special Division memorandum – felt:

> ... for obvious political reasons that it was undesirable that these prisoners be brought to an adjacent country. Accordingly, in the effort to dissuade the British Government from making the transfer, SD devised the Department's 1446, June 27, to London insinuating that reprisals might result. . . For reasons which are again obvious, neither London nor the British Government is aware that the correspondence did not arise as a result of a report from Berlin.

It was a far cry from the seemingly disinterested negotiations the State Department had conducted between Britain, France and Germany only a short while before. They, of course, involved people who were safely separated from the United States by the Atlantic Ocean. Now it appeared that those people were to arrive in 'an adjacent country'; Long's 'obvious political reasons' presumably included pandering to a xenophobia of the kind he had found so distasteful elsewhere. The episode was an accurate omen of the speed with which the United States would succumb to internal suppression when war came, as well as of additional difficulties it would create as Britain tried to untangle its own confusion. At the time, it served merely to deepen the Foreign Office's neurosis over its inability to affect the course of events.

The Home Office was suffering from the same feeling of impotence. In an attempt to reduce the feeling, it had just installed Sir John

Moylan in a new post. Moylan had been responsible for aliens in the Home Office during the First World War, and had since been receiver for the Metropolitan Police, in which he had overseen the finances of the entire London force. But as Moylan revealed to Warner on 26 June, he was not sure what his 'line of country' was to be; Newsam told Warner the following day that he wasn't really sure either, but it would include 'the selection of civilian internees to be sent abroad to the Dominions'.

Newsam's answer offered the glimmerings of an alliance between the Home and Foreign Offices, despite the animosity between them over the restrictions on aliens. Both had started to receive requests for the release of Italians arrested in June; William Gillies of the Labour Party took up the cases of the two Treves brothers and their cousin, and of the two officials of the Italian League for the Rights of Man, Magri and Anzani.

The Ministry of Aircraft Production – headed by Lord Beaverbrook – was lobbying both ministries over an Italian engineer named P. M. Salerni, who had invented a new transmission device which was being developed, under his guidance and on behalf of the ministry, by a British company. In March 1940, Salerni had made a risky journey to Italy to observe trials of his invention, and had brought the results back to London. He had lived most of his life in England, had a British-born wife and was vouched for by Sir Edward Barry, a Maidenhead JP. None of this, of course, had saved him from being interned on 10 June.

The Ministry of Aircraft Production asked the Home Office on 27 June if Salerni could at least be allowed to carry on his work in an internment camp, and requested that officials from the ministry be permitted to visit him there. The writer of the letter was clearly worried on another score. As he told the Home Office's A. I. Tudor: 'I understand that you anticipate success in preventing his shipment to Canada which would otherwise take place in the very near future. I hope there is no possibility of a snag arising on this point.'

That day, Harold Farquhar of the Foreign Office visited Sir John Moylan to see if they could work out a common approach to deportation. Farquhar first made some surprising discoveries. Moylan reported that MI5 had traced fewer than 750 of the notorious 1,500 'desperate characters' who had been so prominent in the internment plans: and that only 3,250 Italians of the 10,000 expected had been interned. Moylan had not yet discovered which camps they were in, and he doubted whether MI5 would be able to classify them satisfactorily, as it 'still clung pathetically to membership of the Fascio as [the] one and only criterion of what constituted an undesirable or a dangerous character'. Afterwards, Farquhar delivered a gloomy forecast: 'All we can do for the moment is to keep in close touch with Sir J. Moylan and hope that we will be able in a reasonable time to produce some sort of order out of the existing chaos.' Farquhar admitted that it was all 'a little late in the day'.

It was indeed. While Gillies and the Ministry of Aircraft Production searched anxiously for their protégés, and the Home and Foreign Offices took the first tentative steps of their *rapprochement*, the arrangements for the next shipment to Canada were irrevocably in motion. As early as 21 June, the War Office had sent MI5's celebrated list of 1,500 dangerous characters to the five camps where Italians were housed, with instructions to the commanders to find them within twenty-four hours, as the ship was due to sail on 25 June.

The Italians who were produced contained a natural preponderance of those described by the puzzled Special Branch Inspector at Lingfield as 'connected with the catering trade', including Zavattoni of the Savoy, Bianchi of the Café Royal and Zangiacomi of the Piccadilly. Serafino Pini was picked out, too, one of eighty-eight Italians taken from the squalid camp of Warth Mills in Bury. Most were indeed members of the Fascio in Britain, including the waiter arrested by Detective Constable Mark in Liverpool: most, but not all. The remainder included those very Italians other ministries were frantically seeking, like three of the anti-Fascists cited by Gillies, and the aircraft engineer Salerni. But even with these obviously erroneous inclusions, only just over 700 Italians supposedly on the MI5 list could be found.

The War Office postponed departure until 30 June and ordered the empty places to be filled by Category 'A' Germans and Austrians. Four hundred and seventy-eight were produced. One hundred and twenty-three were German merchant sailors captured at sea. The others were civilians who, so the Cabinet was later told, 'had either been placed in Category "A" by special tribunals appointed by the Home Office or were among those persons interned as being members of the Nazi organization or Nazi sympathizers'.

It was, at best, an ambiguous description. Two hundred and

forty-two of the Germans and Austrians selected for shipment came from Swanwick, whose inmates comprised merchant seamen like Captain Burfeind and the crew of the *Adolf Woermann*, and a good many avowed Nazis, as well as non-refugee Germans like Bruno Fehle, who had never joined the Nazi Party. A smaller group came from Huyton – the two young men, Leopold Kohn and Hermann Bondi, were not included – and the remaining 185 were from the Seaton camp in Devon. They included political refugees like Karl Olbrisch, the socialist who spent four years in German prisons and concentration camps before escaping, and anti-Nazi trade unionists such as Louis Weber and Valentin Wittke. Seaton also held, as we have seen, Germans and Austrians who were wholly or partly Jewish and had for one reason or another fallen foul of their tribunals or MI5. But the last week of June 1940 was not a time when those decisions would be reassessed. Among those now told to collect their belongings and be ready for a journey of unspecified length and destination were Erwin Frenkel, Peter Jacobsohn, Franz Eichenberg and the three Radok brothers, Uwe, Rainer and Jobst.

As dawn broke on 30 June, Uwe Radok, viewing the countryside from a train speeding north, thought that England looked its best. The fine old trees standing in the lush fields were especially beautiful, and Uwe felt that he understood why the British cherished them as symbols of steadfastness. Seaton had learned of Dunkirk and the fall of France, followed by the wave of internments, and was understandably worried about an invasion whose consequences could be more dire for Jewish refugees than for the British themselves. Although no one had yet announced where they were going, rumours abounded: one said that a shipment of internees had already sailed for Canada, and Uwe reckoned that was not altogether an undesirable prospect, given Britain's predicament. The rumour gained strength when the train ended its journey in Liverpool and its passengers were marched off towards the docks.

Bruno Fehle, coming from Derbyshire, arrived in Liverpool on another train. The mood among the Swanwick internees was different from Seaton's: the Nazis said that the British were panicking and predicted happily that the Germans would soon invade. Fehle's preoccupations were personal. He was deeply worried about the fate of his wife and children, having learned they were now interned in the Isle of Man. He had not been permitted to send word of his departure from Swanwick, not that he knew where he was going anyway. He had hoped he would be joining them on the Isle of Man, but when he saw a large passenger liner berthed at the quayside, he knew it was not to be. He judged she was about 18,000 tons, and he could see the silhouettes of two guns on her decks. The portholes were covered over; there were boards along the side to enclose the promenade deck, and Fehle caught a glimpse of barbed wire. He thought she looked like a coffin.

Her name was the *Arandora Star*.

17 The Last Torpedo

The *Arandora Star,* her owners boasted, was the most luxurious cruise-ship afloat. Built by Cammell, Laird at Birkenhead for the Blue Star Line in 1927, she was first intended for the company's passenger and cargo run to South America. After a year or so, Blue Star decided to convert her into the 'world's most delightful cruising liner'. She was fitted with the most modern equipment for a sybaritic life at sea. The Blue Star brochures vaunted her 'large, airy and dainty staterooms', the beds with their 'best Vi-sprung mattresses', the 'electric elevator' between all decks, and the cinema that showed 'performances of the latest "Talkie films" with experienced photographers in charge'.

Blue Star also considered her, without shame, to be the world's most exclusive liner. Whereas the great Cunard *Queens* carried second and third-class passengers, the 15,000-ton *Arandora Star* accepted only first class. Each winter she took a mere 420 of them in search of the winter sun to the Pacific and the Caribbean. In the spring and autumn she cruised the Mediterranean and the Atlantic coast of North Africa. In summer, she ventured to the 'northern capitals' of Oslo, Stockholm and Copenhagen, putting in at Germany's North Sea ports *en route*.

Thomas Cook always had a representative on board to arrange shore excursions. Thus passengers on the 1930 winter cruise could take a car ride on Barbados 'past miles of sugar plantations'. In the eastern Mediterranean that summer Cook's laid on an ambi-

185

tious tour of the Holy Land, with visits to Jerusalem and Damascus. The company was clearly aware of the anxieties such a venture might arouse, being careful to emphasize: 'Those taking part are assured that adequate precautions are taken against their missing the steamer, and where necessary, one or more spare cars are available in the case of breakdown.'

The captain of the *Arandora Star* throughout the 1930s was Edgar Moulton, a tall, courteous man, popular among the passengers, respected by his crew. The main characteristic shared by his passengers was their wealth. They included royalty, like King Carol of Romania; the nobility, including Lord Nuffield; men of commerce such as Sir Montague Burton, head of the Burton chain of tailors, who took his secretary with him to continue his business, and paid the stewards a shilling to take messages to the radio operator; men of letters like George Bernard Shaw; and entertainers such as Max Miller, who undoubtedly enjoyed the good life on board, but also visited the 'Pig and Whistle' – the crew's bar – to buy drinks all round.

One of the *Arandora Star*'s more modest voyages occurred in 1935, when she spent three days in the English Channel at the time of the Royal Navy Review. She had a reserved anchorage at Spithead, from where, on 17 July, passengers could view 'the impressive sight of H.M. the King in the *Victoria and Albert* leading the British Fleet to sea for exercises'. The *Arandora Star* then embarked on a brief cruise up the Channel, with a gala dinner and dance in her green-and-ivory ballroom that night. The lowest price was 8 guineas, approximately four weeks' earnings for a coal-miner at that time. Her apotheosis was the winter cruise of 1936 to Miami, Cuba and Honolulu, lasting seventy-five days. Blue Star called it 'The Cruise'. 'The homeward run is interesting in the extreme, for stops will be made at San Francisco and Los Angeles, allowing ample time for visits to Hollywood and Pasadena . . . a wonderful cruise, packed with interest and enjoyment in continual sunshine.' Prices began at 153 guineas for a passenger sharing a twin-bedded stateroom, to include all meals but 'not the bar'. The most exalted offering was a Regal Suite: there were two, the Balmoral and the Windsor, with their own bathrooms. They cost 605 guineas per person.

Nobby Fulford joined the crew of the *Arandora Star* in 1933. He came from a seafaring family in Southampton; his father and his uncles were all sailors, and when he left school at fourteen in 1923, it was the natural thing for him to do. His first voyage was as a bell-boy on Canadian Pacific's *Empress of Britain;* soon afterwards he transferred to the Royal Mail Line, graduating to first-class waiter and then barman's mate. When he moved to the Blue Star Line and the *Arandora Star*, it was as a fully fledged barman. His first voyage was to the West Indies, and he took charge of the smoke-room bar.

The bar was open from 9 a.m. until the small hours, although Fulford took a siesta each afternoon to prepare himself for the long night session. By far the most popular mix was champagne cocktail; drunkenness among the liner's expensive clientele was not uncommon. Captain Moulton showed that he understood Fulford's problems, for on his morning tour of the ship he would always ask: 'Any trouble last night?' Fulford was paid around £8 a month to start, raised to £9 after several years. The crew's quarters, although an improvement on most, were badly ventilated and very cramped. Six or eight men shared Fulford's cabin: as it was way down in the hull, the porthole could only be opened when the sea was dead calm or in port. But Fulford was in a better position than most of his shipmates. If a steward knew of a spare passenger cabin, he would offer it to Fulford, who would repay the favour in kind.

The *Arandora Star* proceeded in its self-sustaining way of life through the international crises of the 1930s: Abyssinia, the Spanish Civil War, the Anschluss, Munich. Her brochure for 1939 displayed unhesitating optimism about the year ahead. Twelve sunshine cruises were advertised, beginning with the customary long voyage to the West Indies and ending with the 'Africa Sunshine Cruise' on 22 December. The programme continued without interruption until August, when the liner was due to visit The Faeroes, Iceland, the Norwegian fjords, Denmark, Sweden and then Danzig and the Kiel Canal, ending in Southampton on 31 August. As war neared, she omitted the last two calls and returned to Southampton on 26 August. Time had caught up with the *Arandora Star.*

That week, the Blue Star office in Regent Street – where a model of the *Arandora Star* stood proudly in the window – was besieged by Americans desperate to get home. On 1 September, the *Arandora Star* sailed for New York with 441 passengers. She was two days out of Southampton when war was declared, and the crew spent the rest of the voyage painting her funnels a dull grey and shading her portholes and windows dark blue. At night she was blacked out and smoking on deck was forbidden. Meanwhile, the British government was taking control of Britain's merchant vessels. They were to comply with all instructions from the Admiralty, and the Ministry of Shipping was soon created to allocate their parts in the war effort. The *Arandora Star,* still commanded by Captain Moulton, and with most of her normal peacetime crew on board, returned to Dartmouth to await her orders.

At first the government experts who inspected the *Arandora Star* in Dartmouth were nonplussed. Her conversion into a cruise liner had made her top-heavy, unsuitable to act as a merchant cruiser. In December, she was chosen to take part in anti-submarine trials in the English Channel. By then, U-boats had sunk almost 100 British ships, and the *Arandora Star* was fitted with nets designed to catch torpedoes short of their target. The trials seemed to be successful: the nets trapped all the dummy torpedoes fired at her, and only barely reduced her speed, from 15½ to 14½ knots. The nets, however, never came into widespread use.

The *Arandora's Star*'s next posting was less glamorous. She was assigned to Gibraltar, where she was to serve as headquarters for a censorship office to inspect all mail carried by Italian vessels passing through the Strait. Extensive alterations on her were already being carried out, and a large contingent of censors was being recruited, when someone reappraised the entire grandiose scheme. On 22 May, the chief censor, already in Gibraltar to meet the *Arandora Star,* was told by the War Office to go home. He defiantly removed 800 sacks of mail from the SS *Conti Grandi* the next day, but by 28 May the scheme had been abandoned.

The *Arandora Star* was now directed to more serious matters. While almost every available merchant ship was sent to Dunkirk, she and some others were ordered to Norway, where the remnants of the Norwegian expedition were being evacuated from Narvik. It was a coast she had often passed on her summer voyages to witness the midnight sun; she survived several bombing attacks and was even more fortunate to cross the North Sea unscathed. Her convoy, bearing 10,000 troops, would have run into the main German naval squadron but for an act of great heroism by the destroyer *Acasta,* one of the escorts. The *Acasta* attacked the renowned German battle-cruiser *Scharnhorst* and was sunk with all lives save one. But she damaged the *Scharnhorst,* which had to withdraw, and the convoy reached home safely.

The *Arandora Star* unloaded her soldiers at Glasgow and then headed south almost without pause to help rescue the British army in France: 330,000 men had been saved at Dunkirk, but many others were trapped in the south and west. She took 300 men on board at Quiberon, landed them at Falmouth, and returned to the Bay of Biscay. With German planes overhead, she put in at Bayonne and St Jean de Luz to take on Polish troops and British refugees. By 24 June, she had 3,000 on board and headed for home. Her grateful passengers disembarked at Liverpool three days later.

Nobby Fulford had not been on the *Arandora Star* during the anti-torpedo trials or the bizarre Gibraltar episode, but had joined her again on 30 May, in time for Narvik. He found that many of the rich fittings which had decorated the public rooms had been stripped out; the cabins were as luxurious as ever, but with extra mattresses spread over the floors. He became a canteen manager, opening his bar at intervals to sell drink and cigarettes to the extraordinary variety of wartime passengers the *Arandora Star* carried. At Narvik she took on both British soldiers and German prisoners of war, and Fulford was on deck to see two vessels near-by sunk in aerial attacks. She was most crowded during the evacuation in the Bay of Biscay, when Fulford enlisted the aid of Polish troops to carry fresh stocks up to the bar. He was discharged from the *Arandora Star* in Liverpool on 29 June and returned, after a brief shore leave, twenty-four hours later.

The *Arandora Star* had been armed both fore and aft, and the crew were used to the sight of her 4.7-inch cannon, a useful weapon against sea attack, and her 12-pound anti-aircraft gun. But they were now concerned by the addition of barbed-wire barricades on the promenade deck. They seemed an unnecessary hazard, and the ship's chief officer, F. B. Brown, reported that Captain Moulton had complained about them, to no avail. There were British soldiers on the ship and an officer asked Fulford if he would help them check the passengers as they came aboard. They were German and Italian prisoners, Fulford learned, understanding that they contained a mixture of civilians and captured seamen. Two guards were ordered to count them at the head of the gangway and Fulford pointed out which men were members of the *Arandora Star*'s crew.

There seemed little method in the allocation of accommodation. The Italians were divided into two groups: X1 were sent to 'A' deck, the lowest, while X2, which included Serafino Pini, were given cabins on 'D' deck, the highest. The three Radoks had a cabin together on 'B' deck. Peter Jacobsohn, with a customary show of youthful arrogance, tried to commandeer a lower-deck bathroom for himself, shutting himself in and placing a note on the outside saying 'Private – Keep Out'. A British officer soon turned him out; Jacobsohn was given a sleeping-bag and told to lie under one of the temporary shelters that had been erected on the open decks. Erwin Frenkel found a space there too. Franz Eichenberg had a cabin, and so, eventually, did Bruno Fehle. He spent the first night in the ballroom with the rest of the Swanwick contingent. For some reason a group of Italians was moved in on the morning of 1 July, and Fehle was given one of the best cabins on 'D' deck, with its mahogany panels and ornate lights still in place.

The *Arandora Star* sailed from Liverpool at 4 a.m. on 1 July. Her peacetime capacity had been 450, plus approximately 200 crew. Including her crew and the British guards, she now carried almost 1,600 men. But it was far less than the 3,000 she had brought back from the Bay of Biscay, and the discomfort was eased for the internees by the friendliness of the British, and some unexpected benefits. Uwe Radok was soon to begin a diary, and his entry for 1 July records:

> At full speed through the Irish Sea, zigzagging. In the morning still the coast of Wales, then soon on the right, the Isle of Man, later Ireland left, Scotland right. . . Gradually one almost starts to enjoy the cruise, just as the unaccustomed better food.

Another Seaton internee named Gerhard Miedzwinski also described his voyage on the *Arandora Star* in an account written a month or so later. Aged twenty-nine, Miedzwinski was a Jewish engineer from Silesia who had come to Britain in 1936. He was given an 'A' at his tribunal in October 1939 because, he believed, he was denounced by the father of the girl he was living with in Tooting, south London. Like Uwe Radok, Miedzwinski enjoyed 1 July:

> The soldiers were nice chaps, just returned from Dunkirk; we soon made friends. . . We could move freely and we saw a British submarine following some distance behind. Then a flying-boat came over to exchange the time of day with light signals. All was quiet. The ship's doctor, a delightful old man, an old sea-

dog, offered us cigarettes. . . We had a nice time that day; food was of a nearly forgotten quality, we even obtained drinks from the stewards – yes, we had stewards for our comfort. In the evening we drank a lot, pink gin and beer, played a gramophone, and generally had the best time since our internment. How considerate of the Government to move us to Canada, we thought. . .

Night fell on a rolling but unbroken sea. Towards midnight, the *Arandora Star* rounded Malin Head, the northernmost point of Ireland, and headed due west.

Gunther Prien was going home. It was three weeks since he had left Germany at the command of U-47. Weighing 750 tons, 218 feet long, with a surface speed of 17 knots, submerged of 7.6 knots, and a range of 9,100 miles, she was a U-boat of class VIIB, the latest and most lethal addition to the German submarine fleet. Already on this voyage Prien had sunk eight ships, beginning with the 5,000-ton cargo ship *Balmoral Wood* on 19 June, and including several oil tankers. He had one torpedo left.

Prien was known in Germany as the Bull of Scapa Flow. It was he who, on 14 October 1939, had threaded a way through the supposedly impregnable defences of Scapa Flow to sink the British battleship *Royal Oak*, with the loss of 833 lives. The British had been unable to believe their eyes and supposed Prien must have learned of a route, and the movements of the *Royal Oak*, through treachery. The truth was that Prien and Admiral Karl Dönitz, Commander-in-Chief of the U-boat fleet, had plotted the incursion together, taking advantage of flaws in the British defences and of Prien's courage and nerve. Prien did not learn that his victim was the *Royal Oak* until he was outside Scapa Flow and heading for home. When he docked at Wilhelmshaven, Dönitz told him that Hitler had sent his private plane to fly him to Berlin. The next day Hitler presented him with the *Ritterkreuz*, the highest order of the Iron Cross. Prien was the first naval officer to be so honoured.

An American journalist who observed Prien at a press conference the same day judged him 'clean-cut, cocky, a fanatical Nazi, and obviously capable'. He was a tough disciplinarian, but his crew respected him for the strength of his achievements. In the spring of 1940, U-47 took part in the Scandinavian skirmish with the Allies, but Prien met only frustration. He fired at several British warships from close range but his torpedoes failed to explode through a fault in their mechanism. The fault was diagnosed by the end of May, and Prien was able to share in the period U-boat commanders knew as the 'Happy Time', when Germany's U-boat pack sank Allied shipping almost unmolested, and Britain came perilously close to losing the war. In June, Britain lost fifty-eight ships; Prien made his contribution of eight with only thirteen torpedoes.

At midnight on 1–2 July, Prien was on the surface of the Atlantic to the north-west of Ireland. His speed was 9 knots, his course 20°, and he was heading for the gap between the Shetlands and The Faeroes, where he would turn south again for the North Sea, and Germany. As dawn broke, Prien noted in his log that there was drizzle with moderate visibility. At 6.29 a.m., British Summer Time, he saw a passenger ship to the east. She was coming towards him and moving 'reasonably fast'.

Prien dived and observed the ship through his periscope for twenty-five minutes. He estimated her speed as 15 knots, and at 6.55 she was only 3,500 metres away. She was armed with a large-calibre cannon, 'easy to recognize' on the stern, and another gun on the bow. Was she neutral or foe? The *Arandora Star*'s course gave her away. 'I recognize her as enemy from her zigzags,' Prien wrote.

Prien's position was 56°17′ N, 11° 05′ W – 200 miles west of the Scottish mainland, with the nearest land, the Bloody Foreland of County Donegal, 125 miles away to the south-east. The wind was light and from the south-west; the sea was calm, with a light westerly swell; the sky was cloudy and visibility good. At 6.58 and 28 seconds, Prien fired his last torpedo. The range was an ambitious 2,500 metres. Ninety-seven seconds passed, and then Prien saw a column of water arise from his victim amidships. It was a perfect hit.

Prien made another observation at 7.15. The ship had stopped; boats were being lowered from both sides, and some were already in the water. Prien descended to 20 metres and resumed his normal course. At 7.40 he looked through his periscope again. The liner had disappeared.

Prien's torpedo had struck the *Arandora Star*'s after engine-room on the starboard side. The engine-room flooded at once to sea-level, and those of the ship's crew inside who had survived the initial blast were drowned. The ship's turbines were wrecked and her main and stand-by generators put out of action. That explained the sudden darkness in which Nobby Fulford had found himself, deep in the boat; and also the loss of communications throughout the ship, which meant that no emergency orders could be issued. These factors undoubtedly added to the confusion on board the *Arandora Star* in the thirty or so minutes that passed from the torpedo's impact to her final plunge beneath the Atlantic. Whether that confusion became panic, we shall examine later. For precisely what occurred in that desperate half-hour is disputed to this day.

It is in moments of deadly peril that human observation and memory are least reliable. People recall the same incident in radically different ways as a result of their natural desire to render order from chaos. The sinking of the *Arandora Star* is no exception. We traced and interviewed eleven survivors of her last voyage. In Chapter 1 we presented four of their accounts, concentrating on recollections that were sharpest and have not been contradicted elsewhere. One theme that strongly emerges is that those who survived did so because, whether by reason or instinct, they took quick and decisive actions to escape from the stricken liner. Thus Nobby Fulford, asleep in the crew's quarters, knew that he had to get out, and up, as soon as possible; ten years on the *Arandora Star* told him where safety lay. Erwin Frenkel had been a powerful water-polo player before the war and had the confidence to leap overboard at an early stage, rewarded by finding a place on a life-raft. The three Radok brothers came together again in this moment of crisis and took a cool decision to leave the ship rather than wait for a life-raft that might still have room. Serafino Pini had the good fortune to be among the Italians on 'D' deck and slid into the water with time to spare.

Others on board the *Arandora Star* tell similar stories. Peter Jacobsohn first believed she had been struck by a mine; then he accepted the general verdict that she had been hit by a torpedo. Still wearing his pyjamas, he fumbled with his life-jacket until another internee came to his aid. He tied the jacket tightly, telling Jacobsohn that otherwise it would ride up when he hit the water and break his neck. Jacobsohn watched a line of seamen jump overboard in turn, then followed them. He swam towards a lifeboat that he glimpsed on the crest of a swell, but it disappeared. He tried without success to climb on to a wooden bench, and then saw an Anglo-Austrian internee named Holmes drift by elegantly propped up on a plank. Jacobsohn greeted him courteously:

'Good morning, Mr Holmes!'

'Good morning, Mr Jacobsohn,' Holmes replied.

Jacobsohn was beginning to lose hope when he found a life-raft. It already held Erwin Frenkel and the smartly dressed gentleman who had preceded him into the water, an antiquarian book-dealer named Martin Sulzbacher. It seemed more than full, but Sulzbacher insisted that Jacobsohn be taken on board. Jacobsohn sat on the raft in his pyjamas as water lapped over his legs.

Bruno Fehle had luck on his side. After the explosion, he headed along the promenade deck but came to a barrier of barbed wire. On the top deck above was a lifeboat, and he saw a man trying to reach it by climbing the coils of wire. Fehle thought of doing the same, but then the lifeboat was lowered and he jumped down into it, jarring his back as he landed. The boat slid safely into the water. Its coxswain, from the liner's crew, took swimmers on board until it was filled. He told Fehle that as the *Arandora Star* had sunk in a shipping lane, rescuers should find them soon.

Franz Eichenberg was getting dressed when the torpedo hit. Still acting as camp leader, he shouted to others to go on deck and promptly followed his own advice. Like Serafino Pini, he slid down a rope from a davit and was soon hauled on to a lifeboat. Gerhard Miedzwinski did the same and swam to a lifeboat, lucky to find a place as it was almost full. He counted over 100 men and sat next to a British sailor whose hand was swathed in a bloody rag, having lost a finger in the lifeboat's pulley. Miedzwinski later described the death of the *Arandora Star*:

> Our eyes were glued to the sinking *Arandora Star* where pande-
> monium reigned. Slowly she settled down, stern first. A huge
> beam tore loose and swept along the ship's side, squashing the
> men hanging on the ropes in its path. Down, down she went,
> faster and faster; her bows rose; we saw people running up the
> steepening decks like flies. Suddenly, a mighty hiss, a cry – and
> all was over.

Not all who escaped from the *Arandora Star* survived until rescue came. Some swimmers were hit by life-rafts and deck furniture thrown from the decks above. Others suffocated in the heavy black oil that spread across the surface. The luckiest were those who reached lifeboats. Uwe Radok watched corpses float past, their yellow faces lifted high by their lifejackets. Least fortunate were the men who could not find room on the rafts or boats, and had

to cling to them or to ship's debris in an effort to stay alive. Even
though it was a calm summer day, the cold was deadly to some,
and those on the rafts could only watch as others slipped their
holds and drifted away. It is said that a German father, on seeing
his only son die as they clung to a raft, let go his hold to die too.
Hans Margis, a refugee from Berlin, tells of a journalist named
Moszkowski who became weary of the struggle for space on a tiny
raft. He told his companions: 'I've enjoyed my life, you save
yourselves,' slid into the water and drowned. Mr Holmes, who
had greeted Peter Jacobsohn so coolly from his plank, also died.

The first intimation of rescue came two hours after the sinking.
The radio station on Malin Head had received an SOS from the
Arandora Star and an RAF Sunderland flying boat found the survivors, dropping a box containing food, cigarettes and a message
to say that help was on the way. At 1.30 the Canadian destroyer
St Laurent arrived to find, in the words of its captain, H. G. de
Wolf: 'Ten lifeboats, all fairly well filled, formed a group. The area
to windward for two or three miles was littered with rafts and
small wreckage, to which were clinging many survivors, singly and
in small groups.' De Wolf stopped his ship in the centre of the area
and dispatched his boats:

> with instructions to pick up individuals from the water and
> those with poor support while the ship was manoeuvred among
> the rafts and heavier wreckage, picking up groups of three or
> four. This part of the work was painfully slow. Very few survi-
> vors were able to help themselves to any extent, and in many
> cases it was necessary to put a man over the side to pass a line
> around them and hoist them bodily inboard. Some were very
> heavy. Those taken from the water and from light wreckage
> were covered in oil fuel.

The *St Laurent* completed her task by 4 p.m. and turned east for
Scotland. Without exception, the *Arandora Star* survivors praise the
Canadians for their kindness and humanity. Uwe Radok wrote:

> Conversation with the young Canadians. They are, of course,
> used to this sort of thing and find nothing remarkable in the
> fact that here helpless prisoners of war are involved. But other-
> wise all these people are extraordinarily nice. . . It appears we
> are going to Glasgow.

The destroyer arrived at Greenock on the mouth of the Clyde

at 6.30 a.m on 3 July. Four more men had died on the journey and the survivors were landed at Albert Harbour. The first estimates of the death toll showed that roughly two thirds of some 700 Italians on board had died, and about one third of the almost 500 Germans. For the crew, the figures were 42 dead out of 174, while the army guards had lost 37 out of 200.

Italians lost from the world of cuisine included Zangiacomi and Maggi of the Ritz, Zavattoni of the Savoy, Benini of the Hungaria, Sovrani of the Normandie, Borgo of the Café Anglais. Among others were Ernani Landucci, the waiter arrested by Robert Mark in Manchester; Clement Fiorini from Rusholme, who had lived in Britain for forty years; Gaetano Pacitto, the naturalized British subject, with British-born wife and children. Anzani, secretary of the Italian League of the Rights of Man, died. So did Piero Salerni, the Italian engineer working for the British government.

Among the German dead were the socialist Karl Olbrisch and the trade unionist Louis Weber; the Austrians included eleven men listed by François Lafitte as anti-Nazis, and the figures later showed that almost half the 185 on board from Seaton had died. The proportion from Swanwick was much lower.

Of the British, Captain Moulton, his second officer, Stanley Ransom, and fourth officer Ralph Liddle, all died. They were posthumously awarded the Lloyd's Medal for bravery at sea, and the citation stated: 'having done all they could to save life and having no boat or raft to save themselves, they took to the water as the vessel sank'.

The British press soon found an explanation for the high casualties among the Italians. 'Aliens Fight Each Other in Wild Panic' proclaimed the *Daily Herald* on 4 July. 'Internees' Panic Lost Many Lives' agreed the London *Star*. The *Daily Express* report was typical:

> Soldiers and sailors . . . told of the panic among the aliens when they realized the ship was sinking. All condemned the cowardice of the Germans, who fought madly to get into the boats. 'The Germans, fighting with Italians to escape, were great hulking brutes,' said one soldier. 'They punched and kicked their way past the Italians. We had to restrain them forcibly.' The Italians did not stand a chance against the Germans, according to a seaman. 'The Germans made it clear that nobody was going to stand in their way of being rescued. But the Italians were just

as bad. The whole mob of them thought of their own skins first. The scramble for the boats was sickening.'

On 9 July, the Shipping Minister, Ronald Cross, gave indirect support to these stories when he told the Commons: 'Lifeboats and life-rafts more than sufficient to accommodate all passengers and crew were provided.' The implication, of course, was that the passengers were to blame for not saving themselves – and this was the precise argument of the Foreign Office note to the Swiss Legation and Brazilian Embassy on 4 July advising them of the disaster. 'More lives would probably have been saved had not many of the prisoners of war and internees refused to make use of the rafts which were at once thrown overboard when the ship was torpedoed.'

It can be pointed out somewhat harshly that allegations of panic come uneasily from the army guard, the group with the highest survival rate of all. And fortunately the highly coloured and prejudiced reports published by the British press are not the only evidence with which to assess the more controversial aspects of the last desperate moments of the *Arandora Star*. The Admiralty's Shipping Casualties Section had the specific role of interviewing ships' survivors as calmly and quickly as possible. Its representative reached F. S. Brown, chief officer and highest-ranking survivor of the *Arandora Star*'s crew, in Greenock on 4 July, and his account is now kept in the Public Record Office. So is a composite report based on Brown's version and those of the ship's chief engineer and Major Drury of the military guard. The account by Gerhard Miedzwinski provides further evidence, as does the diary kept by Uwe Radok. He began it on the *Arandora Star*, making his notes on toilet paper. He started it again on being returned to Britain, rewriting the few pages that had been lost. Most valuable of all is a remarkable document compiled by Bruno Fehle on 10 July. Having injured his back, he was taken to the Mearnskirk Hospital in Glasgow. He and three other survivors were so distressed by the British newspapers that they drew up a 1,200-word memorandum to record what they had seen for themselves. The four internees, each of whom attested to its truth, were of widely different backgrounds: their names were C. Krönig, from Seaton; H. Kreuzer, from the pay-camp at Paignton; R. Vicchi-Borghese, an Italian gynaecologist; and Fehle himself, from Swanwick. Fehle

guarded the memorandum safely for forty years; it has never before
been published.

From these documents and our interviews, it is possible to dispel
most of the myths about the sinking. It is immediately clear that
the reports of fighting among internees were false. Brown told his
interviewer: 'There is absolutely no truth in the statement that
German prisoners were pushing the Italians out of the way, nor
did I notice any fighting between the Germans and the Italians.'

The combined British report was almost as definite: 'All the
aliens had appeared on the upper deck and greatly hampered the
crew in the launching. There was, however, little or no panic
among the internees.' And Fehle's memorandum stated:

> We wish to put on record that all reports about unpleasant
> incidents of fighting between the shipwrecked during the period
> of rescue are untrue and lack basis or foundation. The ship's
> crew and the internees assisted each other in a most friendly
> and helpful spirit; and when taking people into the boats from
> rafts, wreckage, or those who were swimming, no differentiation
> whatsoever was made.

There were other less satisfying reasons for the high death-toll
among the Italians. In the first place, many were middle-aged or
elderly men used to comfortable existences, in contrast with the
Germans and Austrians who had already survived much in their
lives, or were fit and experienced seamen. And, of course, a large
contingent of Italians had been allocated to the lowest deck, from
which they were least equipped to escape.

When the slow and tardy did arrive on deck they found that
there was no room left on the lifeboats. These, too, are a focus of
controversy. Simply stated, there were not enough of them. The
Arandora Star carried fourteen boats, with a capacity of not more
than 1,000. Her load that day was 1,564. The Shipping Minister,
Cross, had been careful to tell the Commons that the lifeboats *and
life-rafts* were 'more than sufficient', but the reality, as described
by Chief Officer Brown, was different. He agreed that about twenty
rafts had been thrown overboard, but commented; 'the three big
rafts were filled up and the small floats were practically useless'.
He added damningly: 'It was impossible to have saved any more.'
The overall result was described by Fehle:

> Many people, especially sick and older ones and those from the

lower parts of the ship, could not reach the open decks or could not make up their minds to jump overboard. The majority of these stayed on board and finally went down with the ship clinging to the railings and in this way, many lives were lost. There were many Italians between them, as they were mostly of middle age or older.

If there was no fighting and little actual panic on board, there was undoubted confusion. All internee survivors agree on the cause. No boat-drill had been staged. Fehle wrote: 'No instructions whatever were given for the possible event of being shipwrecked, i.e. no boat drill was held, no one instructed in the proper use of a lifebelt, no instructions were given as to how to proceed in an event of emergency.' Radok concurs: 'Ship definitely overcrowded, no idea regarding boats etc., it will take days before anything is organized.'

It is clear that a further reason for the death-toll is that not all the fourteen lifeboats were successfully launched. Brown thought that *twelve* reached the water, one having been smashed in the initial explosion, another capsizing while being lowered because it had damaged davits. The Fehle memorandum says the total was only *ten*, and is almost certainly right, for this was the number counted by the commander of the *St Laurent* when he arrived on the scene.

But who launched the boats? Fehle makes the remarkable claim that six were lowered by 'officers and men of the *Adolf Woermann*'. The British reports are consistent with this, for Brown could only account for six boats launched by the ship's officers responsible, while Major Drury was not aware of six boats on the starboard side being lowered at all. Several survivors recall that Captain Burfeind had already inspected the lifeboats, and believe that he and his officers marked out those in best condition. The Swanwick casualty rate bears this out: 193 out of 242 survived. They did not include Burfeind himself, who was last seen assisting Captain Moulton on the bridge. The two men stayed there until the last moment, and shared death together in the water.

One vital question remains: the barbed wire. Brown said that Captain Moulton had complained about it in Liverpool and added that it 'greatly hampered' the crew in their work. Another crew member who survived, steward Ted Crisp, says that when he went to his lifeboat station, there was 'wire everywhere'. In 1960, the novelist Alistair Maclean took up this point to allege in a long article in the *Daily Express* that the barbed wire was the 'tragic reason . . . why hundreds died'. This emotive claim does not find support today. Five survivors from the *Arandora Star* whom we asked about the barbed wire could not remember seeing any at all. Of those who did, Serafino Pini recalled seeing only one man trying to get through it. Miedzwinski considered it no more than a token: 'Only very little barbed wire was there.' Bruno Fehle described seeing a man trying to climb *up* the wire, and his memorandum is the most specific on the point, recording that double fences of barbed wire blocked the promenade deck at each end. It was, however, possible to reach the deck via gangways from the deck below, and Fehle did not report that the barbed wire had caused any casualties. The best consensus is that the 50 per cent casualty rate on the *Arandora Star* was caused by a combination of the initial explosion, the shortage of boats and the lack of boat-drill. Reports of panic were drastically exaggerated and those of fighting totally false.

There is one more story to which it is worth alluding: no fewer than three survivors told how they had come across a British soldier standing to attention while the ship settled in the water and all else were trying to save their lives. Each survivor said he had asked the soldier why he was standing still, to be told that he had not yet been given orders to do anything else. Here the versions vary. One survivor said he left the British soldier standing where he was; another that he said, 'I will give you your orders – now save yourself'; a third that, on being reasoned with, the soldier shouted 'Bugger Hitler!' and jumped into the sea. A search of the documents provides no iota of evidence to support this story. It is pleasant to think it might be true.

Once back on dry land, the survivors met with varying fates. Nobby Fulford was put on a train to London where he was met by an official of the Blue Star Line. That night he was back home in Southampton, to find that his wife had received two telegrams simultaneously, one warning her that the *Arandora Star* had been sunk, the other telling her that her husband was safe. Bruno Fehle and the other internees who reported they were injured were taken to hospital. Serafino Pini and the other Italians were marched to a school in Greenock where they were found by members of Glasgow's Italian community. A priest offered Pini a British army battledress which must have belonged to a medical orderly as it had a red cross on the back, but Pini said he did not want to wear British uniform now. In London, his wife Lisa received a telegram telling her that he had survived. As it was the first word she had had since his arrest on 10 June, this enigmatic message left her somewhat puzzled.

Uwe Radok and the other Seaton survivors were put in a large and draughty warehouse with a concrete floor. Their skins were stained with black fuel-oil, which vigorous scouring with Lifebuoy kitchen soap removed. That night Uwe wrote: 'All are like dead and sleep like beasts.' In the morning, he and his brothers were handed a postcard to sign with their names and numbers. They addressed it to their parents in Königsberg. The card already bore three neatly typed words: 'I am safe.' They were forbidden to write anything more.

One last question that is frequently asked remains to be dealt with. Gunther Prien did not know who was on board the *Arandora Star*. By July 1940, the war at sea between Britain and Germany was total; the fact that the liner was behaving as an 'enemy' was sufficient cause for her to be sunk. At midday on 3 July, Prien learned from Germany's monitoring of British radio that her name was the *Arandora Star*. But he had not heard who she was carrying by the time he returned to Kiel on 6 July. When the news broke, German propaganda turned it against Britain for sending German prisoners to sea in the first place. The fact that they had been killed by a German torpedo was conveniently obscured. Prien himself died when the U-47 was sunk by British depth-charges in the Atlantic in March 1941.

18 A Great Future Overseas

News of the *Arandora Star*'s sinking reached the Cabinet on 3 July. It came at a most inconvenient point. Neville Chamberlain had already prepared a paper about the progress of deportations, in which he reminded his colleagues that since 11 June he had been making 'every effort – on the direction of the Prime Minister' to send as many internees abroad as possible. Now 'certain difficulties' had arisen. The Home Secretary wanted 'care . . . taken to select suitable internees for shipment', and to spare people who were doing war work, had wives or children in Britain, or had been interned in error. The Foreign Office had reported the American protest over deportation and the risk of German reprisals. Now, Chamberlain added, the *Arandora Star* had been sunk.

The Cabinet's interest in the fate of the *Arandora Star* was largely confined to whether the German and Italian governments should be told, and whether a public announcement should be made in Britain. These questions were left to Halifax, the First Lord of the Admiralty, and Duff Cooper, the Minister of Information. Chamberlain was more concerned that two other ships were due to leave for Canada almost at once, and formally asked whether they should proceed. His own clear opinion was that the sailings should go ahead without delay; his reasons were principally those of administrative convenience. A time-table was 'already arranged' and it should be 'adhered to'. As for Anderson's idea to vet deportees more thoroughly, this would 'necessarily take some time', and it was even possible that as a result, 'we should be unable to fill the accommodation available in these vessels'. The Cabinet took Chamberlain's side and agreed that the next ship, the SS *Ettrick*, 'should sail as arranged'.

It would have been difficult to stop her. As one of the few files on internment released by the War Office relates, eight officers and 377 men of the 201st Prisoners of War Company were already on the *Ettrick* in Canada Dock, Liverpool. The company had received orders at Aldershot to be ready from 27 June to 'proceed as ship guard for Prisoners and Aliens to Canada'. The company left Aldershot at 10.15 p.m. on 2 July and boarded the *Ettrick* at 9 a.m. the next day.

The *Ettrick* had arrived only a day or so before. Launched by the P. & O. Line in 1938, she had been designed as an 11,000-ton troopship to work on permanent government charter, and was thus ready for her wartime role. In June 1940, she had joined the *Arandora Star* in the Bay of Biscay, and evacuated 2,000 people from St Jean de Luz, including King Zog of Albania, his family, and his Crown Jewels. They were landed at Plymouth on 26 June, and the *Ettrick* headed for her next assignment in Liverpool.

There were 2,600 Germans, Austrians and Italians in Liverpool too. Nine hundred were prisoners of war; the remainder were internees. One was Hermann Bondi, who had been brought there from the Isle of Man the previous day. Although rumours abounded, the internees had received no official announcement of where they were going. They started to board the *Ettrick* at 1 p.m. As she was carrying roughly double her intended capacity, it was hardly surprising that the commander of the 201st Prisoners of War Company, Captain E. Howell, had great difficulty in allocating accommodation. 'Far too many Prisoners and Aliens for quarters available,' he recorded in his war diary. The *Ettrick* sailed at 7.30 p.m., and unlike the *Arandora Star* was provided with a destroyer escort for the first thirty-six hours. The greatest discomfort was caused by rampant gastro-enteritis, but Bondi was spared this as he spent much of the voyage being sea-sick instead.

A further ship, the *Sobieski*, an 11,000-ton Polish passenger liner that had been built only the previous year, sailed from Glasgow on 4 July. She carried 1,550 Germans and Austrians – 1,000 'B' and 'C' internees, 550 prisoners of war – who doubled up in the cabins and slept on tables and floors. An internee named Dr Glucksmann, who had been arrested in Cambridge, thought the

Polish stewards unpleasant – they once made tea out of salt water, he complained – but found the British guards 'as usual friendly and understanding'. By 15 July, some 6,750 internees and prisoners of war had arrived in Canada. What happened to them there we shall take up in a later chapter. For now, it is more important to note that they were very far away from the kind of men Canada had been led to expect.

On 10 June, the hastily assembled Whitehall delegates had told Canada's Charles Ritchie that Britain's 'most urgent need' was to get rid of:

2,633 internees of Category 'A'
1,500 Italians
1,823 prisoners of war

The figures for internees were roughly those Chamberlain gave to the Cabinet the following day. He said there would be 2,500 Germans and 1,500 Italians, which would absorb the 'most dangerous characters' among the internees. There would also be 3,000 prisoners of war. The presentation in both cases supported the notion that Britain was disposing of the internees who represented the greatest threat if invasion came.

The reality proved rather different. By 15 July, the following groups (in round figures) had arrived in Canada:

1,700 merchant seamen in Category 'A'
2,700 internees of Category 'B' and 'C'
  400 Italians
1,950 prisoners of war

The British government had the excuse – which it later used – that the sinking of the *Arandora Star* had compelled it to send a replacement ship. From Chamberlain's presentation to the Cabinet on 3 July, it seems likely that the War Office was planning to send the *Sobieski* as well as the *Arandora Star*, for the references to the *Arandora Star*'s sinking were clearly last-minute additions in Chamberlain's paper. But even if the *Arandora Star* had reached Canada and the *Sobieski* had not sailed, the figures would still have been different from those given to Ritchie and the British Cabinet. They would have been as follows:

2,200 internees of Category 'A' (seamen and civilians)
1,700 internees of Categories 'B' and 'C'
1,100 Italians
1,400 prisoners of war

Ritchie and Cabinet had been misled. And the figures given to both had conveniently supported the notion that Britain was disposing of the internees who were the greatest threat should invasion come. Whether this was deliberate deception or a simple arithmetical mistake, we cannot tell.

It is clear that other mistakes were being made. The *Duchess of York*, the first ship to sail, was supposed to contain only Category 'A' internees: but, as we have seen, among those on board were 400 from Categories 'B' and 'C', many of them like sixteen-year-old Kurt Tebrich and his companions from Lingfield, classed as refugees from Nazi oppression. (Tebrich forgivingly concluded that his inclusion was a mere clerical error.)

Chamberlain was still making mistakes in Cabinet on 3 July. Having broken the news of the *Arandora Star*, he said that the next ship, the *Ettrick*, would contain Category 'B' internees: in fact its passengers included many 'C's, among them Hermann Bondi, another undoubted refugee from the Nazis. But even the Category 'B's were a departure from Chamberlain's presentation of 11 June, when he spoke only of Category 'A's being deported. But no one at Cabinet on 3 July either noticed or cared.

The Canadian government did not learn of the switch in categories until 8 July, when the Canadian High Commissioner cabled his government to say that the 'B' and 'C' men were on their way. It is unlikely that anyone in Ottawa yet appreciated the difference. In any case, they were all on the high seas by then, and Canada, like the British Cabinet three weeks before, had been presented with a *fait accompli*. For the Canadian government, in the long run, the alteration did not really matter. The main result was that those Canadian officers and soldiers who had been led to expect a dangerous consignment of spies and saboteurs, found that the men they were to guard included a high proportion of doctors, lawyers, pianists and Talmudic scholars.

While the shipments went ahead against Anderson's desire to at least select the deportees more carefully, the Home Office was at last fighting back on another front. The first stage in the mass internment of Category 'C' Germans and Austrians began on 25 June; and the Home Office ordered the second stage, taking in German and Austrian men living outside London, on 4 July. But Alexander Maxwell had now regained his writing form. His customary letter to chief constables contained a list of more than a dozen groups who were exempt. The categories make it clear that the Home Office had heeded many of the complaints about the earlier all-embracing phases of internment. Those now spared included people under eighteen at school or living with British families; the 'invalid and infirm'; people performing work 'of national importance', which included mining, ship-building and engineering; skilled workers in agriculture or forestry; those about to emigrate; those employing at least twelve British workmen; and parents with sons in the British forces. In addition, the police were not to intern where this would cause 'gross hardship'.

Six days later, the Home Office enacted the third and final stage, telling the Metropolitan Police to arrest all Category 'C's in London, subject, of course, to the same exceptions. But a simultaneous letter to the rest of Britain's police showed a further softening of approach:

> If internment in your area under Stages One and Two is not yet complete, the Secretary of State will be glad if you will instruct your officers that when an arrest is effected the alien should be given a reasonable time for settling his affairs and collecting such belongings as he can be permitted to take with him. In addition, each alien should be asked, when he is brought to the police station, whether he desires to advance any reasons why he should not be interned. In any cases where the alien makes statements which appear to suggest that he may fall into one of the exempted categories he should be retained in police custody or should be temporarily released while the necessary enquiries are being made.

Despite these peripheral modifications, each successive wave of arrests brought a further 3,000 or so men into custody. The Home Office may none the less have felt some satisfaction at being able to affect the course of internment once more. The Foreign Office remained unhappy. Having done its feeble best to stop the deportations, it was now embroiled in their unseemly consequences, which included a sordid row over exactly how many internees had died on the *Arandora Star*.

On 4 July, the Foreign Office formally notified the Swiss Legation and Brazilian Embassy – protecting powers for Germany and
Italy – of the sinking. It added the best gloss it could, besides
claiming that more lives could have been saved but for the internees' own hesitation. It stated:

> Every effort was made to save the lives of those on board the
> ship; rescue ships were at once despatched to her aid and despite
> the fact that the attack was made without any warning, 264
> Italians and 322 Germans were saved. . . Those saved all
> appeared grateful for the care shown them on board the rescue
> ships.

It gave a copy of the note to Joseph Kennedy, who cabled it to
Cordell Hull without comment. But on 5 July, the American
Embassy in London received a cable from its Rome counterpart,
reporting that Italy was 'highly exercised' over the *Arandora Star*,
and asking if Britain had told the International Red Cross that she
was about to sail. The Foreign Office admitted the next day that
it had not. Sir George Warner was already under pressure from
the Red Cross delegate, Haccius, on the same point. Haccius was
in Manchester when he learned of the sinking and immediately
sent Warner a telegram about further shipments:

WITH REGARD TO SAFETY BRITISH PW IN GERMANY
AND AIMS OF 1929 CONVENTION WILL YOU SEE
THAT EVERY PRECAUTION FOR CROSSING DANGER
ZONE IS TAKEN STOP BELIEVE BILATERAL AGREE-
MENT ADVISABLE AND POSSIBLE STOP

On 6 July, Red Cross headquarters in Geneva offered to act as
an intermediary with Germany 'in order to limitate risks of transfer
[*sic*]'.

The Foreign Office took up the Red Cross suggestion with some
enthusiasm. It soon ran into opposition. The Admiralty was adamant that it would not give the enemy information about the
movements of its ships. It did suggest that vessels carrying prisoners and internees should fly a warning flag, and this appealed
to the Foreign Office at first, not least for the possible propaganda
benefit. Displaying hitherto unsuspected cynicism, Sir George
Warner said it would be 'additionally discreditable' to Germany
if she sank a boat flying the special flag. He conceded, on the other
hand, that the flag could imply that all other ships were fair game.

Another official observed that the problem was 'one of German-Italian making and arises solely out of their disregard of their international undertakings or the dictates of humanity'; by implication, the problem was theirs to solve. The suggestion petered out at the end of July, long after the last ship had left.

Just how many had died on the *Arandora Star,* and who they were, was taxing the Foreign Office even more. When Warner wrote to the Brazilian Embassy on 4 July, he promised more details as soon as possible. When he tried to obtain them, he found the War Office in utter confusion. According to the first figures issued on 4 July, 270 Italians and 243 Germans had died. Two days later, Sir Alan Hunter, head of the Prisoners of War Department and a member of the Swinton Committee, gave Sir George Warner entirely different totals: the dead now numbered 225 Italians, 292 Germans, one Pole, and four stateless persons. He also sent Warner a list of their names.

Unable to reconcile this information with the earlier figures, Warner telephoned the War Office, to be told that casualties had been listed as survivors, and vice versa. Warner, who had already sent the lists to the Swiss Legation and Brazilian Embassy, now had to retrieve them. When he complained to the War Office about the muddle, Hunter blandly replied: 'It is obvious that a complete and final list is a difficult thing to produce under these circumstances.' In the end, the Foreign Office made its own calculations, concluding that out of 478 Germans on board, 175 were lost and 303 saved; for 712 Italians, the figures were 486 lost, 226 saved.*

While the Foreign Office was preoccupied with this grim arithmetic, the main action was once again elsewhere. The last ship had departed for Canada; but arrangements were almost complete

---

* This calculation is drawn from a printed but undated 'Embarkation List' to be found in FO 371 25210. It cites passengers by name and internment camp, and states whether they survived or died. It is probably the same list referred to by Anthony Eden in a parliamentary answer on 23 July 1940 as about to be placed in the House of Commons Library. In his report to Cabinet in October 1940 on the *Arandora Star,* Lord Snell gave different figures for embarkation. He said there were 473 Germans and 717 Italians; but happily this gives the same grand total, 1,190, as the Foreign Office list. But Lord Snell smartly sidestepped the more difficult question of how many had died. The Foreign Office list should not, however, be taken as the final word, for the *Arandora Star* veterans who perused it said that several listed as casualties had in fact survived. In 1979, Bernard Wasserstein, in *Britain and the Jews of Europe 1939–1945,* stated that 453 Italians and 146 Germans had died, but these figures appear merely to have been taken from *Anderson's Prisoners,* published by Gollancz in 1940.

for a new shipment to Australia. Having readily consented to accept internees, the Australian government had been waiting for more details, and on 27 June Sir Geoffrey Whiskard, the British High Commissioner in Canberra, provided them. He told Australia's Prime Minister, Robert Menzies, that Britain had 6,000 internees 'immediately in mind', and asked how many more Australia could take.

Menzies did not respond at once. Instead, he circulated Whiskard's cables to his Ministers of Defence and the Interior, and the Attorney-General. Open opposition to the internees was later to emanate from these quarters, and it seems that some reservations were now voiced, for on 2 July Menzies told Britain that 6,000 was the *maximum* Australia was prepared to accept.

In London on 3 July, Chamberlain, having told the Cabinet that the shipments for Canada should go ahead, revealed that a ship was due to leave for Australia on 7 July. She was the 11,000-ton *Dunera*, owned by the British India Steam Navigation Company, and launched in 1937. Like the *Ettrick*, she had been designed as a troopship, to hold 1,500 passengers. Chamberlain told the Cabinet that she would take 3,000 internees on her two-month voyage to Australia.

No one in the Cabinet raised any questions over the possible hardships of such a voyage, nor over the internees who would take it, even though they were all in Category 'B' and 'C'. After his gerrymander over the Canadian sailings, Chamberlain was prepared to show the Home Office some generosity. To meet Anderson's objections, he offered to delay the *Dunera*'s departure for Australia for a few days, 'in order to enable the internees who are to sail in her to be more carefully selected'. This slight concession was reflected in a modification of the approach to the deportees themselves. Previously they had been dispatched without any choice in the matter: this callous method was replaced by a different form of persuasion.

Henry Teltscher, from a Jewish family in Austria, arrived in England in November 1938. Aged seventeen, he was forbidden to accept paid employment, and spent a year as a student in Manchester. In January 1940, he started to work as an unpaid trainee in a textile factory in Lancaster. His tribunal, which he thought 'very pleasant and very gentlemanly', gave him a 'C'. Teltscher read about the loss of the *Arandora Star* in the press and was interned a day or so later. He was taken to Huyton, where he spent several nights in one of the camp's tents, by now almost afloat in a sea of mud. Then word went round that a boat was shortly leaving for Australia or Canada and the camp commander was looking for volunteers. According to Teltscher, 'We were told that if we went on it we would be released as soon as we arrived.' As Teltscher had contemplated emigrating to Australia before the war, he volunteered.

There are many repetitions and some variations on this theme. An internee named Walter Fliess, also at Huyton, thought he was volunteering for Canada, and recalls being promised that his wife would be able to join him. Others remembered being told that there was 'a great future overseas in store'. In the camp of Onchan on the Isle of Man, the Canadian postal address was officially announced. There, and at Ramsey, internees hoping to emigrate from Britain, principally to the United States, were told they would not be placed in a worse position by going abroad. On 9 July, the women at Port Erin were told by Dame Joanna Cruickshank, the camp commander, that, if their husbands went to Australia, they and their children could soon follow.

That the internees remained uneasy about these blandishments is evident from an anguished telegram sent by a group of married men at Onchan to Anthony Eden, Secretary of State for War. It read:

IN THIS VERY LAST HOUR WHERE WE ARE TO LEAVE THIS COUNTRY WHICH RECEIVED US ONCE AS FRIENDS WE MARRIED INTERNEES OF ONCHAN INTERNMENT CAMP ISLE OF MAN IMPLORE YOU TO ASSURE US THAT UNDER ALL CIRCUMSTANCES SHALL WE BE TRANSPORTED WITH OUR WIVES AND CHILDREN TO THE SAME DESTINATION STOP IF AN EMERGENCY SHOULD ARISE WE WANT TO SHARE THIS EMERGENCY TOGETHER WITH OUR DEAR ONES STOP PLEASE REALIZE THAT WE HAVE LOST EVERYTHING FREEDOM FATHERLAND PROPERTY STOP DO NOT TAKE FROM US THE VERY LAST WHICH PRESERVES OUR WILL TO LIVE STOP LEAVE US OUR WIVES AND CHILDREN TO LIVE OR DIE WITH TOGETHER
                THE MARRIED INTERNEES OF ONCHAN CAMP

Their distrust was amply justified. None of the promises was fulfilled.

Further shipments to Australia were undoubtedly contemplated. Chamberlain said as much to the Cabinet on 3 July, and in Australia Sir Geoffrey Whiskard told Robert Menzies that Britain certainly wished to take up the remaining 3,000 places on offer. But only the *Dunera* ever sailed, and in Chapter 22 we examine why the plans were altered. For the moment it is necessary to consider the position of the camp commanders themselves. It seems unlikely that they were all consciously party to deception on so massive a scale, and almost certainly they, too, believed that other ships would be leaving for Australia and/or Canada. François Lafitte, who interviewed several welfare officials on this point, probably comes nearest the truth when he suggests that the commanders, who had quotas to fill, were culpable of exaggeration rather than deceit. When asked what conditions overseas would be like, they provided the answers the internees wanted to hear.

It should also be said that many internees, fearing the consequences of an invasion, were quite willing to go abroad. One was Leopold Kohn, who, having been sent from Huyton to the Isle of Man, had been picked to go to Canada on the *Sobieski*, even though he was Category 'C'. By the time he arrived in Glasgow, the *Sobieski* was full to overflowing and he was sent back to the Isle of Man. Several days later he was simply told to pack his belongings again for the *Dunera*. Kohn cheerfully complied.

The Foreign Office made no attempt to prevent the *Dunera* from sailing, although its officials should have known from Chamberlain's announcement to Cabinet that she was due to leave. But they did not know that her passengers were to include most of the survivors from the *Arandora Star*. After two nights in the draughty warehouse described by Uwe Radok, the German and Austrian contingent were taken by train to Edinburgh, and then by bus to a camp of tents somewhere in the countryside. Radok found their treatment at the hands of the Scottish guards 'rough at first, with little cordiality'; he was still expecting to be sent to Canada, or perhaps Wales. By now there were 251 of them, for some fifty, including Bruno Fehle, had been taken to hospital.

They left the camp for Liverpool on 10 July. Around 2,100 internees had been brought there from the Isle of Man, together with 202 Italian survivors from the *Arandora Star*, including Serafino Pini, who had been quartered at Arrowe Park, Birkenhead. The

Arandora Star men were rigidly segregated from the rest, being placed first in a barbed-wire enclosure on the deck of the *Dunera*, and then led to the lowest level of her stern, with no bedding of any kind. Uwe Radok was by now feeling reconciled to his fate, and noted distantly: 'The escorts are very strange, regard luggage as their property and take even wrist watches and fountain pens.' He found that he could sleep on the bare deck without difficulty.

One fear, however, remained. What if the *Dunera* was attacked, like the *Arandora Star*? Radok could not help noticing that he and the others were virtually barricaded into their quarters, with only a narrow exit via a stair-well which was guarded constantly. He noted: '. . . getting out in serious circumstances won't work'. Then, on 11 July, he achieved resignation to even the most dire possibility.

> All things considered no one would care two hoots about us. For a while that is very worrying and then suddenly all becomes insignificant; one can't do more than kick the bucket, half that important, really. Strange relaxation of tension alone from that reflection. . .

To avoid the fate of the *Arandora Star*, the captain of the *Dunera* chose an elaborate and circuitous route out of Liverpool. It was the peak of the U-boats' 'Happy Time', and the south-western approaches were virtually closed. The U-boats also plundered around the north coast of Ireland, and to escape their attentions the *Dunera* sailed almost due north for a time, parallel to the coast of Scotland. At eight o'clock on the morning of 12 July, she had reached a point some twenty miles west of the island of Barra in the Outer Hebrides. That was where Oberleutnant zur See Harms, commander of U-boat U-56, was lying in wait.

Through his periscope, Harms estimated that the *Dunera* was steaming on a course of 314° at a speed of 14 knots. He made his calculations carefully. He selected two electric torpedoes from the armoury of the U-56 and, anticipating the *Dunera*'s position, set them on paths of 242° and 243° respectively. The spread would double his chances. The *Dunera*'s draught was 7 metres: Harms set the torpedoes to explode at 4 metres. At 8.06 a.m., the *Dunera* was 1,500 metres away, well within range. Harms fired. The two torpedoes left the U-56 dead on course and sped at 30 knots towards their target.

19   A Soldier's Letter

We shall describe later how the *Dunera* survived that seemingly lethal attack. For it is a consequence of the deportations themselves that the story of internment is about to be widely dispersed, with the action taking place in three continents. For the moment it is necessary to return to Liverpool, where a young soldier named Merlin Scott had just completed a spell of guard duty. His prisoners were the Italian survivors from the *Arandora Star* who were held for two days in Arrowe Park, Birkenhead. Scott had escorted them on to the *Dunera* – he thought they were bound for Canada – and was very disturbed by what he had seen. On 11 July he sat down to write a letter home.

> I thought the Italian survivors were treated abominably – and now they've all been sent to sea again to Canada. The one thing nearly all were dreading, having lost fathers, brothers etc. the first time. Many valuable men I think have been packed off. We had a certain Martinez who had been head of the Pirelli Cable and Tyre factories and who knows more about armaments than most – there were many others who had just been rounded up without any sort of inquiry.
>
> When they got down to the ship their baggage was naturally searched, but what I thought so bad was that masses of their stuff – clothes etc. was simply taken away from them and thrown into piles out in the rain and they were only allowed a handful

215

of things. Needless to say various people, including policemen! started helping themselves to what had been left behind.

They were then hounded up the gangway and pushed along with bayonets, with people jeering at them. It was, in fact, a thoroughly bad show. I think largely due to some of those useless hard-bitten bogus Majors who were standing around in large numbers!

Masses of telegrams came for them from relatives nearly all just saying 'Thank God you are safe', and they were *not* allowed to see them.

Although written in English they had to go to a Censor's office, and as the ship has now sailed, I know they will never get them. Some of them said they had had no mail for six weeks.

Merlin Scott's father was an assistant under-secretary at the Foreign Office. When David Scott showed his son's letter to his colleagues, the effect was explosive. For no one in the Refugee or Prisoners of War Sections had any inkling that the survivors from the *Arandora Star* had been packed off to sea again. On 13 July, Harold Farquhar was sent round to the Home Office to see if Scott was correct. Farquhar met Sir John Moylan, and – 'after some difficulty' – discovered that Scott's letter was true.

Farquhar was appalled. He wrote later that day:

To the best of my belief and knowledge, no one in the Foreign Office was informed of this action and I have the authority of Sir John Moylan for stating that the Home Office were also not consulted in the matter. If only half of the statements in this letter can be proved, it discloses a shocking state of affairs. . .

Merlin Scott left Liverpool soon after writing to his father and was posted to Africa with a regular battalion of the Rifle Brigade. There he distinguished himself in action, being recommended for the Military Cross, before being killed at the age of twenty-one during the Eighth Army's first advance into Libya in 1941. Many of his letters home from Africa were later included in the Rifle Brigade's official history. But it can be argued that his letter from Liverpool was the most important of all. For it helped towards the forming of an alliance between the Home and Foreign Offices that was to prove decisive in the course of internment in Britain. Harold Farquhar recommended that Scott's information be incorporated into a detailed letter of complaint from Lord Halifax to Sir John Anderson, and that is precisely what occurred.

The letter was drafted by Nigel Ronald, an official of counsellor rank, who had helped try to resolve the chaos over the repatriation of Italians and now drew on the observations and complaints of others involved. On 27 June, Richard Latham of the Refugee Section had vehemently denounced MI5. In a memorandum proposing a new committee on political refugees, he wrote:

> MI5, the department of the Security Service charged with the examination of the loyalty of individuals to the Allied cause, and in consequence, *inter alia* with the investigation of the *bona fides* of refugees, under the stress of recent currents in public opinion and under the influence of high authority in the War Office, has adopted the rule of thumb that any person of foreign nationality is to be presumed (almost, it would seem, irrebuttably presumed) to be hostile, while any person of British nationality is presumed to be loyal. This amounts to a confession of failure, for this department exists for no other purpose than the examination and judgment of individual cases.

Latham became even more angry a week or so later when he discovered that MI5 had imprisoned two Swiss refugees in Pentonville following a bizarre sequence of events including a 'Catch-22' of sheer perfection. The two men, named Eggler and Schmid, were working in Belgium when Germany invaded. They started to cycle home to Switzerland, but were arrested by French troops as suspected parachutists – Eggler was wearing a rucksack – and handed over to the British. They were taken to Dunkirk, where the British army was in the throes of evacuation, and shipped to Dover. There the immigration authorities refused them permission to land. As by then traffic across the Channel was strictly one-way, there was no prospect of returning them to France and MI5 ordered them to be sent to Pentonville Prison instead. They had been there a month before the Swiss Legation complained to the Foreign Office about their plight. On 9 July, Thomas Snow, head of the Refugee Section, asked the Home Office for their release. Six months later they were put on a boat for *Portugal*, but what had happened to them already did much to stoke Refugee Section's rage.

Ronald gathered further fuel from a visit paid by Farquhar to MI5 at Wormwood Scrubs on 10 July. Farquhar met a senior officer, Captain Guy Liddell, and explained that he had been sent originally to discuss MI5's methods of classifying Italians at the start of the war, but this was now 'rather past history'. Instead he would like Liddell to explain why 'various prominent and well-known figures in the hotel and restaurant business in London' had, among others, been dispatched to Canada.

Liddell blamed the Home Office. He and a colleague named Curry told Farquhar that the Home Office had asked for 'a list of suitable people to transport to Canada'. This proved to be the notorious list of fascist members, which they said the Home Office had passed to the War Office. But the War Office had been unable to find more than 700 men on the list in internment camps. Farquhar reported:

> What happened then they do not quite know but they suspect that the military authorities just filled up the number haphazardly by picking out any Italian between the age of 16 and 70, whether members of the Fascio or not.
>
> MI5 [Farquhar concluded] . . . cannot help us to sort out the sheep from the goats, and have no properly constituted dossiers against individual Italians. It is with them a question of hit or miss. If a Fascist, dangerous, if not, harmless.

The buck-passing by MI5 was paralleled in a major debate on internment and deportation in the Commons the same day. Although there had been numerous parliamentary questions, it was the first opportunity for MPs to discuss the subject in full. They did not waste it. Eleanor Rathbone, Major Victor Cazalet and Josiah Wedgwood, three MPs who had taken up the cause of refugees, spoke passionately of the plight of the sick and old in camps, the irony that anti-Nazis should be interned, and the difficulty relatives had found in tracking internees after their arrest.

But the MPs themselves had great difficulty in pinning down who was responsible for deportation. Sir Edward Grigg, Joint Under-Secretary of State for War, told them that 'the movements of internees has nothing whatever to do with the War Office'. When Miss Rathbone turned to Osbert Peake, Under-Secretary at the Home Office, he replied: 'The question of sending refugees and internees overseas is a decision that is not taken either by the Secretary of State for War or the Home Secretary.'

The trail on which the MPs had embarked led to the Home Defence (Security) Executive. Peake, of course, could not reveal that. In reply to the persistent question, 'Who is responsible?' he said: 'It is a decision taken by a Committee of the Cabinet, presided over by the Lord President of the Council.'

That statement was in itself a rare admission that the Cabinet even had such a committee, information which is usually denied to the British public to this day. Since the Lord President of the Council, Neville Chamberlain, was not present at the debate, MPs could not press the matter further. But it is worthwhile pointing out that Peake's answer was hardly consistent with the information Farquhar had extracted from MI5. And the muddle and evasions provided more grist for Ronald's mill.

In his 2,000-word draft, Ronald expressed his feelings almost without inhibition. He included a passing knock at Churchill – 'you will remember that the Prime Minister was strongly of the opinion that the largest number of prisoners of war and internees should be sent overseas as soon as possible' – but reserved his strongest vituperation for the War Office.

> As I see it there is a great danger that as things are at present, the decision in matters of this sort is passing, if it has not already passed, into the hands of the military authorities in charge of the internment camps. They do not always seem to know who is in which camp. They cannot know anything definite about individuals, and, when directed to produce a given number of internees for transport to Canada, they make the selection perforce at random. They can have no conception of the political considerations involved, nor yet of the psychological effects on foreign public opinion of any error of judgment into which they may slip. Many ugly stories have reached me and no doubt you too regarding conditions in these internment camps, and are naturally leaking out to American and other journalists.
>
> This is not the place to enlarge on the dangers of this, but if, on top of these allegations, it becomes known that the military authorities are left a perfectly free hand to decide who is to be kept in internment and who liberated, I fear there is a real danger of a most damaging scandal.

Ronald included a reference to the Italian aircraft engineer Salerni – the Foreign Office learned of his death on 13 July – and concluded by asking that Anderson should read the letter from Merlin Scott. As is usual when a ministry is staking out its position, Ronald's draft was polished by many hands. Warner and Cadogan approved it, and Farquhar made additions. So did Halifax himself, who was particularly struck by Scott's letter, and penned an emphatic postcript: 'It speaks for itself – and discloses a state of affairs that we should all find it quite impossible to defend.' Halifax sent the final version to Anderson on 15 July.

For the Home Office, the letter arrived at a most opportune moment. During the long Commons debate on 10 July, Sir Edward Grigg had made an unexpected admission on the War Office's behalf. Far from defending the army's right to keep control of internment policy, Grigg had asked for the MPs' sympathy for its plight. He described how, in the midst of its expansion and its preparations for a possible invasion, the army had suddenly been asked to provide some twenty internment camps. Grigg added: 'While it has done its best, I should like to say here in the clearest terms that the business of looking after the internees is not the business of the Army, and I very much hope that the Army may, in due course, be relieved of it.'

The Home Office could have pointed out that the responsibility for the camps had not suddenly descended on the War Office, but had rested with it since the decision of the Committee of Imperial Defence in 1923. It did not. For it now saw Grigg's penitential statement as its chance to regain control over internment policy. And if we are more positive than hitherto about Home Office motives, it is partly because one of the few files about internment released to the PRO covers this happier turn in its fortunes. It is also because the questions in the Commons about the *Arandora Star* had restored the debate on internment to the public domain. And instead of being returned to the confines of the Home Defence (Security) Executive, that debate was resumed in Cabinet on 11 July.

The Home Office had first to deal with a threat on its flank. In its deliberations on internment following the Commons debate, the War Cabinet asked Clement Attlee, Lord Privy Seal, to report how conditions in camps might be improved, and how aliens could be used to the nation's benefit. The Home Office was quick to impress on Attlee its point of view. Newsam and Moylan prepared a memorandum suggesting that the War Office should continue to provide the accommodation, camp commanders and guards, but should 'be relieved of their present responsibility for the conditions of internment and the treatment of internees'. They were firm that any new body to govern internment should come under civilian control and be answerable to the Home Secretary. Anderson sent the memorandum to Attlee on 13 July.

Attlee prepared his proposals by 16 July. The Home Office found he had concluded that 'the problem of sorting out aliens into their various categories . . . is not work appropriate to the Home Office or the Fighting Services'; Attlee suggested a 'special organization' to take on the task. Maxwell commented: ' . . . while the Home Office would be glad to be relieved of the work, it is difficult to see what Minister other than the Home Secretary could be made responsible.'

The War Office was now clearly out of the running. On 16 July, Anthony Eden, Secretary of State of War, answered questions from MPs about the *Arandora Star*. He was as discomfited as his junior Minister Sir Edward Grigg six days before. He told the Commons that all on board the *Arandora Star* were either Italian fascists or Category 'A' Germans, and that none were refugees. Eleanor Rathbone said that over the Italians, Eden was simply wrong; while George Strauss pointed out that the Germans and Austrians included well-known anti-Nazis. Eden, who told the Commons that he was relying on assurances from his officials, lamely replied that he would look into the question again.

Thus, with the War Office in a weak position and Attlee's proposals to be considered by the Cabinet on 17 July, the Foreign Office offer of an alliance was most welcome. Anderson was happy to agree with Halifax's analysis of where the blame for deportation lay, even if it did contradict what Grigg had told the Commons on 10 July. The 405 Italians sent on the *Ettrick*, Anderson said, had been chosen by the War Office, who regarded themselves as 'covered' by earlier Cabinet conclusions. The Italians for the *Arandora Star* had been 'selected' by MI5, and if this epithet ducked the point, Anderson knew who to condemn for sending the survivors on the *Dunera*. 'The decision to send these people to Australia was taken by the War Office authorities who, no doubt, regarded themselves as covered by previous Cabinet decisions that Italian Fascists should be sent overseas.'

Anderson also told Halifax that Merlin Scott's complaints were a matter for the War Office, which was making inquiries. He concluded: 'I hope I shall have your support.'

Although Anderson's reply was dated 19 July, it would be surprising if he had not intimated its contents to Halifax before the crucial Cabinet meeting of 17 July. When Attlee proposed his new 'special organization', Anderson said that the Home Office already had a small department headed by Sir John Moylan to take care of the problems of internment, which could, of course, 'have associated with it' the new body Attlee suggested.

But support for general internment in Cabinet seemed solid: the minutes noted a feeling that, 'further examination of the Category "C" enemy aliens was unlikely to result in the release of any substantial number.' Attlee was asked to raise the subject again the following day.

On 18 July, the Cabinet was due to meet at 11.30 a.m. Earlier that morning, the Cabinet's Home Policy Committee heard an extraordinary contribution from its chairman, Neville Chamberlain. At Churchill's request, he had enacted deportation without hesitation. But since then he appeared to have undergone a remarkable change of heart. Although absent from the Commons debate on 10 July, he told the Home Policy Committee that he was 'greatly disturbed' by the 'large number of complaints'. He had heard that among those interned were invalids, diabetics, TB patients and others who were chronically ill; also that relatives of some internees had been unable to find out where they were being held. Anderson told Chamberlain that the police had ignored orders not to arrest invalids 'in the rush of the moment', and that the War Office had been 'at their wits' end' to find accommodation.

Chamberlain's dramatic conversion proved decisive. He was now aligned with Halifax, which gave Anderson the support of two of the most senior members of Cabinet. Chamberlain repeated his observations at the meeting at 11.30, and the Cabinet agreed that the 'internal management, though not the safeguarding', of the camps should be transferred from the War Office to the Home Office. Far more important, it concluded that 'persons who were known to be actively hostile to the present régime in Germany or Italy, or whom for other sufficient reasons it was undesirable to keep in internment, should be released'. As an act of expiation, the Home Office was to order an inquiry into the selection methods for the *Arandora Star*.

The Cabinet had reached these momentous decisions just one week after Merlin Scott sat down to write his letter. They came just in time. Internments had been halted at 27,200, sparing the government the shame of exceeding the figure of 29,000 set during the First World War. Interning 27,200 people had been no easy matter. It was going to look simplicity itself against the task of releasing them again.

20   Regrettable Things Have Happened

Of the 27,200 men and women interned in Britain, 7,350 had been deported, and 650 drowned. That left 19,200, who were now scattered throughout Britain, from Seaton in Devon to the remote parts of Scotland – there was one camp at the head of Loch Eck in Argyllshire, and another in Knapdale, near Lochgilphead on the shore of Loch Fyne. By far the largest proportion was on the Isle of Man, which had expanded from its modest beginnings in May to become virtually a prison island, with the capacity for over 10,000 internees.

The Manx people reacted at first with some hostility to the internees, inspired partly by the abrupt requisitioning of the board-ing-houses and private homes at Ramsey and Onchan. They also took a lead from the Isle of Man's governor. When the Tynwald debated whether to intern the island's own tiny German popula-tion, he roundly declared: 'The only good Hun is a dead Hun.' At this point most of the dozen or so Germans on the island opted to go into internment voluntarily. However, the Isle of Man soon saw that its interests coincided with those of the internees; the rent paid to guest-house keepers and hoteliers was the only source of income in the absence of the tourist trade, and by harvest-time, farmers were allowed to employ internees at a shilling a day.

Richard Broh, the Jewish journalist expelled by Goebbels, had arrived on the Isle of Man from Kempton Park on 5 June. Many people jeered as he walked along the Douglas quayside, and one shouted: 'Bloody Nazis.' He was taken to the camp at Onchan, formed by a double barricade of barbed wire that encircled the houses of Royal Avenue. The camp had already taken in 1,000 men who were glad to escape the squalor of Warth Mills, and a further 250 from Huyton. Onchan was very crowded indeed, with most men sleeping two to a bed, and others on the floor. Five hundred departed for Canada and Australia, but on 11 July their places were filled by a large influx of Category 'C' men, bringing the total back to almost 1,500.

New arrivals were greeted with a notice in English and German from the commander of all the Isle of Man camps, Lieutenant-Colonel S. W. Slatter:

> It is my wish that every man who enters internment on this Island shall be assured that nothing avoidable will be done that might add to his discomfort or unhappiness.
>
> It must be obvious to you all that a uniform code of discipline is essential if a community of men are to live together success-fully. That code will be mine and will be obeyed. There is, however, a good reason for every order and there will be no aggression. The Officers and troops who are given charge of you are men of understanding. In any case, it is not a British char-acteristic to oppress the man who is unable to retaliate, and you will find no one anxious to foster a spirit of enmity which, within the confines of an Internment Camp, can achieve nothing. . .
>
> The measure of your co-operation and good behaviour will decide the measure of your privileges and the consideration shown for your welfare. In all events, you are assured of justice.

Onchan's commander, Major R. G. Marsh, also posted the War Office instructions for the conduct of the camp, but its inmates soon demonstrated that they were determined to impose a pattern of their own. Within days they inaugurated the Popular University, with a time-table of classes and lectures to fill the week: English was a popular subject, and among others were Russian, Spanish, telegraphy, advertising, the theory of numbers and first aid. They held a concert in August with *Lieder* by Schubert, arias from Puc-cini, songs from a youth choir, dancing and an excerpt from *A Midsummer Night's Dream* (Erich Freud played the joiner). They mounted an art exhibition and published a cyclostyled newspaper, the *Onchan Pioneer*. In the second issue, dated 9 August, they announced the promotion and departure of the commander with the salute: 'Three cheers for Major Marsh – a man of great tact and understanding.' The island commander, Slatter, evidently took a jaundiced view of camp newspapers, for he warned that they should not be 'mere vehicles for grouses and political matters'. Perhaps the strongest 'grouse' concerned communication with the outside world. For some weeks internees were forbidden any newspapers, and while this order was relaxed in July to permit *The Times, Daily Telegraph, Sunday Times* and *Observer*, the BBC was still banned.

Letters were another source of complaint. As at the start of the war, internees were allowed to write only two letters a week on army-issue 12-line notepaper, a regulation endorsed by a stern warning from Onchan's new commander, Captain The Lord Greenway: 'Writing across the lines is forbidden and the writing shall not be unduly close. . . Any infringement of the above orders is an offence which will be punished.'

The limit had been imposed for the sake of the Censorship Office in Liverpool, which had been overwhelmed. Letters were taking three weeks to reach their destination, and one internee calculated that the backlog must have reached 100,000. Richard Broh was unhappy that news from his wife was so delayed, but the greatest distress was felt by the men at Onchan whose wives and children were held at the women's camps at Port Erin and Port St Mary. Even though they were only a dozen miles away, letters between them were also routed via Liverpool.

Richard Broh, who had been chosen as spokesman for one of the Onchan sections, was particularly moved by the plight of a German named Werner Marx. His wife Dorothea was in Port St Mary, while their eight-year-old son Klaus remained in England. Marx was half-Jewish; he had left Germany at an early stage to set up a business in England, his family joining him in 1934. They had started naturalization proceedings, but their application was frozen at the start of the war. They appeared before a tribunal in Manchester on 27 May 1940 – and were both put into Category 'B' and told to be ready for internment the following day. Despite Home Office orders to the contrary, Mrs Marx was not told that she could take her son with her. She arranged for him to be looked after by friends, and on 28 May was taken to Strangeways Prison, Manchester. She spent four weeks there, and another two in Holloway, before being sent to Port St Mary early in July. Not until then did she know that her husband was on the island too, and

she received some very English letters from her son: 'the stocks
and pansies are all dead but the sweet peas are very fine. . . Love
and kisses from Klaus.'

Werner Marx joined the other married men of Onchan who
were pressing strongly to see their wives, and eventually a visit
was promised for the last weekend in July. The men were taken to
the Ballaqueenie Hotel in Port St Mary, their wives greeting them
with bouquets of flowers gathered from the fields. Collinson's Café
at Port Erin was also used as a venue. Later, monthly meetings
were arranged in Derby Castle, Onchan, where husbands and
wives were permitted to spend two hours together almost unsuper-
vised. In August meanwhile, Dorothea and Werner Marx decided
to send for their son, and Klaus joined his mother at Port St Mary
on 2 September.

Two miles south of Onchan was Hutchinson's Camp, formed
from a group of houses around a square that overlooked the main
town of Douglas. One of the men held there was Hellmuth Weissenborn, an artist and teacher who had left Leipzig with his wife
in distressing circumstances in 1938. His wife was Jewish, though
he was not; that did not stop their German maid from denouncing
him to the Gestapo for anti-Nazi remarks she had overheard. Even
though Weissenborn lost his job at the Leipzig Academy of Arts,
he wanted to hang on, but his wife implored him to leave. They
lived in furnished rooms in Notting Hill, and Weissenborn made
a bare living from illustrations and etchings. They both received
a 'C' at their tribunal, and Weissenborn was interned in the last
wave of arrests early in July.

He had not been in Hutchinson long before he received divorce
papers from his wife. She told him she intended to go to the United
States to live with her family; her parents had always disapproved
of their daughter marrying a non-Jew, and had not spoken to him
since their wedding. Weissenborn tried to soften this blow by
immersing himself in the cultural and intellectual life that Hutchinson, like Onchan, quickly established. There were frequent con-
certs and lectures, and Weissenborn added his own artistic flourish
by scratching mythological scenes in the blackout paint on the
camp's windows. Other artists followed this impetus, and there
was soon a range of improvised creative activities, with scraps of
lino eagerly garnered to serve as printing plates, and printing ink
mixed from margarine, soot and pencil graphite. Weissenborn
became one of the camp cooks, and his vegetarian soup, distilled

from the remains of earlier meals and served at teatime, was especially popular.

If the men on the Isle of Man were managing to exert some control over their lives, the women of Port Erin and Port St Mary were finding a stern adversary in the Home Office camp commander, Dame Joanna Cruickshank. With 4,000 women and several hundred children in her charge, she applied the rules rigorously and allowed the women little margin to participate in decisions. On the days when married women were to meet their husbands, she posted a notice forbidding them to wear trousers. Renate Scholem, who was becoming politicized and more bold, clashed with her several times, while Irmgard Fehle forced a major confrontation. As Dame Joanna paid scant regard to the delegations who attempted to see her, Mrs Fehle and a group of women decided to turn the censorship procedures to their advantage. They wrote letters to the mainland detailing their grievances in the knowledge that these would be summarized and sent to the Home Office. When Dame Joanna summoned them to her office and accused them of betraying her, they knew the ploy had worked. Life in the camps improved soon afterwards.

Karl Wehner was in Central Camp, Douglas; his wife had been interned at the end of May, and he was in the party of men who rode down to the women's camp at the end of July. Later that summer he fell foul of a further attempt to recruit him by MI5. On orders from the camp commander, a soldier escorted him to a Douglas hotel where a rather meek man introduced himself as a member of a civil liberties group and said that he could help obtain Wehner's release. When a puzzled Wehner started asking questions, the man came abruptly to the point: 'We need someone we can trust in the camp and who can keep us informed about the Nazis and their activities.' Wehner said he was prepared to answer specific questions but not to become a permanent informer. The man warned him: 'I hope you change your mind. You have twenty-four hours to give me a reply in the affirmative.'

Afterwards Wehner saw the camp's own intelligence officer, who became angry and muttered: 'What's this bloody interfering devil up to?' Wehner had stumbled into a bitter and long-running rivalry that existed between the military intelligence officers appointed to each camp and MI5, who pursued their own activities independently and of whom the mild 'civil libertarian' was undoubtedly a member. MI5's power over recalcitrant internees' lives became very clear within a week when Wehner was transferred to Huyton. He interpreted the move as a punishment, and was sure the British still regarded him with suspicion when Huyton's commander – who happened to be Lieutenant-Colonel Slatter, recently transferred from the Isle of Man – told him enigmatically: 'I can respect no man who has no loyalty to his country, especially the country of his birth.'

Bruno Fehle meanwhile was making a Cook's tour of virtually every internment camp in Britain. After being discharged from Mearnskirk Hospital in Glasgow, he was moved to Donaldson's School in Edinburgh, where he was intrigued by the small-scale furniture and fittings provided for the former deaf-and-dumb inhabitants, particularly the minute lavatories. From Edinburgh he proceeded to Prees Heath, where he slept in an army bell-tent, around which he and the other internees were told to dig a trench in case of air raids. The food was the best yet, for it was prepared by a noted Italian chef named Bolonini, supplemented by delicacies sent to the camp by Italian families. Then he spent a brief spell at Huyton at about the same time as Karl Wehner, finally being sent north to Knapdale in Argyllshire. There were about 150 in the group whom the British tagged as Nazis; although there were few party-members in the group, Fehle was prepared to concede that they were largely anti-British. They lived in Nissen huts which were warmed by stoves fuelled from the surrounding woods. He was questioned by the army intelligence officer when he arrived, who seemed to regard him with hostility. But he relaxed his attitude when Fehle told him that he had been on the *Arandora Star*. Fehle was quite gloomy about his chances of release, and felt certain he would have to wait until the end of the war, whichever way it turned out. But he was almost alone in his attitude of resignation. At all other camps, and especially on the Isle of Man, the paramount question for almost every internee was: 'When will I be released?'

The first public announcement came on 23 July, when Anderson told the Commons that Category 'C' internees would soon be able to apply for release. On 31 July the Home Office published a White Paper listing eighteen headings under which release could be sought. In effect, they were a restatement of the exemption groupings contained in Maxwell's earlier letter to the police, with one or two added. By then Attlee had presented a revised paper to the Cabinet in which he concentrated on the question of alien manpower – it was clearly absurd that Britain should be deprived of the 'potentially useful' and should suffer the 'loss of valuable services' in its fight. On 1 August, in Cabinet, Churchill agreed that it should 'now be possible to take a somewhat less rigid attitude in regard to internment of aliens'. Soon afterwards he told a bemused House of Commons that he had always thought the 'Fifth Column danger. . .somewhat exaggerated in this Island'.

Further apologies came from the Duke of Devonshire, speaking for the Home Office in the Lords on 6 August, when he said that internment had been forced on the government by the military authorities, and carried out in 'a situation of extraordinary difficulty and gravity'. The final atonement was reserved for Sir John Anderson. In the Commons debate of 22 August, he spoke of 'the very greatest reluctance and regret' with which he had departed from the policy he had declared at the start of the war.

> I am not here to deny for a moment that most regrettable and deplorable things have happened. . . They have been due partly to the inevitable haste with which the policy of internment, once decided upon, had to be carried out. They have been due in some cases to the mistakes of individuals and to stupidity and muddle. These matters all relate to the past. So far as we can remedy mistakes, we shall remedy them.

The first fifty category 'C' men to be released from internment sailed from the Isle of Man on 5 August. They were followed by 100 women and children, and by the end of the month almost 1,000 internees had been allowed home. A German dentist from Paddington magnanimously told a reporter from the *News Chronicle*: 'Everything in the camp was fine. Everything reasonably possible was done for us.' An Austrian psychiatrist, released so that he could continue with his research, said: 'We are all grateful for the kindness shown us by the authorities including soldiers whose job it was to guard us. The commandant was very fine.'

The releases were ostensibly decided upon by a plethora of committees set up out of the Cabinet discussions of July and early August. The cases of Italians were reviewed by a four-man committee headed by Sir Percy Loraine, the former British Ambassador to Rome. Another committee chaired by Sir Robert Dummett, a senior London magistrate, considered all Germans and Austrians in Category 'B', still a sore point among internees. As the first tribunals had doled out far more 'B's than had been intended, the

Home Office had appointed an advisory committee in March 1940 to look at these cases again. It had completed a quarter of its work when mass internment rendered such fine distinctions useless. The Dummett Committee was to start this work anew.

The Foreign Office appointed a committee to advise on welfare among internees and 'measures for maintaining the morale of aliens in this country so as to bind them more closely to our common cause'. Its chairman was the Earl of Lytton; its vice-chairman Sir Herbert Emerson, the League of Nations Commissioner for Refugees. Committees of eminent academics and scientists were to decide which of their interned colleagues could be released for 'work of national importance'. Later this bracket was expanded to include those who had made 'outstanding contributions to Art, Science, Learning or Letters', which required further committees drawn from the Royal Academy, the Royal Institute of British Architects and the PEN Club. Lord Justice Scott chaired a committee to consider lawyers, while musicians were scrutinized by a panel headed by Vaughan Williams. Finally a three-man committee under Mr Justice Asquith advised the Home Secretary on the general principles of internment policy and such proposals for change 'as he may refer to them from time to time'.

It might appear from this abundance of committees that power had been diversified among them. In fact they could only *recommend* releases, with the Home Secretary having the final word. And the majority of release applications were not referred to committees at all, but were decided solely by Home Office officials. Having wrested back control over internment, the Home Office was not about to see it dispersed again. At the same time, it had forged a more equitable partnership with MI5. This had come about as a result of the enduring row over the function and efficiency of MI5 culminating in an important constitutional decision by the Cabinet on 22 July.

In the Foreign Office, Richard Latham had continued his fulminations against MI5. An irked Gladwyn Jebb had demanded 'chapter and verse' for his strictures and Latham was happy to oblige. He compiled an indictment of the security services that must rank as one of the most vitriolic attacks ever made by one government department upon another.

Latham accused the security services of utter failure in their principal task of vetting individuals on the basis of the evidence in each case. This, Latham charged, was due to:

(a) The lack, in most of the personnel of MI5, of experience in weighing evidence; (b) the further lack, in most of them, of a political background adequate to enable them to judge the cases where evidence is indirect; (c) stupidity; (d) poor organization.

In place of individual security, Latham charged, MI5 had merely imposed arbitrary rules of thumb which had led to injustice and chaos. The Home Office had been placed 'in the anomalous and humiliating position of having to administer and to acknowledge as its own a policy which it did not desire, the details of which it did not frame. . . ' At the heart of the matter, Latham judged, was MI5's 'secret and largely irresponsible status'. He concluded: 'The Security Services are not publicly responsible to Parliament through any Minister, and public responsibility through a Minister is in the last resort the only kind of responsibility which is known to our constitution.'

Latham's paper was circulated rapidly in the Foreign Office, even Cavendish-Bentinck adding an apologetic note, admitting that he was 'to a small degree responsible, as Chairman of the Joint Intelligence Committee, for the stricter policy which was adopted as regards aliens since the May or beginning of June'. The 'muddles' had arisen, he explained, because:

> it is not possible to build up an efficient counter-espionage organization in a few weeks. For years, MI5 have been starved of funds, and after war broke out they did not succeed in recruiting officers of the calibre which a counter-espionage system requires if it is to do any good. The Gestapo has reached its present admirable pitch of efficiency as a result of 7 years' work.

Although Gladwyn Jebb recorded no immediate comment on Latham's diagnosis, it seems to have struck home. Three days later, on 22 July, the Cabinet reviewed the accountability of MI5. The sensitivity of the discussion that day can be judged by the remarkable lengths taken to conceal it since. MI5 featured as item 10: in the Cabinet minutes in the Public Record Office, this is marked 'Not open to public inspection'; and even in the agenda the heading has been blacked out. The discussion was based on Cabinet paper WP (40) 271, but the file that should contain this says only that the relevant pages 'are not open to public inspection and have not been filmed'. But an unguarded reference by Churchill in Cabinet on 7 November discloses what decision was reached. The *Arandora Star* was being discussed again, and the efficiency of the security services had been raised once more. Churchill pointed out that, 'subject to the Ministerial responsibility of the Lord President of the Council, Lord Swinton had been entrusted with executive control of MI5.' A note in the margin shows that this decision was taken on 22 July.

Cavendish-Bentinck was in no doubt that MI5 was now subject to the ministerial responsibility that Latham had sought. On 29 July, he wrote that MI5 had been 'put under the complete control of Lord Swinton, who whilst not officially a member of the Government, had more or less the same powers as a Cabinet Minister'. That was by itself a remarkable admission of Swinton's standing. MI5, of course, had been represented on the Swinton Committee from the start, and we have argued that MI5 saw the committee not as a restraining influence, but as providing sanction for its own unbridled and lawless behaviour. The significance of the 22 July decision was not that MI5 was formally placed under the committee's control, but that the committee was now answerable through Chamberlain to Cabinet for MI5's actions. It was an important transfer of power that was to lead eventually to MI5 being made directly responsible to the Home Secretary.*

After 22 July, the Home Office was able to settle into a smoother working relationship with MI5. The partnership was at its most comfortable when it was removed from the scrutiny of the various release committees; and in February 1941, the 'high official of the Home Office' who briefed the American Embassy in London (our guess is that this was Frank Newsam) revealed just how it worked. The Home Office referred all release applications to MI5, who now had a dossier on each internee; the application was turned down if MI5 said that the release would entail 'immediate or potential danger'. The Home Office almost invariably heeded MI5's advice: ' . . . practically complete reliance is being placed upon the data available from MI5 covering the alien's security record'.

---

* After the war, the Prime Minister inherited the responsibility for MI5 from the Swinton Committee. In 1951, Sir Norman Brook recommended that the responsibility should be transferred to the Home Secretary. A directive by Sir David Maxwell Fyfe, then Home Secretary, effected this in September 1952. However, as Lord Denning observed in his report into the Profumo scandal in 1963, 'considerable misapprehension' about ministerial responsibility for the Security Service remained.

The Home Office also helped to establish a *modus vivendi* when an application fell into one of the groups covered by the various release committees, with one exception. The Home Office would send MI5's recommendation to the committee and ensure that MI5 agents did not have to appear in person. If the committee required clarification of MI5's information, a Home Office man would attend instead. Furthermore, 'he would not be subject to cross-examination and such testimony would probably be given to the Committee in confidence and in the absence of the alien concerned or his representative.'*

The exception was the Loraine Committee, which considered the release of Italians. As former British Ambassador to Rome, Sir Percy Loraine remained loyal to the Foreign Office, which sought to influence the conduct of internment through its own Council of Aliens. The council's secretary happened to be Richard Latham, who was still penning strictures against MI5. He took a most uncharitable view of the cosy relationship the Home Office and MI5 had established, which he described as 'rather like the relation between the Vichy Government and the Third Reich'. (MI5 was the Third Reich.)

The Loraine Committee was the only one that dealt directly with MI5, and Latham was soon issuing dire warnings. 'I cannot stress too strongly the danger of accepting blindly the recommendations of MI5 or even the facts stated in MI5 reports, unless they are supported by detailed corroborative evidence. What we have seen of the work of that department of MI5 which deals with aliens discloses a notable incapacity for weighing evidence and a tendency to conceal this incapacity by unnecessary recourse to secrecy.' It is hardly surprising that the Loraine Committee was immediately plunged into the dispute over what constituted a true fascist. The Home Office was compelled to mediate, persuading MI5 to accept that 'membership in the Fascist Party does not disqualify for release'. This left ample scope for disagreement in individual cases, which occurred with depressing frequency.

This problem apart, the releases continued in a stream, meeting Anderson's expressed and characteristic desire that there should not be 'too violent a reaction from the policy previously enforced'.

* This method clearly provided a model for the 'Commissioners' Courts' set up in Northern Ireland thirty years later, when it was considered vital that a detained person should not be able to see a prosecution witness or an intelligence agent giving evidence against him.

By early October, over 4,000 men and women had been freed. Almost all were in Category 'C', which left internees such as Karl Wehner pessimistic about their prospects. Those entitled to be most optimistic included Richard Broh, Hellmuth Weissenborn and Renate Scholem.

However, they were not the only cases that needed attending to. While the British government was congratulating itself on the new liberal policy it had adopted, there remained the unfortunate matter of the 5,650 civilian internees who had been deported. The most pressing problem was posed by the 3,100 men who had been languishing in Canada since the middle of July.

21 A Cynical Excuse

The men who had been deported to Canada were confused by their reception. When the *Duchess of York* arrived in Quebec on 28 June, its passengers were told to discard their gas-masks and to board a Canadian Pacific train waiting on the quayside. Armed guards kept curious onlookers at bay, though this did not prevent the *New York Times* from reporting that many were Nazis who had behaved 'exactly as one might expect of their breed – they sulked and indulged in boasts and insults and in general earned the crew's forthright opinion of them as skulking, swaggering louts'. The report was reprinted in the *Manchester Evening Chronicle*, which brought an anguished protest to the Foreign Office from M. Haccius: it was *peu utile* – 'of little use' – to the Red Cross in their efforts for British prisoners in Germany.

On the train each man received a large cardboard box. Kurt Tebrich found riches inside: bread, onions, sardines, fruit, cheese, condiments – even cutlery and a mug. Each carriage had a stove to heat water for coffee. That night he slept in a bunk lowered from the ceiling, and in the morning washed in more hot water from the stove.

After two and a half days, the train arrived at the village of Nipigon on the northern shore of Lake Superior in Ontario. The passengers were marched to a disused mining camp surrounded by barbed wire. Somewhat lulled by the train journey, they were disconcerted at being meticulously searched by guards armed with rifles and bayonets. They were installed in wooden huts that contained no furniture or bedding, and an officer bearing a revolver told them that the guards had been instructed to kill anyone who tried to leave or even look through the windows. When one disbelieving internee attempted to do so, several shots flew over the hut. The officer returned to warn that next time there would be no half-measures.

The *Ettrick* disgorged her 2,600 passengers, who included Hermann Bondi, in Quebec on 13 July. They were first placed in an army camp on a spectacular site overlooking the St Lawrence river. They, too, were thoroughly searched – with the difference that the guards kept everything of value that they found. Soon afterwards they were moved to a camp near the city of Sherbrooke in southern Quebec. It was a former railway yard and the conditions were primitive, with constant long queues for the latrines and showers.

The *Sobieski*, which had called at St Johns, Newfoundland, on 12 July, reached Quebec on 15 July, and her 1,550 passengers were also searched and robbed almost as soon as they disembarked, losing even hairbrushes and nail-scissors. They were taken to a camp in a sports stadium at Trois-Rivières, a town on the St Lawrence midway between Quebec and Montreal. It, too, was surrounded by barbed wire, overcrowded and devoid of furniture.

Canada had been caught out by the indecent haste with which the deportees had been bundled across the Atlantic. Canada's Director of Internment Operations, General Edouard Panet, had mercifully not taken up the suggestion that they should be consigned to the desolate North-West Territories, which extended above the Arctic Circle. Showing much drive and ingenuity, he found camps in the far more congenial south, and soon put their evident shortages to rights. Within days of their arrival, the men at Nipigon were supplied with mattresses, blankets and pillowcases; the huts were furnished with tables, chairs and stoves, and a complete range of modern kitchen equipment was provided. Soon the internees were settling down to lavish meals of eggs, bacon, steak and fresh vegetables in such abundance that they could remove the surplus to consume in their huts. To complete the picture of luxury, the meals were served by stewards captured from German luxury liners who even dressed for the occasion in their white uniforms.

The Sherbrooke camp was also equipped with ample bunks and

sanitary facilities, while early in August the *Sobieski* men were transferred from Trois-Rivières to a purpose-built camp at Fredericton, in New Brunswick, which had heated and ventilated huts with their own lavatories and showers.

General Panet also attempted to group his charges according to whether they were seamen, prisoners of war or civilian internees. But he soon discovered that these gradations were insufficiently fine, and that many of the civilian internees were far from the kind of men Britain had led him to expect.

The civilians at Nipigon had been the first to disabuse their guards. Some had asked why they were being guarded so rigorously, to be told that this was the treatment deserved by parachutists, spies and saboteurs. The Canadian officer who gave them this information even asked if he could buy Nazi insignia as souvenirs. While the civilians promptly started manufacturing swastikas and Iron Crosses, they also explained to a disbelieving camp commander exactly who they were. The news soon reached Panet. He sent a pained note to Canada's Secretary of State: 'Cable 808, dated June 10, and others led us to believe that the internees were to be dangerous characters. This has not been found in all cases.' He was more pointed in a letter to the British liaison officer, writing that many of the internees were 'of the refugee type, and include a large number of schoolboys, college undergraduates, priests, rabbis, etc. . . . It is considered that these people should not have been sent to Canada.' Panet's surprise was soon echoed in London. On 16 July, the High Commission official, Charles Ritchie, noted in his diary: 'I now hear that the ferocious internees whom the British Government begged us on bended knees to take to Canada to save this country from their nefarious activities are mostly anti-Nazi refugees. . .' The High Commissioner, Vincent Massey, wrote a pained letter to Caldecote on 22 July. 'A number of questions have now arisen regarding the internees transferred to Canada which appear to require some fuller clarification,' he began. He reminded Caldecote that Canada had been told the internees were a security risk to Britain. 'As you know, the Canadian Government only accepted this responsibility in view of this urgent request.' Now Massey had been told by the Home Office that 'a number of internees sent to Canada are, in their opinion, innocent refugees'. If this were true, then Canada faced 'responsibilities of a character which they had certainly not contemplated when they consented to receive those internees'.

Caldecote could only offer one excuse: the *Arandora Star*. It had contained 1,200 Category 'A' internees and Italian fascists, who would have gone to Canada. Caldecote also explained that the *Arandora Star* was carrying tents to accommodate 1,000 men whom Newfoundland had agreed to accept. The men in question had been on the *Sobieski*, which had indeed put in at St Johns, but as Newfoundland had no alternative accommodation to offer, they had continued to Quebec instead. Caldecote also told Massey that Canada should have learned the truth about the internees earlier from their MI5 dossiers, but these, too, had been on the *Arandora Star*. This was the most remarkable assertion of all, and supposed that the War Office and MI5 had managed to gather all 7,950 dossiers on the men on the four boats in question, including the *Ettrick* and *Sobieski* which had not yet sailed.

The excuse was less than comprehensive, and Caldecote had no alternative but to apologize: 'The United Kingdom authorities greatly regret that the inclusion of "B" and "C" category internees among those sent to Canada was not explained to you at an earlier date, but I hope that no serious difficulties will arise in connection with their internment in Canada.'

He enclosed a long memorandum of more detailed explanation from the Home Office. It confirmed that most of the 'B' and 'C' men were refugees from Nazi oppression, and hoped that Canada might apply to them 'a system of less rigid custodial treatment'.

The suggestion appealed to Panet. He asked the Canadian government if he could remove all guards from the civilian camps and establish them as 'Refugee Republics'. Canada's State Department liked the proposal, but it was blocked by the Ministry of Defense. For it was feeling other pressures, from south of the Canadian border.

The US State Department, it should be recalled, had abandoned its liberal stance over internees as soon as it discovered that some of them were to be brought to the American continent. It lost no time in seeking reassurances about them from Canada. At the State Department's request, an official of the American Legation in Ottawa visited General Panet on 8 July. Panet told him what he wanted to hear: 'Orders have been given to all guards to shoot any prisoners who attempted to escape, after a first warning shall have been given. . . Heavy barbed-wire barricades are being used at all of these camps, and most of them have been placed in inaccessible regions whose exact location is being kept secret as far as possible.'

Panet, who did not yet know who the internees comprised, added that they would all be sent back to Europe at the end of the war. The US Attorney-General told Cordell Hull that Panet's assurances were no more than 'reasonably adequate'. And American fears were soon realized when several prisoners escaped from their camps, one getting far enough to be recaptured by US immigration officers. The American Ambassador to Canada, Pierrepont Moffat, requested a meeting with Canada's Under-Secretary of State for External Affairs, Dr Skelton, who told him that Canada would conduct an inquiry into the escapes and 'a thorough investigation of the whole internment system'. Skelton blamed the British for what had gone wrong, and was not above minor deception to support his case. The British had sent at least 2,000 more men than Canada was expecting, and 'the unheralded arrival of additional numbers put a heavy strain on available facilities'.*

Moffat reported this to Hull, and reassured him on another point. The American Legation in Ottawa was 'under constant pressure from American citizens (usually with strong political backing) to persuade the Canadian authorities (a) to release prisoners of war or internees usually with a view to their obtaining visas to enter the United States, or (b) to permit them to have interviews with the prisoners'. But as Moffat informed Hull, he had devised a neat response to those pestering the legation. As 'no direct American interest was involved', they were told to inquire instead at the Swiss Consulate in Montreal or the Japanese Legation in Ottawa, the protectors of German and Italian interests in Canada. 'In default of instructions to the contrary I shall assume this meets with the approval of the Department.'

The State Department had accurately discerned that emigration to the United States would help Britain in its problem over the deportees. In its long memorandum, the Home Office had, indeed, pointed out that many of the deportees either had American visas already, or wished to obtain them – one estimate was that around 1,000 of the 3,100 civilian internees in Canada had registered to emigrate to the United States at some stage. The Home Office politely wondered if Canada could help them to enter the United

* On the other hand, Skelton's assertion can be taken to support the view that Britain had intended to send *four* liners, including the *Sobieski,* all the time.

States. But Canada knew only too well how the State Department would react at even the hint of that proposal. Canada could see only one solution: the British should send an official to Canada to sort out the mess for themselves.

After several further conferences in London between the Canadian High Commission and the various British ministries involved, the official was chosen. He was Alexander Paterson, a 56-year-old Home Office Commissioner with a reputation for reforming zeal, who had also played a pioneering part in setting up boys' clubs in London's East End. He would sail for Canada on 7 November. Canada, of course, was not the only country to which internees had been sent. There remained the 2,550 men who had been deported to Australia. They had arrived early in September, and the stories now reaching Britain about their voyage were very unpleasant indeed.

22 'Drown Like Rats!'

By only a fraction did the *Dunera* avoid sharing the fate of the *Arandora Star*. Moments after the U-56 fired, Oberleutnant Harms observed the *Dunera* make a 40° turn to starboard. It is clear that the turn was merely a standard precautionary manoeuvre, and not the result of a lookout's warning. The electric torpedoes Harms had selected were notorious for leaving no tell-tale wake; and, in any case, the *Dunera*'s turn, from 314° to 354°, took her precisely into the path of the two torpedoes bearing down, on courses of 242° and 243°, from the north-east. But the turn was sufficient to upset the delicate geometry of Harms's calculations. The torpedoes were travelling at twice the *Dunera*'s speed, and thus reached the new point of intersection some twenty seconds ahead of her. On the best calculations, they missed by some 100 to 200 metres.

Harms did not know just how close he had come to sinking the *Dunera*, making the brief, rueful observation in his log that the torpedoes had passed ahead of the *Dunera* and exploded harmlessly some way beyond. Those on board the *Dunera* had little doubt that disaster had been very near. *Dunera* passengers today speak of hearing a rasping or grating noise, followed by a louder, more substantial sound that some believe was one of the torpedoes exploding close by, others that it had even struck the *Dunera*'s hull and bounced off without exploding. (The electric torpedoes were fitted with magnetic detonators that were still proving unreliable.)

Some were at first merely puzzled by the sound. But the *Arandora*

Star survivors deep in the *Dunera*'s stern knew at once what it portended. Most leapt to their feet and rushed to the stairs that led to safety. At the top, their way was barred by a door. Erwin Frenkel was in the leading group and had helped plan for this exact contingency; one of the group charged at the door and succeeded in breaking one of its panels. A British bayonet speared through from the far side, wounding his arm, and a soldier shouted: 'Drown like rats!' Another *Arandora Star* man named Hans Margis heard this too.

Uwe Radok had been waiting for this very moment, recording in his diary beforehand his 'persistent vision of the explosion and the subsequent panic'. When it came, he did not join the men fighting on the stairs to escape. He and an internee named Felix Gutmann simply looked at each other and shrugged. Then Radok climbed into his hammock to wait for the end.

When the panic had subsided it was replaced by proliferating rumours about what had happened. By one account, the British sailors had seen a torpedo pass directly *underneath* the ship. Those who believed that the torpedo had actually struck the *Dunera* found support when they learned of buckling in the ship's plates around the galley, which the crew had shored up. The Germans from the *Adolf Woermann* organized a watch-keeping rota in which Radok and the others took part. Radok conceded: 'In this situation the Nazis come into their own. . . By and large, it is easier to sleep when one knows other people are keeping guard.' Gradually Radok regained his composure. 'One gets used to the ship's motion and in part, to the condition.' It was barely disturbed even on 16 July when there was a search and he calmly noted: 'Afternoon handing over of valuables, also razors etc. Won't see any of that again, probably.'

Most of the passengers on the *Dunera* lacked Radok's ability to retreat once more into a protective shell. The large majority, numbering some 2,100, were Category 'C' men, many of them arrested in the final round-up that began on 25 June. While Radok and his companions had already spent at least six months in captivity, the new internees were still struggling to come to terms with their predicament when they were put on the *Dunera*. The events of the first hours and days of the voyage vastly multiplied their shock.

What happened on the *Dunera* has been so well established that it is not even a matter of dispute. There is no shortage of survivors from the 2,550 men on that voyage, and many wrote accounts of

it afterwards. The most valuable is a document named the Dunera
Statement. It is similar to the *Arandora Star* memorandum of Bruno
Fehle, in that it was compiled by a group of men determined that
the truth should be recorded and preserved.

They wrote it soon after they arrived in their Australian internment camp, and they consulted widely among their companions.
It is true that self-interest played some part, as we shall see later.
But the authors had one major advantage over Fehle. He had
attempted to make sense of the events of one appalling hour. The
outrage of the *Dunera* lasted for almost two months. The Dunera
Statement is the source for much of the following account.

The first 500 men to arrive at Liverpool docks for the voyage came
from Huyton. As they arrived they were subjected to an 'exceed-
ingly rough search'. Items without value were thrown on to the
quayside, but:

> valuables were stuffed into sacks or disappeared openly into the
> pockets of the searching soldiers. Soon rows of empty wallets
> were lying on the floor. . . No receipts were given except by one
> single searching group. Appeals to the officers standing by were
> fruitless. Attempts of protest were quickly suppressed.

No group boarding the *Dunera* escaped similar treatment. The
statement adds: 'All these searches were carried out without any
discrimination, accompanied by acts of violence, and resulted in
the loss of an enormous amount of money, valuable articles, toilet
necessities and important documents which have never been
recovered.'

The next shock came when the internees were directed to their
accommodation, packed to almost twice its supposed capacity.

> The congestion was such that people slept at night on mess
> tables, and on the floor during the whole voyage. . . During the
> day when no hammocks were allowed, staircases and every inch
> of floor space was constantly packed. . . For weeks the hatches
> were kept battened down. Neither daylight nor natural air ever
> reached the decks. The portholes remained closed the whole
> time.

The overcrowding was made worse by the natural reaction of
dazed men to their first days at sea. Leopold Kohn was the young
trainee pastrycook interned in Suffolk and taken to Huyton. From

there he had been shipped to Douglas on the Isle of Man, then taken to Glasgow for the *Sobieski*, returned to Douglas because she was full, and finally sent without choice on the *Dunera*. He had lost his baggage, but he at least had the fortune to be given a hammock in a cabin holding several hundred men. The consequences for those on the floor beneath were not pleasant. Kohn spent the first two and a half days of the voyage being sea-sick. On the first night, no one was allowed out of the cabin, and buckets were provided as lavatories. They soon overflowed and the deck was awash with a mixture of vomit, urine and excrement.

When use of the lavatories was permitted, they presented a no more attractive prospect. They were flushed with a powerful stream of salt water which swilled the contents over the edge of the bowl – the statement drily records that 'the mixture of salt water and excrement made the use of some seats impossible'. There was almost no lavatory paper. In the army fashion, the cubicles had no doors, so that those struggling inside were in full view of an impatient queue. Conditions became even more foul when attacks of diarrhoea spread through the ship.

Some of the complaints in the statement's grim catechism are major; others minor but no less irritating. Most of the ransacked baggage had been consigned to the hold, which caused a great scarcity of toilet accessories such as toothbrushes and combs. For the first five weeks, shaving was forbidden. (Peter Jacobsohn had managed to procure a razor and shaved regularly. He told the officer who inspected him that he was unable to grow a beard, but eventually his story cracked and the razor was confiscated.) There was one piece of soap per week to each ten men, who also had to share a towel. There was one exercise period on deck of fifteen to twenty minutes each day, with internees of all ages walking or running on instructions, often accompanied by a string of oaths and sometimes by blows from rifle-butts as well. There was no boat-drill, and the Dunera Statement notes that, had the liner gone down on 12 July, there would have been 'complete disaster'. And all the time the thefts continued.

Sometimes troops carrying bayonets appeared in the cabins at night 'to unfasten wrist-watches, tear off wedding rings, and search for valuables, forcing the persons affected to keep quiet by the threat of violence'. The Italian Serafino Pini preserved his wedding ring by attaching it to his penis by a length of wire. One morning, the 350 men on No. 2 Troop Deck were ordered to take an unexpected bout of exercise. They returned to find that items like gloves and scarves had disappeared and that coat-linings were slit open. Afterwards the spokesmen for the internees on Lower No. 3 Deck collected all their remaining valuables and asked an officer to keep them safely.

> He gave his word of honour as an officer to look after them and return them at the end of the voyage. Two closed canvas bags filled with articles were thereupon handed to him. Neither the bags nor the articles contained therein have ever been seen again.

The culminating misery for an internee named Jakob Weiss came when he discovered that his visa for a country in South America had been destroyed in the looting. He committed suicide by jumping overboard.

Against all this, the *Dunera*'s actual destination might have seemed unimportant. To the men cooped below decks, the fact that they did not even know where they were going added powerfully to their bewilderment and disorientation. Some, of course, believed they were going to Canada, but this became increasingly hard to sustain.

As a mathematician with navigational training, Uwe Radok was attuned to the shifts in the *Dunera*'s direction. When she sailed north he had written: 'We are taking a wild course – one can't see from it where we are heading.' On 16 July he noted she was heading south: 'If Canada we ought to see land the day after tomorrow or at least be near to it.' And on 18 July: 'We'll have to turn west soon if it is to be Canada. . . Reinforced rumours that it will be Australia.' Radok began to make abstruse trigonometrical calculations to determine the *Dunera*'s position, covering several sheets of precious lavatory paper with figures, using the changing length of the days as his starting point. Internees on another deck fashioned a pendulum and judged their direction by the changing angle of the sun's shadow. For a time, Jamaica was mooted as a possibility; Peter Jacobsohn suggested Bermuda. When the *Dunera* anchored outside the port of Freetown in Sierra Leone on 24 July, there could no longer be any doubt that they were bound for Australia.

The *Dunera* continued on her southward passage, calling at Takoradi on the Gold Coast on 27 July, Capetown on 6 August. Radok was disappointed that Table Mountain was wreathed in mist, but the next morning the cloud had disappeared. When the *Dunera* sailed that evening, Capetown 'presented a very beautiful sight, the town below the rock in the dusk'. The *Dunera* turned east, and during an interlude on deck Radok watched flocks of albatross skimming the waves, then landing elegantly like seaplanes. 'In the evening in moonlight,' he noted, 'the same birds still there.'

At last the tensions of life on board eased a little. Some guards became more friendly, one passing on snippets of war news, another joining the internees in some improvised music. The internees displayed humankind's limitless capacity for extracting the maximum benefit from the least promising circumstances. Below deck, queues were organized for those wishing to look out of the only portholes that would open – they were in the lavatories, and each man was allowed twenty seconds. One amateur astronomer who looked up and spied the Southern Cross said his whole journey had been made worth-while.

Henry Teltscher had been assigned to the ship's galley and helped win the occasional bonus for his companions. The *Dunera* had taken on crates of African fruit which were distributed on longed-for 'fruit days'. Oranges were especially precious: internees who received a rotten one could trade it in, and Teltscher ensured that the same rotten orange was circulated many times. He also took part in an operation planned with military precision, when a man dropped a crate of oranges so that it burst open, and every orange and fragment of wood was hidden among a crowd of internees within seconds. The galley was barricaded with barbed wire, and Teltscher was watched longingly as he helped prepare the food. An old man begged a morsel of raw fish and chewed it with evident relish, the bones protruding from his mouth and saliva glistening on his beard.

In the third week of August, cynics among the passengers perceived that Australia must be near. Razors were distributed and the passengers ordered to make themselves look presentable; men aged fifty-five and over, and those who were sick, were permitted to take an hour's fresh air each day. As if in response, an excited rumour swept the *Dunera* that all internees would be released in Australia. On 27 August, the port of Fremantle in Western Australia came in sight. 'Australia looks good,' Radok wrote. 'Trees of all kinds, in addition sun . . . A street with life, cars, incredible. In the evening everything lit up, like peacetime.' But rigid discipline was restored, and Franz Eichenberg was put in a cell after losing his temper while reminding the British of their undertaking to return all valuables on landing. The internees were also disappointed in their hope of prompt release – it might come 'in a few months'.

On 3 September 1940, the *Dunera* slid gently over the mirror-like surface of Melbourne Bay and tied up at Prince's Pier. It was fifty-four days since she had left Liverpool, and a year to the day since the war began.

The *Arandora Star* men disembarked and a train soon carried them to the township of Tatura, 110 miles to the north. Their new home consisted of corrugated iron huts set on a hill; the Germans and Austrians were divided from the Italians by the customary barbed wire. They were greeted that night by a cold and fine starry sky, and grew accustomed to the solid ground beneath their feet. 'One can slowly start to learn that not every bang is a torpedo,' wrote Uwe Radok. He found the Australian servicemen running the camp 'extraordinarily nice'.

The *Dunera* continued north to Sydney, docking on 6 September. The 2,100 men still on board were also taken by train direct from the quayside to their place of internment. The journey lasted thirty hours, most spent crossing the arid, treeless Nullarbor Plain. Kangaroos bounded away from the train as it passed. Their destination was Hay, a railway terminus on the Murrumbidgee River, celebrated in the line, from an Australian folk-song, 'Hay, Hell, and Booligal', as one of the least hospitable places on earth.

The camp was built around a former air-strip, with a double barbed-wire fence, four watchtowers armed with machine-guns, and thirty-two wooden barrack huts set in a fan formation. Within days, Hay's fearsome reputation was borne out. The temperature soared to over 100°F and the notorious 'Bricklayer' wind began to blow with gathering strength from the north. Clouds of soil and sand swirled around the camp, penetrating every corner. The dust-storm was followed by tropical rain – and then the sun returned, casting a mirage of flowing water from the Murrumbidgee River to bewilder the men from Europe even more.

Ten thousand miles from home, the internees at Tatura and Hay might have felt with justification like castaways, abandoned by the world to whatever now befell them. But, during their two-month voyage, their fate had become the subject of a flurry of anguished cables that passed almost daily between London and Canberra. They covered a multiplicity of problems, of which the

first and most basic was that no one knew how many men had
sailed on the *Dunera*.

Britain had originally told Australia that the first ship would
contain 3,000 internees. On 9 July, Whiskard informed Menzies
that 'about 2,700 men' would be sailing the next day. In mid
voyage the figure was reduced again, when Caldecote told Massey
that it was now 2,367. The true total was not established until the
Dunera arrived at Fremantle and officers from the Australian navy
counted for themselves. They sent the result to Menzies' office,
where an official added the mournful note that, while the British
had said that '2,367 persons sailed on the *Dunera*, this message
shows that 2,543 arrived'.

The arithmetic was of more than academic significance. It
related to a matter of much greater importance, not least to the
Dunera men themselves: the promise that their wives and families
could join them soon afterwards. The British government did
intend to dispatch one or more liners to Australia after the *Dunera*.
Chamberlain had said as much in Cabinet on 3 July, and Sir
Geoffrey Whiskard told Menzies on 9 July that further ships would
be sailing for Australia on 15 and 16 July. How many could sail
on them would depend on how many had left for Australia already.
But while enmeshed in its calculations, the British government's
plans hit a major snag. The problem was New Zealand.

On 26 June, Caldecote had sent New Zealand his by now standard request for assistance. New Zealand seemed ideal and Caldecote confidently expected a positive reply. With some surprise
he learned that the New Zealand government considered that the
country's 'limited size . . . and small population' made it unsuitable. Caldecote asked the British High Commissioner in Welling-
ton, Sir Harry Batterbee, to press the point. On 2 July, Batterbee
reported his conversation with Peter Fraser, New Zealand's Prime
Minister. Fraser had argued that 'the presence of a large number
of prisoners in New Zealand would be likely to tempt Hitler to try
to induce Japan to rescue them and also might facilitate Japanese
operations. This view seems to me rather far-fetched but it is
apparently sincerely held by the Prime Minister and I was asked
to put it to you.'

Caldecote was disinclined to accept New Zealand's refusal, and
pressed ahead with his plans for sailings to the Antipodes. At that
point he believed that 2,700 men had gone on the *Dunera*. He asked

Whiskard to tell Menzies that two more ships would be departing on 15 and 16 July. They would carry 4,500 men, women and children: 3,300 would be put off in Australia, while the balance of 1,200 would go on to New Zealand. But Caldecote now discovered that New Zealand meant what it said. And it was not so much Japan that was the stumbling-block, but the United States. Evidently guessing where the problem lay, the British government asked its US Ambassador, Lord Lothian, to make soundings in Washington. They were relayed to New Zealand on 14 July. The next day Batterbee reported that Fraser was 'especially relieved by views expressed by His Majesty's Ambassador at Washington as to probable United States reaction. He fully appreciates the reasons for anxiety about Japanese attitude.' The plans for sailings were postponed.

On 27 July, Stanley Bruce, Australia's High Commissioner in London, sent Menzies a memorandum from the British Dominions Office. Similar in tone to the one prepared for Canada, it attempted to explain that most of the men on the *Dunera* were not exactly the subversive characters they had been painted. It was true that the *Dunera* carried 450 survivors from the *Arandora Star*, including Category 'A' Germans and Austrians who were 'dangerous or potentially dangerous', and who should be kept 'under strict custody'. But the fact that the remaining 2,100 passengers had been interned 'involved no reflection on their loyalty and disposition' towards Britain. The memorandum diffidently wondered if this group could receive a system of 'less rigid custodial treatment'.

Soon after making this painful admission, the British government was confronted with the promises with which many married men had been induced to sail on the *Dunera*. In a letter to *The Times* on 6 August, an Isle of Man internee named Zinnemann said that twenty-two men left 'under a guarantee given to them in the name of the Command that their interned wives in Port Erin would accompany them in the same convoy. . . Furthermore, letters from Port Erin dated July 10th say that all women there had been told exactly the same day that their husbands would leave for overseas and it was hoped to reunite them there at a later date.' On 13 August, Osbert Peake of the Home Office parried questions about the letter in the Commons. The government evidently now attempted to fulfil the promise, for on 16 August Menzies was told that Britain proposed to send 188 wives and 204 children of *Dunera* men to Australia. But by now Menzies himself was in great difficulty.

Throughout the twentieth century, Australia had maintained unbending control over immigration, characterized by the unashamed racism of its 'White Australia' policy. It was also ruthless towards those it regarded as potentially hostile. In 1934, the learned Czech author Egon Kirsch arrived in Melbourne to attend an anti-war conference. Immigration officials asserted that he had communist affiliations and refused him permission to land. Kirsch jumped on to the wharf, broke his leg, and was taken to hospital. The government decided to deport him under the Commonwealth Immigration Restriction Act of 1901, the cornerstone of its immigration policy. The act stopped short of barring would-be entrants for the colour of their skin, but stipulated instead that they must pass a dictation test in 'any European language'. Immigration officials gave Kirsch a test in Gaelic. He failed.

Although in 1938 the Australian Prime Minister, Joseph Lyons, said that in principle Australia would accept 5,000 Jewish refugees from Europe, the restrictive strain dominated. This became rapidly clear when it was learned in Australia that the *Dunera* was on her way. On 31 July, the Department of the Interior asked Menzies to confirm that the *Dunera* men would be deported at the end of the war. On 6 August, Norman Makin, member for Hindmarsh (Southern Australia), warned the Australian House of Representatives that the internees would 'constitute a ready-made Fifth Column' at which the people of Australia were 'gravely disturbed'. Menzies revealed his discomfiture when he sent a 'personal and secret' telex to Bruce in London on 31 August, asking him to stop the British government from referring in public to the dispatch of internees to Australia.

When Menzies received the British requests that the 'B' and 'C' internees should be treated more leniently, and that their wives should be allowed to join them, he sent copies to his ministers. The Army Minister was pondering his reply when he learned that the family of one *Dunera* man was already on its way. He drafted a telegram asking the British government to stop further departures immediately, to which the Minister of Defence Coordination added that wives and families should be prevented from coming, even at their own expense. Menzies obediently dispatched the cable to Bruce on 13 September, instructing him to tell the British that

Australia had only accepted civilians for internment and was not prepared to release them into normal life.

The British government received Bruce's message just as it was beginning to attend to the chaos in Canada. There, of course, about 1,000 deportees were hoping to emigrate to the United States and the British government guessed that the same applied in Australia. In fact, 400 of the men on the *Dunera* had laid similar plans, including 100 who had reached the final stages of the United States's lengthy immigration procedures. Australia was duly added to the agenda of a meeting held at the Home Office just before Alexander Paterson left for Canada, and was discussed at length on 12 December. But it was clear by then that Australia's problems would be even more intractable than Canada's. The first official news of the voyage of the *Dunera* had just arrived.

In Australia, it had been known for some time that things had gone badly wrong. Doctors who went on board the *Dunera* at Fremantle prescribed extra milk and eggs for the emaciated patients they found. They, or other officials, evidently discussed matters with the British army commander, Lieutenant-Colonel W. P. Scott, with the internees' allegations. For while the *Dunera* was *en route* from Fremantle to Melbourne, Scott sat down to compose a memorandum for the Australian authorities. It is possibly the most revealing document of the entire internment saga.

Scott first explained what had happened to the internees' baggage.

> As there are over 2,000 bags and a like number of document cases, all unlabelled, it is absolutely impossible to sort out the property of any internee going ashore at Port Melbourne. This will be appreciated when I inform you that embarkation at Liverpool was made in such inadequate time that to tabulate this baggage was out of the question. Moreover, as the voyage progressed, bags had to be forced open in order to obtain linen and clothing which after fumigation and washing, was distributed piecemeal to the internees. This was an urgent necessity owing to large numbers becoming lousy. It will be a simple matter for detention authorities at Sydney to distribute baggage on identification by internees when the balance may be returned to Melbourne.

He turned to the question of the internees' valuables:

The same applies in this paragraph. Valuables have been placed in a sack and sealed. Two valuable items of jewellery are under separate cover. As I have already pointed out to Capt Heighway, search of internees was commenced on shore by the Dock and Military Police in conjunction with my Command, but there being such urgency to sail owing to escort and convoy anxiously waiting, that it had to be continued to the best advantage on board ship.

It will be appreciated that in the difficult circumstances of sorting out internees in their respective groups, that certain articles are possibly missing but in my opinion this of course is unavoidable. I have asked Australian Authorities to support my urgent request to the British Authorites that they should in no circumstances permit internees to have more than one kitbag per head and that all valuables should be handed to Conducting Officers in a sealed parcel for which receipt may be demanded.

Scott evidently felt uneasy about these explanations: perhaps he felt he had not done himself justice, for he now added some further observations.

I would now like to give my personal views on
a. Nazi Germans, b. Italians and c. German and Austrian Jews.

a. Having warned this group prior to sailing of my methods should trouble arise through them, their behaviour has been exemplary. They are of a fine type, honest and straightforward, and extremely well-disciplined. I am quite prepared to admit however, that they are highly dangerous.

b. Italians. This group are filthy in their habits, without a vestige of discipline, and are cowards to a degree.

c. Can only be described as subversive liars, demanding and arrogant, and I have taken steps to bring them into my line of thought. They will quote any person from a Prime Minister to the President of the United States as personal references, and they are definitely not to be trusted in word or deed.

Scott addressed his report to the Prisoners of War Information Bureau of the Australian Imperial Forces. However, it was by no means the only account of the voyage.

Once on dry land, the *Dunera* men themselves set about record-ing their version of what had happened. They had a pecuniary interest in doing so, for almost all had lost possessions or valuables, and were naturally hoping to be recompensed at some stage. None the less the circumstances in which the Dunera Statement was composed make it an impressive document.

The 2,100 men sent to Hay in New South Wales had been divided into two camps, called rather mysteriously 'No. 7' and 'No. 8'. The men of No. 7 camp soon organized themselves on democratic lines. They elected as camp spokesman a twenty-five-year-old economics graduate from the London School of Economics named Andreas Eppenstein, and then formed a camp council from representatives of each of the camp's thirty or so huts. Eppenstein asked half-a-dozen of the hut representatives to help him prepare the statement, and soon amassed far more evidence than he needed. He selected the items that appeared most widely corroborated and compiled a memorandum some 5,000 words long. He included four individual statements, which were recorded by lawyers among the internees, and attached an illustrated cover which showed the camp of Hay viewed as if through a porthole. He presented the Dunera Statement to Hay's commander.

It was not long before the statement had the desired effect. A stream of visitors of ascending status arrived at Hay, inquiring whether the statement was true. First came officers of the Australian army, who were trying to sort out the mountain of damaged and unmarked baggage which had been dumped on the Sydney quayside, and they asked Eppenstein to help compile a list of all that was missing. They were followed by the Director-General for Public Health in New South Wales. Then came Sir Frederick Jordan, Chief Justice of New South Wales, who had been appointed 'Official Visitor to Internment Camps in New South Wales' under the terms of the Geneva Convention. Jordan had at first been reluctant to become involved in the disagreeable happenings on the *Dunera* as they were hardly on his territory. He eventually made a report to the Army Minister which was promptly referred to Menzies. Finally, late in November, Sir Geoffrey Whiskard asked Eppenstein for a copy of the Dunera Statement. On 2 December, Eppenstein happily obliged.

It was thus clear in London that Paterson's counterpart in Australia would require considerable determination, tact and forensic skill. The man chosen was Julian Layton, a major in the British army who had a diverse and useful range of experience. Layton was a stockbroker who had already been to Australia on business. He was also Jewish, and had been involved in the refugee welfare movement before the war. He had made numerous visits to Europe to help refugees to obtain the correct papers to enter Britain, and worked closely with the Home Office to validate their credentials. In Austria, he had dealt directly with Adolf Eichmann, whom he had found chillingly courteous and efficient. Layton was in Vienna in November 1938, and Eichmann telephoned him on the eve of *Kristallnacht* to warn him to stay out of the way.

When the war began, Layton had acted as liaison officer between the War Office and the refugees at Kitchener Camp in Kent. At one time he had hoped to join army intelligence, but had instead accepted a commission in the Pioneer Corps, a decision which he had since regretted. He had already formed a jaundiced view of the workings of MI5, blaming them for much of the confusion over the sailings, and in particular the promises and inducements that had not been borne out. MI5 had angered Layton on another occasion, when a member of the British Royal Family died, leaving a notable collection of valuable German books, stamped on the flysheet with a royal seal. The books reached Layton with the suggestion that they should be distributed among German internees on the Isle of Man. When Layton asked the War Office for permission to do so, he was referred to MI5, who refused. Layton appealed to Frank Newsam at the Home Office, who wrote to the Isle of Man commander, instructing him to receive the books. But before they were distributed, every flysheet was torn out to obscure their origin. A noted academic among the internees told Layton later he need not have bothered – the collection was so well known that it was obvious where the books had come from. Layton manfully withheld just one book for himself, selecting it for its inscription, 'To my daughter Louise – from dearest Mama'. Mama was Queen Victoria. Layton later owned up to Newsam, who said he was surprised that Layton hadn't kept more.

In early December, Layton's brief for Australia had already been drawn up. But before he left a new heading was added: 'Claims for Compensation by UK Internees for losses of personal effects during the voyage of H.M.T. *Dunera* to Australia.' Layton sailed from Britain in February 1941, and expected to be in Australia for a year. It was almost four years before he came home.

23 The Other Side of the Hill

At the end of 1940, as Julian Layton prepared to depart for Australia, almost 10,000 internees had been released in Britain. Richard Broh was one of them. A Home Office committee visited the Isle of Man to consider anomalous cases, and the mythical 'B' which had led to his arrest at the end of May was formally replaced with a 'C'. Broh was now entitled to apply for release. As he scanned the list of groups in the Home Office White Paper of 31 July with its subsequent additions, he realized there was very little open to him. He was not a scientist, doctor, dentist, person of academic distinction, researcher or skilled worker in agriculture or forestry; he had no sons in the British forces, and he could not claim that he was a case of 'special hardship'. His best chance lay in Group 12: 'Internees who are accepted for enlistment into the Auxiliary Pioneer Corps.'

The Pioneer Corps enjoyed a sad reputation as the dumping ground of the British army; all human dross, it was once unkindly said, was there. It was the natural home of illiterates and former criminals; when the War Office agreed to accept internees, they were assigned there too. Many internees had attempted to enlist in fighting regiments at the start of the war. In the autumn of 1940, only the Pioneer Corps was open to them. The pay for privates was 2s 6d (12½p) a day.

The first announcement that category 'C' internees could join the Pioneer Corps was posted in Onchan Camp on 19 August, and its reputation was evidently proving a deterrent. There was an unsavoury hint of blackmail in the next notice to appear, on 17 October:

> A small number of internees are delaying their applications for the A.M.P.C. in the hope of being released under some category of the White Paper. . . In this they may be disappointed as firms engaged in work of national importance have shown no particular desire to re-employ aliens now in internment and medically fit for service in the Auxiliary Military Pioneer Corps. . . In their own interest internees should be informed that delay in making up their minds whether or not they wish to join the A.M.P.C. may result in their internment for the duration of the war. It is proposed to close recruiting after the 30th November.

About 4,000 internees joined the Pioneer Corps by the end of the year. Broh was one, and just before Christmas he left the Isle of Man for a training camp at Ilfracombe. Aged forty, he spent several weeks square-bashing with men half his age, and was posted to the 165th Pioneer Corps at Newbury, where his work consisted largely of cleaning lavatories, unloading lorries, digging ditches and humping coal.

Hardly at peak fitness, Broh found the work especially arduous to begin with, and when a young lieutenant threatened to send him back to the Isle of Man, dumped the sack he was carrying and challenged him to do so. The officer backed down. Broh stuck to his task for two years, but was eventually discharged on grounds of ill-health. He went home to Streatham and spent several months recuperating before looking for civilian work. He had made 159 unsuccessful applications before the London and North-Eastern Railway gave him a job as a coal clerk at Spitalfields Station. He spent the rest of the war counting sacks instead of carrying them.

Hellmuth Weissenborn left the Isle of Man soon after Broh. He qualified for release under Clause 20, which spoke of 'Persons of eminent distinction who have made outstanding contributions to Art, Science, Learning or Letters'. Weissenborn did not have to perform the indignity of submitting his work to the committee composed of members of the Royal Academy, for the appeals of artists were handled on their behalf by groups of sympathizers in London. Weissenborn did not even know he was being considered when, two days after enjoying a Christmas lunch of roast goose at Hutchinson camp, the commander told him he could go.

The rules for release drawn up by Lieutenant-Colonel R. Baggallay, overall commandant of the Isle of Man, were predictably precise. At 4 p.m. the day before, the internee had to deposit his luggage with the orderly officer for inspection. He had to be ready at 6.30 a.m. the next day, and collect his baggage at 7. He was not allowed to telephone or to send a telegram from the island without permission, and was strictly forbidden to take out of the camp any parcels or letters on behalf of any other internee.

Weissenborn did as he was bid, clutching his travel ticket on Douglas Pier. At Liverpool he dutifully reported to the Aliens' Registration Office by Lime Street Station, and then caught a train to London. There he wearily obeyed the instruction that 'every released internee shall on arrival at his destination, no matter what the hour, day or night, report without delay at the office of the Aliens' Registration Officer'. Finally Weissenborn reached his flat in Notting Hill, gratefully finding that his landlady had kept it vacant. His wife, of course, was not there; his divorce was completed, and she had departed for the United States. Weissenborn joined the ARP soon after his release and took regular turns firewatching from the roofs of office buildings. He embarked on a new phase in his artistic work, making etchings based on his sketches of war-damaged London.

Renate Scholem meanwhile was continuing her education in the women's camp, learning maths and German literature, and once going on a geological expedition to look for quartz in an ancient mineshaft on Bradda Head. The women internees had now developed their own social life, which ranged from bridge tournaments whose habituées wore evening dress, to long political discussions on the nature of socialism. Renate was becoming more militant, and objected when recruiting officers from the Women's Army Corps arrived. Renate made a fiery speech outside the recruiting room, demanding the freedom to enlist of her own choice and not as a condition for release. She was hauled before Dame Joanna Cruickshank, who threatened that she would be reclassified 'A' and would stay on the island for the rest of the war. Soon afterwards, the Red Cross told Renate that her father had been shot for leading a protest against food racketeering in Buchenwald.

Renate was released in the spring of 1941 after the MP Josiah Wedgwood had taken up her case. Back in Hampstead, she told her mother that she no longer wanted an English education, because if the British regarded her as an enemy alien, then so did she. She was turned down for war-work and became a night wait-ress at Lyons' Corner House on Tottenham Court Road. She started to attend meetings held by various radical German and Austrian groups that were springing up, and was visited by an officer of the British Security Service – she didn't know whether from Special Branch or MI5 – who told her that she'd had a good education and shouldn't spoil her chances. She ignored the warn-ing and moved into a commune run by the 'Free German Youth' in Belsize Park. She helped to organize the Free German League of Culture, where she learned to act.

In late 1940 and early 1941, releases continued at a rate of nearly 1,000 a month. Meanwhile, other official cleaning-up was in prog-ress. The first such step came in October 1940, when Anderson was replaced by Herbert Morrison, the arch-schemer and stalwart of the London Labour Party. Morrison continued Anderson's pol-icy on releases, steered by Maxwell and Newsam. He won the lion's share of internees' gratitude for their freedom, while Ander-son reaped most of the blame for the early chaos. The hysterical xenophobia of the press had given way to equally passionate den-unciations of internment, with one of the most incisive a broadsheet entitled 'Why not lock up General de Gaulle?' from the brilliant pamphleteer Michael Foot. Lafitte's *The Internment of Aliens* followed and the policy was even enshrined in the hapless Anderson's name when Gollancz published a diatribe entitled *Anderson's Prisoners*.

The judgment was unfair, but it contributed to Anderson's downfall. The catalyst, however, was the public's hostility to his decision not to provide deep shelters for protection against air-raids. When in charge of civil defence preparations before the war, Anderson had felt that deep shelters would encourage defeatism. The bombs that rained on London in the Blitz made that decision seem harsh, and Anderson handled the issue badly. He guaranteed the enmity of the press by hectoring a gathering of newspaper editors, and the people of London took matters into their own hands by occupying the tube stations at night. Churchill came to see Anderson as a political liability, and announced on 8 October that he would be replaced by Morrison, whom he praised as a 'long-trained parliamentarian'. Anderson took over from the failing Chamberlain as Lord President of the Council, and his disappoint-ment was clear in a letter to his father: 'One must just do what comes one's way and make the best of it.' In an uncharacteristic display of emotion, he told his parliamentary secretary: 'I should like to have seen the job through.'

In November, Brigadier Harker was sacked and his place at the head of MI5 taken by Sir David Petrie. He continued Kell's recruitment policy and won the respect of both the brilliant amateurs and his professional officers for his ability to protect the service from interference from men like Ball. Under Petrie, MI5 returned to more conventional and painstaking methods of counter-intelligence.

On 27 November, the Cabinet attempted to lay the *Arandora Star* to rest. Lord Snell had presented his report, limited in its brief to the 'method of selection' of those on board. Although the report provides an invaluable account of the preparations for the *Arandora Star*'s sailing, its criticism was limited. Snell pointed out that 'the need for speedy action, and for sending aliens overseas in large numbers, was repeatedly emphasized in Minutes from the Prime Minister calling for periodic reports on the progress achieved'. The War Office had proceeded on the principle that the most dangerous characters should be deported first; all Germans and Austrians on board were category 'A' and Snell saw 'no reason to question the machinery of classification'. His main complaint concerned the Italians.

> MI5 apparently took the view that those who had been only nominal members of the Fascist Party, and those who were ardently Fascist, were equally dangerous. The result was that, among those deported, were a number of men whose sympathies were wholly with this country. I cannot regard this lack of discrimination as satisfactory. . .

Snell then recoiled from his outspokenness. Apart from the blanket classification itself, little had gone wrong. For Signor Anzani of the Italian League of the Rights of Man to have been on board was a clerical error, 'largely due to the fact that the work was carried out under great pressure. Taking the broad view of the programme for deportation, I do not consider that this number of errors is a cause for serious criticism.'

While Snell resumed his inquiry into Huyton camp, which was published a month later and was strikingly more critical, the Cabinet pondered how to dispose of the *Arandora Star* report. Discussion was brief. The Cabinet 'was reminded' that MI5 had been placed under the Swinton Committee (a move we examined in Chapter

20). The Cabinet was also reminded that, although Parliament had been told of Snell's inquiry, no undertaking had been made to publish it. 'Public interest in the matter seemed to have died down, and it would be a pity to revive it.' The following conclusion was recorded: 'The War Cabinet took note of the report, and decided that no further action should be taken in regard to it, at any rate for the present.'

Foreign Office officials involved in the *Arandora Star* and its aftermath greeted Snell's report with dismay. 'The whitewash has been laid on very thick,' wrote Farquhar. Their lack of forgiveness reflected the continuing rows with MI5 over the release of Italians, which reached such a pitch in December that Sir Percy Loraine threatened to resign and only the joint intervention of Halifax and Morrison dissuaded him from doing so.

That dispute was promptly replaced by another clash between the Foreign Office and the Home Office, with Richard Latham to the fore once again. The Foreign Office Council on Aliens decided to examine how far the Geneva Convention could be applied to internees. During the tortuous negotiations with the US State Department in the early months of the war, the British government informally declared that it would treat internees no worse than prisoners of war, and the Council on Aliens wanted to make this a binding obligation. When Latham sought the Home Office's views, his letter spurred L. W. Clayton, previously one of the joint secretaries to the CID Committee on the Control of Aliens in Wartime, to a release of pent-up wrath:

> I must confess that it seems to me to be preposterous that the Home Office, during the present period of severe pressure, should be expected to assist this troublesome body in drafting its recommendations. It has consistently lagged behind the Home Office in its consideration of practical questions and it seems fantastic that we should now be asked to suggest, e.g., a standard of rationing in order that the Council may recommend it to us for incorporation in some sort of Internees' Charter.

Clayton's minute was circulated in the Home Office and received signatures of approval from Frank Newsam and Sir John Moylan. But Clayton soon reported that the council had made 'a strong attack' on the Home Office for not having framed rules for the camps. Moylan replied to the council in March, invoking Morrison to declare that 'unification of administration has been the constant aim of the Home Office since the department assumed responsibility for the camps. . . In the day to day management of the camps a good deal has reasonably been left to the discretion of the Commandants.'

It was almost the last time the Home Office heard from Richard Latham. Soon afterwards he was called into the RAF. He became a flying officer and died when his aeroplane disappeared over Norway in August 1943.

Moylan's response sufficed for a while; but the Foreign Office had strayed into an area of contradictions that had remained unresolved since the Home Office had seized on the revelations about conditions in the camps to take control of internment policy. It announced in some glee that it had found 100,000 letters awaiting scrutiny in the Censorship Office in Liverpool. Not wanting to have the chore itself, it abolished censorship instead. But apart from this the Home Office had attempted to leave the mundane details of camp life in the War Office's hands. The camps retained their military commanders and guards, and War Office regulations still applied.

The War Office was not blind to the Home Office's strategy. And a rare glimpse of what military men call 'the other side of the hill' is available from one of the few War Office files on internment released to the Public Record Office. The principle document is a review of 'the murky past of internment camp responsibilities' compiled by Sir Alan Hunter, director of the Prisoners of War Department and one of the founding members of the Swinton Committee. Hunter wrote:

The main difficulty throughout with the organization and manipulation of these camps has been the not un-natural, but entire difference in the point of view of the Home Office and the War Office.

The Home Office arrangements for the 'panic' internments of Mid-Summer 1940, were put into effect at short notice and at high speed, with consequent blunders, often serious in their results, which were aggravated by mis-management attributable to the same causes.

The Home Office lay the whole blame for the change of policy then evident, from 'no internment' to 'intern the lot' on the General Staff. But internment is a Home Office and not a War

Office operation, and it was only reasonable to suppose that there was a skeleton (at least) plan in existence.

The public outcry that arose from the blunders and misman-agement admitted above had the effect of causing the Cabinet to decide that the Home Office should take over 'Internee Man-agement', but that War Office should continue to find the camps and equip them, to safeguard them and to perform all what were described as 'Quartermastering' duties.

The Military Officers, too, were to continue at the camps, in a capacity which can best be described as a crossbreed between a guard and a welfare man.

At the preliminary, and subsequent conferences on this take-over the Home Office Officials undertook to examine the pos-sibility of replacing Military personnel by their own special contingent suitable for the duties.

Not in one single case has this yet materialized!

Further the Home Office management has been almost entirely confined to tribunals and releases, and far from any assistance or taking of responsibility, the arrangement has only, from D.P.W. point of view made safeguarding and 'Security' far more difficult.

Under the circumstances outlined above, and having regard to the serious shortage of man power, it is only reasonable to suggest that the Army should be relieved of its responsibilities and detachments, and that the Home Office (and so far as they are concerned the Ministry of Home Security) should take over full responsibility for management and staffing.

Hunter sent the memorandum to Lieutenant-General H. Wemyss, Adjutant-General to the Armed Forces, and pointed out that if the Home Office took over the camps, the army would gain 'some 193 officers and 2,778 men, who though often of low cat-egory, have at any rate been trained as soldiers'. He suggested that Wemyss raise the matter at the next meeting of the Army Council. Wemyss agreed.

On 12 May, G. W. Lambert, secretary to the Army Council, wrote to Alexander Maxwell to report the council's views. He cited War Cabinet decision of 18 July 1940, 'by which the Home Office were charged with the responsibility for the administration of Internment Camps for civilian internees'. And he told Maxwell that the council 'are therefore obliged to ask Mr Secretary Morrison that the method and date by which he will fully implement the War Cabinet decision should now be given his immediate consideration'.

The Home Office received the Army Council letter with surprising complacency. An official named Holderness saw it as 'little more than a challenge by the PW Dept to cause us embarrassment'. Sir John Moylan believed that the letter was based on 'a suggestio falsi which convinces me that this letter must have been drafted by Col. Coates' – a long-standing adversary in the Prisoners of War Department. The argument turned on what had been concluded at a meeting between the Home Office and the War Office on 27 July 1940. Lambert said the army had agreed to 'keep the camps on as a going concern until such time as the civil authorities were able to make their own arrangements for the provision of a civil staff'. The Home Office claimed that the agreement was only that the Home Office would *review* the staffs later, to decide whether they should be replaced by civilians.

Moylan none the less admitted that the Army Council's request was embarrassing. 'At no time since the transfer of the internal management of the camps on 5 August 1940 has there been any scheme for replacing military staffs by civilians for the simple reason that no one has been able to suggest how suitable civilian staffs could be found.' Holderness did concede that the Home Office had agreed to provide civilian welfare officers to run the camps. 'This we have failed to do, though perhaps the War Office are equally to blame for not having pressed the matter.' He recommended that the Home Office should act quickly, 'if we are to convince the War Office of our good faith in the matter'.

In the end, the Home Office agreed to try to recruit civilians for office and administrative duties. The camps' military commanders remained, although they now had to report to both the Home and War Offices. It was a compromise that was all too reminiscent of the First World War, when the contradictions of government policy were visited upon the commanders themselves. In 1941, the problem was hardly on the same scale, for by the summer there were around 7,000 internees on the Isle of Man, against more than 20,000 in the First World War. And the War Office meanwhile had a far more bizarre problem on its hands.

The Secret Intelligence Service had been recruiting internees to train as agents and saboteurs behind enemy lines. It was ironic that men dubbed enemy aliens should be asked to serve Britain in this way; the training they received was arduous and exacting, and the dropout rate high. The army had the problem of disposing of those men who were rejected halfway through their course.

The Home Defence (Security) Executive considered the matter at a meeting on 20 March 1941, chaired by Sir Joseph Ball. The problem was simply stated. Many of the rejected trainees had ample knowledge of SIS operating techniques; that knowledge must not spread. The most humane solution anyone could think of was to put them back into internment 'until their knowledge became obsolete'. In some cases, this would not be until the end of the war.

The consequences for the internees in question were grim.

> All possible steps should be taken to prevent any visits whatever, (including visits from representatives of the Protecting Power) . . . It was essential to prevent any knowledge, either of the presence in this country of the persons concerned, or the use for this purpose of any particular place, from reaching foreign governments. If they made a particular request regarding a named person who happened, in fact, to be a segregated internee, the Home Secretary should inform them that there was no trace of that name in the index of persons in internment.

Sir Alan Hunter proposed a special camp for SIS rejects on the Isle of Man, but this was deemed unsuitable, as Red Cross delegates or other 'foreign representatives' would be bound to notice it and request a visit. 'Even if such a request were refused the existence of the camp would be given away.' Various alternatives were considered. One was Latchmere House on Ham Common, already notorious as MI5's 'tough' interrogation centre; but it would be hard to maintain total segregation even there. Sir Joseph Ball produced the answer: a separate wing of Stafford Gaol, with room for sixty inmates, was available for the next six to nine months. Meanwhile a new permanent camp would be built (the minutes do not record where). 'This would provide a place,' Ball concluded, 'the purpose of which could effectively be concealed, and from which all visitors could be kept for the duration of the war.'

24 Dear Breck

Alexander Paterson arrived in Ottawa on 18 November 1940. A tall, handsome man of fifty-four, he was endowed with a wealth of experience and practical knowledge from his twenty-five years as a prison commissioner in Britain. He was a hard-living man who chain-smoked and liked good whisky. He was also an active Christian, a regular churchgoer who devoted much of his spare time to organizing boys' clubs in the East End of London. He was fond of young men, and sympathized with their problems.

He was also a good writer, with a sharp eye for detail and a ready appreciation of the ironies of life. When he eventually returned to Britain, he handed Herbert Morrison an account of his work. He called it: 'Report on civilian internees sent from the United Kingdom to Canada during the unusually fine summer of 1940.' It is one of the most elegant and witty official reports to have graced Whitehall. Morrison told him: 'I regard the report as a most valuable and important State Paper because it is so human a document.' Frank Newsam told Morrison: 'In one sense it is a pity that the report is written in such an enjoyably racy style. It can never be published.' It finally saw the light of day when the Dominions Office released it to the Public Record Office under the thirty-year rule. It is the source for much of this chapter.

Paterson was greeted in Ottawa by the newly appointed Director of Internment Operations, Colonel H. Stethem. General Panet had just been promoted and Stethem, his assistant, was elevated to fill his place. The difference between the two men was striking and unfortunate. Paterson saw Panet as a man of personal charm and commanding stature – 'to serve with him is to have the privilege of meeting the incarnation of French Canada'. As for Stethem, 'a mixture of shyness and disappointment was perhaps partly responsible for an unusually ungracious personality and manner'.

Stethem clearly did not like Paterson either. He once kept him waiting in his office for an hour while he dictated and made desultory telephone calls. Then he subjected Paterson to a tirade against refugees, Jews and voluntary agencies. 'It was exhilarating to find that anyone could be ruder than an Englishman on his travels,' Paterson wrote. If he could tolerate Stethem's rudeness, there others who were more vulnerable. Refugees were a 'sick headache' to Stethem, said Paterson. 'He disliked them, despised them, and distrusted them.'

When Paterson reached Canada, the 3,100 civilian internees had been separated from the remaining 3,650 or so merchant seamen and prisoners of war, and allocated to five camps. Paterson was installed in the Windsor Hotel, Montreal, but spent much of his time in the camps, arriving without a top-coat or hat even in the Canadian winter. He observed that food was abundant and camps were well-equipped. But he found that life had become intolerably strict. Machine-guns were on display, there was barbed wire everywhere, and discipline was rigid. He told how a youth had disobeyed the standing order that towels should be spread out in bunks to dry, not hung in the open air. He was given seven days in the camp cells, and had to scrub the floor three times a day. When goaded into abusing a guard, he received a further fourteen days. Paterson attributed the harsh régime to Stethem's intolerant attitudes, but pressure from the US State Department undoubtedly contributed.

It is not surprising that Paterson was welcomed by the camp inmates as their rescuing angel. Many were hoping to reach the United States and others to be released in Canada, but the most positive offer Paterson could make was to send them back to Britain. If an internee opted for that, Paterson had to decide whether he was a security risk and which of the Home Office release clauses he might fit. Even then his decision was not final, for, once back in Britain, internees still had to wait in the Isle of Man for confirmation of Paterson's verdict. In most cases, it was forthcoming.

Paterson was only too aware that he was sitting in judgment on a man's fate; and the internees recognized it too. He wrote:

Many so far lost their emotional control that I had to keep them after the interview was at an end, rather than that their comrades in the queue outside should witness their condition. While smoking a cigarette with me they recovered their composure, but it was then necessary to wait till their cigarette was at an end, for it was not any more desirable that they should face the company with a cigarette in their mouth, than with tears on their cheeks. So the time passed.

Paterson worked fast. On 26 December 1940, the first 287 men sailed for Britain, followed by 274 in February and 330 in June. There were few Italians among them. Paterson had been disconcerted to find that many of the 407 Italians in Canada had strong Scottish accents, and concluded that the Scottish police had interpreted their instructions more strictly than in England. Most could have returned to Britain under a new release clause – number 22 – which applied to internees who had lived 'continuously or almost continuously in the United Kingdom' since early childhood. But a large number elected to stay in Canada rather than risk the Atlantic crossing, or so Paterson felt. The main exception was the small group of Jewish refugees from Italy.

Hermann Bondi returned to Britain in the third ship in June 1941, part of a huge naval convoy that was mercifully not attacked. He was annoyed at having to spend a month on the Isle of Man before being allowed back to Cambridge. Later he became an experimental research officer and helped to perfect Britain's wartime defences, including radar.

Kurt Tebrich went back on the same boat, and as he was under eighteen was one of a few people released as soon as it docked. (Another boy released with him had to say good-bye to his father who, after being with him throughout, was taken to the Isle of Man.) Tebrich stayed with relatives in Oxford, where he worked as a shop assistant, enlisting in the British army as soon as he was eighteen. He spent two years in the Pioneer Corps before joining the Tank Corps in 1944, when fighting units were opened to ex-internees. He landed in Normandy in early August and fought his way steadily east. In May 1945, he was among the first British troops to enter Hamburg, his former home. It was a traumatic moment. Much of the city had been devastated by RAF bombs in

1943, the worst attack causing a firestorm that destroyed the city centre. The area where Tebrich lived had disappeared. Tebrich took part in the Allied victory parade in Berlin, then returned to Hamburg to try to trace his parents. The first prisoners released from the concentration camp of Theresienstadt told him that his parents had been sent to the extermination camp at Auschwitz. Soon afterwards the Red Cross confirmed that they had died. Tebrich stayed in Germany to work for the military government and returned to Britain in 1947.

Paterson left Canada in July 1941. He had just persuaded the Canadian government to create refugee camps with their own commissioner, a former lawyer named Colonel Fordham, while Stethem remained in charge of camps for non-refugees. Paterson prepared a set of draft regulations and Fordham took office on 1 July. It was a notable victory with which Paterson was justifiably pleased. But he returned to Britain with one resounding failure to his name. It concerned his attempts to get internees into the United States.

As we have noted, some 1,000 of the Canadian deportees had hoped to emigrate to the United States, and some who had completed the visa procedures were within weeks or days of leaving Britain when they were interned. In Canada, their predicament occupied Paterson more and more, and he made four separate visits to New York and Washington on their behalf. He had the capable assistance of Chaim Raphael, an Oxford lecturer who had worked with the Jewish movement and knew of Paterson's good works in the East End; their partnership was aided by the fact that both were graduates of University College, Oxford. Together they entered a world of sophistry, evasion and lies.

Paterson had first been optimistic of success. One of the first to try for a US visa was Hermann Bondi, whose parents had gone to the United States in August 1940 and were keen that he should join them. Bondi must have cut a bizarre figure when he was escorted to the US Consulate in Montreal, for he wore a camp uniform consisting of blue trousers with a broad red stripe, and a blue jacket with a huge red circle on the back. Despite his appearance, Bondi appeared to meet US entry requirements, until the US State Department cited the tortuous wording of two Immigration Acts. One said that immigrants could be barred if their sea-passage had been paid by a third party. Another said that entry from 'foreign contiguous territory' was forbidden if the applicant had arrived on what was termed a 'non-signatory carrier' – the United States required all transportation lines bringing immigrants to have registered with it first. In Bondi's case, the British government had paid his passage across the Atlantic; and whether the British government was a 'signatory carrier' appeared a moot point. Bondi's parents hired expensive lawyers to fight his case, while Bondi observed with amused detachment, as he really wanted to go back to Britain anyway. But it was soon clear that these legalisms were skirmishes before a larger battle.

At stake were two conflicting principles. The US consul in Montreal told Paterson that the United States was not prepared to accept men direct from internment. The Canadian government, on the other hand, was maintaining that it had accepted the deportees for internment and was not prepared to release them into civilian life. Like Australia, it had stringent entry requirements, and was sticking to its understanding that the internees would be returned to Britain at the end of the war.

Paterson and Raphael devised an ingenious solution. The would-be immigrants could be given their freedom in Newfoundland, and enter the United States from there. Newfoundland, disappointed when it could not take charge of the 1,000 civilian internees on the *Sobieski,* readily agreed. At Christmas 1940, Paterson went to New York and Washington to explore American reaction. On 26 December, the American Attorney-General, Robert Jackson, told Paterson there were no legal objections to the scheme. On 28 December, the American Under-Secretary of State, Sumner Welles, told Paterson that he was 'very much in sympathy with the proposal' and was 'anxious to do something for the refugees'. Paterson told a group of anxious parents in the lobby of his New York hotel that he was sure their children would be able to join them from Canada soon. While awaiting formal American confirmation, Paterson and Raphael put the final touches to their plans. Raphael selected the first 100 who were to enter, mostly men under twenty-one with first-degree relatives in the United States, and went to St John's to book their accommodation. But weeks passed without word from the US State Department. In the camps, Paterson wrote, 'the disappointment was bitter indeed, and I felt a grave responsibility for their distress'.

At the end of March 1941, Paterson returned to New York. The head of the Visa Branch at the State Department admitted the scheme had run into snags. He said that the American Legion, which stood for the interests of military veterans, disliked the scheme, and its members formed a 'useful minority in Congress'. But he added that Sumner Welles was still sympathetic.

Paterson sought out the American Legion and attempted to forestall its criticism by explaining just who the internees were. On 5 April, he met the US Secretary of State, Cordell Hull, and begged for an answer. Hull said that he was unwilling to make a decision until he had consulted with his foreign-policy adviser, Breckinridge Long, who was then on holiday in Florida.

Long had shown interest in the fate of civilian internees from the time of the United States's negotiations to secure their exchange at the start of the war. He had received the Special Division memorandum in April 1940, which concluded that Britain had the least generous record of the countries involved. But Long had also devised the fraudulent cable to London in June 1940 which implied that the German government was much exercised over the British plan for deportations. Paterson finally met Long on 15 April 1941. Long announced that the United States could not accept internees from Newfoundland or anywhere else. He blamed his decision on 'the opposition which would probably be raised by the American Legion'.

Long's statement was a lie. He had made up his mind to reject the internees almost four months before. The truth is contained in Long's own papers in the National Archives in Washington. The sequence begins with a letter to Long – 'Dear Breck' – from the American Minister in Ottawa, Pierrepont Moffat. He explained to Long that Paterson was in Canada 'to sort out into Nazis and non-Nazis the internees held in Canada for British Government account. He has released about two hundred for return to England and is on the point of releasing some four hundred more. A goodly percentage of the latter do not want to return to England but want to go to the United States.' Moffat reported Paterson's hope that they could be issued with US visas.

Moffat voiced his own doubts on the subject: it was true that a 'great many innocent men were mixed up with dangerous internees'. The Canadians had said that their records were lost on the *Arandora Star*, and that their background information had been reconstructed since. 'Be that as it may, Nazis and anti-Nazis have been pretty well mixed up in camps for the past few months and whether the Nazis have corrupted the anti-Nazis or the anti-Nazis have converted the Nazis is a point on which different views are held.'

Long's reply to Moffat on 16 December 1940 was brief and to the point.

> My dear Pierrepont:
> Thank you enormously for your letter of December 12 about the proposed visits of Mr Paterson. I am communicating it to Justice. My first impression is definitely negative, and I think it is going to stay that way.
> Yours as ever,
> Breckinridge Long

Long sent a copy of the letter to the Immigration Department of the US Department of Justice. On 26 December, Sumner Welles, Under-Secretary of State, told Long of his conversation with Attorney-General Robert Jackson. 'My understanding is that the Attorney-General believed that it would be very difficult to justify the admission into the United States of individuals who have been interned in England or Canada and I imagine you feel, as I do, that opinion is well justified.' That very day Jackson had advised Paterson that he had no legal objections to his scheme, and two days later Welles told Paterson that he was 'in sympathy with the proposals' and was 'anxious' to help the refugees.

Paterson and Raphael, no match for political dealings of such hypocrisy, were not to know that the next three months' negotiations were a mere charade. And when Long finally vetoed the Newfoundland scheme, they searched for another country as a substitute. They hit upon Cuba. Parents of some internees had already taken out Cuban tourist visas on their sons' behalf, hoping they might enter the United States from there. They were not cheap. The unlovely government of Fulgencio Batista granted a tourist visa in return for a bond of $500, and a 'maintenance credit' of $2,000. Raphael secured their identification certificates, and boat tickets to Cuba. As Raphael wryly recorded, 'this involved a great deal of detailed work, always with the possibility, practically a certainty, that in the end the US Visa would not be granted at Cuba.' The first six internees sailed for Cuba, via Trinidad, on 28 May 1941; Raphael's misgivings were entirely justified. For the US State Department was fast preparing legislation to make entry for aliens even more difficult, no matter what route they tried.

The first move came when the member for Louisiana introduced a Bill into the House of Representatives stating quite flatly that no alien interned in a foreign country could apply for admission until a year and a day after his release. The Bill went a long way towards becoming law, but in June was replaced by a more simple and sweeping measure: an Act 'to authorize the refusal of visas to aliens whose admission into the United States would endanger the public safety'. It allowed American officials to refuse entry to any alien whom they had 'reason to believe' might endanger the public safety of the United States.

Although Pearl Harbor was still six months away, the rivalry between Japan and the United States in the Pacific was leading steadily to war. The United States was girding up for the conflict, and the Act of June 1941 formed part of its preparations. Several remarkable documents show that the United States felt it could learn from Britain's experience of combating any threat from within. The State Department abandoned its avowedly disinterested stance of late 1939 for a purely pragmatic interest in the problems of internment. Bluntly stated, the United States asked Britain how to do it.

Soon after Paterson's first encounter with the US State Department, the American Embassy in London was asked to obtain a set of all Home Office instructions for internment. The American chargé Herschel Johnson obliged with no fewer than thirty-five documents, which included all Maxwell's confidential letters to chief constables at the various steps of internment. One particular point troubled the State Department: 'The problem of presenting evidence on behalf of the Government and the cross-examination of Government agents testifying against an alien enemy.' Johnson was happy to advise that 'no difficulties in this respect actually arise in practice' – for, as Johnson explained, 'members of the MI5 Division . . . never appear in person before these Committees'.

Rather curiously, the Home Office reciprocated with inquiries of its own. On 3 March 1942, the US Embassy cabled the State Department: 'Our friends state that it would be extremely helpful in considering their problems with enemy aliens to obtain a clear picture of the methods now being adopted in the United States in connection with these questions.'

It may have been merely polite interest; but perhaps there was a hint of irony in the British request. For it was an appropriate moment to ask. On 2 March 1942, the US army designated large parts of the West Coast as military areas from which anyone could be excluded. Two months later it issued a 'Civilian Exclusion Order' banning 'all persons of Japanese ancestry' from those areas.

There were 112,000 such persons involved, including 70,000 US citizens. General J. L. DeWitt, commanding general of the Western Defense Command, regarded them as 'subversive', belonging to 'an enemy race' whose 'racial strains are undiluted', and constituting '112,000 potential enemies at large'. Most of these 112,000 persons were removed from their homes and interned. DeWitt argued that the subversive threat posed by Americans of Japanese ancestry was proved by the sinister absence of any overtly subversive activities.

The argument had been heard before. In May 1940 the British Joint Intelligence Committee reasoned that 'the absence of sabotage to date' pointed to the enemy's prearranged military plan. For all its diligent inquiries into the state of health of internees in Britain, the United States had missed the most obvious lesson of all.

With the United States blocked, those wishing to stay in North America had one other choice: release in Canada itself. From the start, the Canadian government had sworn that this would not be allowed, and when a Toronto university professor was refused permission for his interned nephew to be educated in Canada, Paterson and Raphael were pessimistic. In February 1941, the government relented sufficiently to release eight men and boys with parents or siblings in Canada, but was adamant that this set no precedent. But shortly before Paterson departed, the Canadian Prime Minister broke the rules in a manner which dismayed his officials and embarrassed even Paterson.

Ruth Draper was an American diseuse, one of that rare species of performer who can hold an entire theatre audience with monologues and solo performances. In the 1930s she had a spectacular love-affair in Italy, and in 1940 discovered that her lover's nephew was interned in Canada. Early in 1941, she gave a performance in Ottawa for the Canadian Red Cross; afterwards the Prime Minister, William Mackenzie King, asked what Canada could do in return. Ruth Draper gave him the full benefit of her dramatic gifts. She told him: 'There is a young innocent boy, whom I have known since he was a baby, being held in one of your internment camps behind barbed wire, without offence, without a trial.' Mackenzie

King was unable to resist such an appeal. He overrode his aides' objections and ordered the boy's release.

After his months of patient diplomacy, Paterson was miffed by so arbitrary an act. He complained to sympathetic Canadian officials that he could hardly announce that releases were available in return for large donations to the Canadian Red Cross. On reflection, he saw that Mackenzie King's decision could be used to advantage – 'as an open door,' he wrote, 'for others'. By the time he and Raphael left Canada, the Minister of Immigration had agreed that 100 students and schoolboys could continue their education in Canada. They were released in time for the autumn term of 1941.

The students were soon followed by several dozen draughtsmen and tool-makers sponsored by the Canadian Ministry of Supply. Other internees were told they could go free if they found individual sponsors of their own. Those with skills were best placed, others used ingenuity instead. A boy named Morawetz, friendless in Canada, found one man with the same name in the Toronto phone directory. He agreed to help. The releases became a flood, and in September 1943 the last refugee camp was closed. By then, 1,537 internees had returned to Britain; the others were in Canada or had departed elsewhere. Soon afterwards, in ones and twos, some began to enter the United States. The Canadian government meanwhile had been tidying up. It split a bill of $1,290.50 for the *Ettrick* thefts with the British government and court-martialled nine Canadian soldiers. (Only one was found guilty, and his conviction was later quashed.) In 1945, Canada reclassified its former prisoners as 'Interned Refugees (Friendly Aliens) from the U.K.' and invited them to become Canadian citizens. Nine hundred and seventy-two chose to do so. The door opened by Ruth Draper had proved very convenient indeed.

25   Ten Thousand Miles from Home

To the men of Hay and Tatura, Julian Layton was a long time coming.

The internees of Hay felt as if they were in the middle of nowhere. The camp was on the rim of an apparently limitless plain, dusty and shimmering in the heat. The only relief to the landscape came from the distant fringe of the Murrumbidgee River, and a solitary sheep-farm, shaded by a gum tree. Hay itself was out of sight, and if a curious inhabitant came to stare, guards quickly shooed him away. With the Australian summer approaching, temperatures were already soaring over 100°F; the night brought bitter cold.

The camp's isolation stimulated an enclosed and self-sustaining life, described by one internee as akin to a small working republic. After the camp's democracy had been established, there was much shuffling of personnel so that like-minded people could live together: communists in one hut, Catholics, Orthodox Jews, actors, homosexuals in others. A force of watch-keepers patrolled at night to prevent elderly men with weak bladders from peeing against the walls, and woke the boilermen and kitchen staff in the morning. Wages were paid for all camp duties, with latrine cleaners earning the highest rate of 3s 6d (17½p). The camp canteen sold luxuries such as sweets, canned fruit and cigarettes – the cheapest were fourteen for 6d (2½p). The camp commander wanted prices as low as possible, but the internees persuaded him to allow a profit which could be redistributed as welfare payments to the sick and elderly. The camp designed its own bank notes, with sheep on one side, a kangaroo and an emu on the other, bordered by barbed wire into which had been woven the refrain: 'We're here because we're here because we're here.'

Inmates made furniture from eucalyptus wood and sandals from old rubber tyres. One man ran a vegetarian restaurant and others painted portraits for modest fees. The cultural and intellectual life was richer even than at Onchan or Hutchinson on the Isle of Man. There were lectures on chemistry, astronomy, atomic research, Shakespeare, Italian, Russian, Chinese. The concert pianist Peter Stadlen gave recitals and transposed orchestral works so that they could be performed by male-voice choirs. A maths professor made a dozen whistles from eucalyptus wood and another internee carved a working violin. They combined forces with Stadlen to perform Handel's oratorio, *Israel in Egypt*. The actors staged *The Good Soldier Schweik* and the anti-war drama *Journey's End*, which left the Australian camp commander, seated as a guest of honour in the front row, in tears.

For the *Arandora Star* men in Tatura, the main drawback to life was not heat but the dust that swirled at the hint of wind. The hut walls had been built with spaces at the ceiling and floor, supposedly so that the dust should enter at the top and exit at the bottom; as Tatura liked to joke, no one told the dust. In his detached way, Uwe Radok enjoyed Australia's climatic extremes, from the dust storms to the chill but brilliant night skies. Erwin Frenkel opened a Viennese-style coffee-house, decorated with a mural for which he paid in kind. In the Italian camp alongside, Serafino Pini became the storeman, dispensing socks, razor blades and dunga-rees. The Collegium Taturensium was founded, with a range of lectures almost as diverse as Hay's; one of the most popular series was on political philosophy, given by a veteran of the Spanish International Brigade. The trade-unionist Valentin Wittke became the camp carpenter and advertised for a carpenter's mate. He set each applicant the test of sawing a fifteen-foot plank from a length of Australian hardwood, and it was a long time before anyone passed.

In Tatura and in Hay one question came to dominate all con-versations: when would freedom come? News of the Home Office White Papers, and the first releases from the Isle of Man, reached Australia by the end of the year. Soon it was learned that Layton was on his way. But, as the weeks passed, he seemed like a myth. At Hay, an actor impersonated him and tricked several men into pouring out their life-stories. Finally, on 11 April, Layton arrived.

Layton had reached Sydney on 25 March. Promoted to major in mid voyage, he presented himself to the Secretary of the Australian army, then travelled to Melbourne, where he booked into the Menzies Hotel and then went to Canberra to meet the British High Commissioner, Sir Geoffrey Whiskard. A cable had arrived from Morrison with the news that there had been questions about the *Dunera* in the House of Commons. There would be a court of inquiry and courts martial, but Morrison wanted 'speedy reparation' to be made. This was now Layton's most urgent task.

Layton was instructed to inquire into the internees' losses and tell the Home Office how much money was involved. Layton boldly predicted that he could complete his task in four weeks. The camp commanders at Hay and Tatura distributed intimidating claim forms that began:

> I, the undersigned declarant hereby respectfully claim compensation or damage to personal effects owned by me and shipped on the S.S. *Dunera* from England to Australia on 10th July 1940, particulars whereof are set out hereunder. . .

They ended with the stern warning that the penalty for a false declaration was four years in prison, 'with or without hard labour'. Layton was overwhelmed by the response. He received 1,600 claims for compensation, ranging from trivial sums for the loss of toilet requisites to £700 for a diamond ring. There were sixteen claims for lost patents or documents, and one author who priced his manuscript at £200 explained that he had received £100 for his previous work but his reputation had doubled meanwhile. On 7 May, Layton wearily reported to Whiskard: 'Have to date interrogated about three hundred claimants.' He suggested that the claims be accepted 'in principle' and asked for assistance to complete the work. An Australian officer continued the interviews, and the British government finally paid out over £30,000.

In May and June, three British officers from the *Dunera* were court martialled, including Lieutenant-Colonel Scott. A sergeant-major was found guilty on ten charges of theft and given one year in prison; a sergeant was found guilty of disobeying a superior officer and reprimanded. Scott was found guilty of 'failing to ensure

a proper inquiry into the violent treatment of one internee'. He
was severely reprimanded.

Layton was now able to return to his original brief: to recommend
which internees should be allowed to return to Britain. First he
effected an important improvement in their lives. Appalled by the
heat of Hay – 'not right for Europeans', he said – he persuaded
the Army Department to transfer the inmates to other camps.
They moved out at the beginning of May, burning their home-
made furniture on a giant pyre after hearing that the camp might
be used for genuine prisoners of war.

Three hundred men who were in the worst health took up
residence at Orange, a town in the Blue Mountains close to Sydney, while the remainder went to Tatura. There Layton started
work in earnest.

Like Paterson in Canada, Layton was badly hampered by a lack
of documentation. Only twelve dossiers had arrived on the *Dunera*
and Layton had the awesome task of considering each case in
turn.* Part of his brief was to nominate men for the British Pioneer
Corps, and the procedure he was instructed to use put heavy
pressure on the internees to enlist.

Layton, again like Paterson, could not authorize releases. Each
week he sent long cables to Newsam in London with his recommendations. The Home Office consulted MI5 and the War
Office, and then cabled Layton a list of the internees who could
return. But internees accepted by the Pioneer Corps could come
back to Britain as free men: those seeking release under the Home
Office White Papers would have to travel under escort or in the
charge of the ship's captain, and wait on the Isle of Man while
their cases were reviewed. In consequence, over 500 of the 724
men who left Australia in 1941 did so as Pioneer Corps recruits.

The first ship to sail was the *Largs Bay*, which left on 2 June
1941 with 139 men. The largest contingent of 338 men went on
the *Sterling Castle*, which sailed on 12 October. Among them was
a young Bavarian named Michael Mellinger, who had gone to
Britain with his mother in 1933, and was interned in London in
June 1940. At Hay he acted in *Journey's End* and took part in the

* The War Office and MI5 had at least one week's notice of the sailing of the
Dunera. That they could produce only twelve dossiers in that time casts further
doubt on Caldecote's statement that dossiers for all 7,950 men bound for Canada
had gone down with the *Arandora Star*. (See Chapter 21, page 240.)

Layton hoax. He had his twenty-first birthday in Tatura. He volunteered for the Pioneer Corps without demur, and before leaving Australia was given a bright red tweed jacket to wear. He enjoyed the long voyage home, even the three weeks spent queueing for the Panama Canal. Like Richard Broh, he learned square-bashing at Ilfracombe, and then to his delight was drafted into a band as a trombonist to entertain troops in Devon. His delight was short-lived, for the band was soon ordered to build a breakwater at Weymouth as part of Britain's sea defences. In 1944, he joined the Engineer Corps, and when he learned that German translators were needed, volunteered for service overseas. He was posted to Burma, where his German was useless, and stayed there for the rest of the war.

Like Paterson in Canada, Layton was also hoping to help those internees who had applied to emigrate to the United States. He soon encountered the same resistance and obfuscation as Paterson, and was further angered when American attitudes even hindered the return of internees to Britain. After Pearl Harbor, the United States refused to allow any ship carrying enemy aliens through the Panama Canal, and there was a hiatus in sailings that lasted from November 1941 until July 1942. But there were also in Australia many who had considered emigrating there in the first place, among them Teltscher and the Radok brothers. Before the war, some had even obtained landing certificates that would allow them to enter as permanent residents.

At first the Australian government stuck to its position that Australia had accepted the men as internees, and internees they must remain. But it soon realized that it had a pool of able-bodied men at its disposal who were having to choose between returning to England or incarceration in Australia, and on 29 August 1941 the Army Minister told Menzies that the problem should be 'squarely faced'. Two events precipitated the change of policy. The first was the fall of Menzies in October, replaced as Prime Minister by John Curtin, the Leader of the Australian Labour Party. The second was Pearl Harbor and the start of the Pacific War. It was absurd that anti-Nazis should be locked up any longer; besides, the internment camps were needed for Australia's own Fifth Column.

On 20 January 1942, the new Army Minister, F. M. Forde, announced that skilled internees would be released for vital war-work, so long as they were not competing with Australians, 'while fit men of military age' could join the labour units of the Australian army. There was no shortage of volunteers. Within a month, 300 men enlisted in Melbourne. They were placed in charge of a Maori officer named Captain Broughton who quickly won their admiration by changing the name of their unit from the Eighth Employment Company (Ex-Internees) to the Eighth Employment Company.

Leopold Kohn was one, having progressed to Melbourne after spending several weeks picking fruit in the mosquito-infested Goulburn Valley, 200 miles to the north. Hoping to join a fighting unit, he was disappointed to find his work consisted of unloading ships in Melbourne Harbour. Henry Teltscher was another; his army career lasted for just one week. After complaining of stomach ache he was sent to a Melbourne hospital. The doctor could find nothing wrong but gave Teltscher a job as a laboratory assistant instead.

At first it seemed that the survivors of the *Arandora Star* were fated by their tribunal classifications of 1939 to remain imprisoned for ever. In February 1942, Forde announced that only 'B' and 'C' internees could apply for release and that the remainder were still seen as 'dangerous or potentially dangerous' and would have to stay interned. But Layton had visited Tatura at an early stage and knew that the 450 *Arandora Star* men comprised a mixture as diverse as the original sailing list, with Italians, Nazis, 'loyal' Germans and political and Jewish refugees. Soon Eichenberg, Frenkel and the Radoks were released too, enlisting in the Employment Company and going to work at the 'break of gauge' stations of Albury and Tocumwal on the border between Victoria and New South Wales, where the incompatible railway lines of each state met, and all goods and luggage had to be shifted from train to train by hand.

Not all enlisted; Peter Jacobsohn had got on the wrong side of Layton at the start and stayed there ever since. He regarded Layton as a 'typical bureaucrat' and resented his pressure to join the Pioneer Corps, although he protested that he was eager to join the regular army. Nor did he want to live in Australia. Serafino Pini was irrevocably regarded as a fascist, and was later moved to a camp at Loveday near Adelaide in South Australia.

Soon Australia's own Japanese, German and Italian internees arrived, arrested after Pearl Harbor and reaching a peak of 6,780 in September 1942.

By the end of 1943, 1,141 internees had left for Britain. Forty-seven never arrived, for their ships were torpedoed. About 750 men joined the Australian Eighth Employment Company or were performing vital war-work. Some 150 emigrated elsewhere, mostly to Palestine, recruited by an ardent Zionist named Benzion Patkin. A dozen or so even managed to reach the United States.

In October 1944, the Australian government announced that former internees who would make 'desirable citizens' could stay in Australia and apply for naturalization. Those who stayed included Leopold Kohn, Henry Teltscher, Erwin Frenkel and the three Radok brothers. Serafino Pini went back to Britain in March 1945, and was allowed home after a further three months on the Isle of Man, meeting his wife Lisa for the first time since 10 June 1940. Peter Jacobsohn returned in the summer and was released in London in September 1945. Franz Eichenberg left for the United States. Julian Layton sailed from Australia in January 1945, and reached home to find that the last chapter in the story of internment was almost complete.

26   Colonel Scott's Diary

On 11 March 1942, Lieutenant-Colonel A. M. Scott opened a new page in his diary. 'To Isle of Man to take over command of Alien Internment Camps,' he wrote. It seemed unlikely to Scott that this posting would be as exciting as his last. For nine months he had been commander of Camp 'Z' in Surrey, with just one prisoner in his care, referred to as 'Prisoner Z'. There was good reason for the obscurity. The prisoner's real name was Rudolf Hess, and he had been there since his dramatic crash-landing in Scotland in May 1941 while British intelligence tried to decide if he was (a) genuine and (b) sane.

Hess was questioned frequently and watched without pause. MI5 and MI6 visited him and his telephone calls to the Swiss Legation were bugged. In the end, British intelligence decided that the answer to (a) was yes, to (b) no. Hess was written off as being of no further use and moved to a hospital in Wales. Lieutenant-Colonel Scott was posted to the Isle of Man.

Scott was evidently a sensible and humane man, and life on the island remained for the most part on an even keel. The principal exceptions are noted in Scott's diary. On 30 March he travelled to Ramsey airport to receive a major-general who was due to inspect his staff. 'However he didn't turn up.' On 15 April, the intelligence staff held a dinner. On 30 April, the start of a tunnel was unearthed: 'Plan to discover culprits fails'; 26 May: the Ministry of Information photographer Bertram Park arrived to spend two

285

days taking pictures; 22 June: 'A visit from the Bishop who wanted to know what spiritual arrangements there were for the Rumanians' (the island's catchment was clearly spreading). 8 July brought 'a little flutter from the fact that the German Consul Herr Deters has been accused by Fraulein Helenbrandt of the woman's camp of having put her in the family way.' The problem was soon solved. 25 August: 'Deters and Fraulein Helenbrandt are to get married.'

By the summer of 1942 there were fewer than 5,000 internees on the island. Only 300 to 400 were 'refugees from Nazi oppression'; most 'C' internees had been released and the Home Office turned to the remaining 'B's. With the falling rolls, some camps were closed and others consolidated. In May 1941, the Home Office had established a 'Married Aliens Internment Camp' at Port St Mary. It did so in the teeth of War Office opposition: the Western Command of the Home Defence Forces, whose area included the Isle of Man, condemnded the scheme as 'highly dangerous in every way', but by then the Home Office was feeling strong enough to ignore such bombast.

The move brought enormous comfort to families like the Fehles, and couples like Karl and Johanna Wehner, who could live together again at last. In 1942, the married camp was moved across the promontory to the lower part of Port Erin. Single women stayed in the upper part. The other main internment camps were at Ramsey and Douglas. Apart from right-wing notables such as Mosley, Ramsay and Domvile, who were kept in Brixton Prison, the Isle of Man also contained most of the 500 British still held under Regulation 18B. They were first quartered at Peel, but later that, too, was closed and they were transferred to camps alongside the internees.

Scott recorded the brief incursion of Japanese internees in March 1942: 100 out of the 500 Japanese living in Britain were arrested but were repatriated by the summer. Scott remained alert for all possibilities, conducting an exercise to see if he could accommodate a sudden influx of 5,000. 'It will not be easy,' he concluded. His newcomers were mainly groups of deportees returning from Canada and Australia, who waited on the island while the Home Office reviewed their cases. There was consternation when one internee hanged himself after the Home Office refused to release him, and Scott asked the editor of the local newspaper to 'keep it as quiet as possible'. M. Haccius from the Red Cross paid regular visits, and in general approved of what he found. He clearly got on well with Scott, dropping in for 'little chats'.

Scott did reveal the occasional moment of despondency. At Christmas 1942, he visited Douglas Hospital and Ramsey for a sing-song and wrote afterwards: 'I must say they were doing their best to have a happy Christmas but to my mind it was all sordid, dark and dismal.' But he was more moved when he wrote about his superiors. There was first the Chester headquarters of Western Command, who informed him that one of his officers was to be deprived of his car as he had failed to meet the regulation petrol consumption of 30 m.p.g., achieving a mere 29.33 m.p.g. instead. Then a brigadier at Chester complained that Scott was making improper use of 'priority' phone calls to the War Office in London. Scott protested that ordinary calls took two hours to come through and was astounded when the brigadier, who had clearly been tapping his line, quoted large parts of his last call verbatim.

Scott reserved his sharpest venom for the Home Office. After the War Office onslaught in 1941, it was taking greater interest in the running of the camps, but the only effect Scott could discern was that he had two masters instead of one. When summoned to London, he would visit the Home Office in the morning and the War Office in the afternoon, and purge his anger in his diary afterwards. His bugbear was a Home Office man named Kirk who had the gift of new appointments on the island. Scott was enraged in September 1942 when Kirk wanted to dismiss three officers and appoint a new commander at Ramsey: 'Stuck my heels in and refused to budge.' But Kirk had his way when he sent a former Police Superintendent to take over another camp. 'He is definitely not the type,' Scott lamented, 'but I am powerless.' Kirk refused to let Scott spend 25s (£1.25) a week to hire a ballroom for internees to receive their visitors: 'Kirk just obstructive – says no on principle.' Scott became more angry when Kirk rejected an alternative. 'Kirk would as usual say nothing until he has seen it on paper. Ass!'

Although the divided command distracted Scott, it was scarcely as disastrous as in the First World War, for the Home Office and MI5 worked steadily through the 'B' internees and the numbers continued to fall. Karl Wehner had just completed the eighth year of his life spent in British internment camps when, at Christmas 1943, he and his wife were released. They had been living together at the Bradda Private Hotel in Port Erin, and watched in dismay as the proportions among their fellow-internees gradually shifted. 'Friends and enemies of Nazism rub shoulders willy-nilly, the latter being the minority,' Wehner wrote in November 1943. 'To my mind it is as if any old Berlin backyard of 1933 or 1934 had been emptied of its denizens who all of a sudden found themselves dumped on top of one another. . .' On their release, Karl and Johanna Wehner went to live in Streatham, south London. Wehner worked for a British press agency, but had to give up his job when the original incumbents were demobilized. He joined a European agency and started to write for German newspapers again.

There had also been a steady trickle of releases for 18B detainees. Mosley was freed in November 1943, when the number held was 316. A year later it was 223, and most of these, Morrison told the Commons on 2 November, though 'technically British', were 'persons of hostile origin or association'. Within another six months, all but fifty had been released.

One of the last internees to leave the Isle of Man was Bruno Fehle. He, his wife Irmgard, and their two sons were among the 1,200 regarded as the irreducible hardcore who could in no circumstance be released. Reunited in the married camp, they lived in the Towers Hotel. They had raised money by selling their furniture which Maple's had stored, and received extra amounts from Home Office handiwork schemes: internees could earn 7s 6d (37½p) a week from moulding chess-sets and lacquering them by hand.

Food in the shops of Port Erin seemed plentiful, at least for those who could pay. Cheese, herring, kippers, and eggs at Easter time, were freely available; cooked meat was not rationed and local butchers sold roast joints; by 1944, pork with thick crackling was a best seller. Prosperous Germans sent their children to King William's, the island's boarding school. Gus Fehle attended the camp school. It had a local headmistress, but most of the teachers were internees, including three German Protestant nuns. They were paid 5s (25p) a week.

In 1943, repatriation was in the air. By then there were 1,800 British internees in Germany and a further 6,000 in occupied France who had been rounded up in December 1940. (The Germans justified the arrests by citing the internment of 'B' category men and women in Britain in May 1940.) Their conditions were lamentable. Scott read a report of a Red Cross visit in 1943, and remarked, 'it makes shocking reading and forms the basis of reply

to many of our grousing internees.' The repatriations were nego-
tiated by the Red Cross and the Swiss government, and the first
exchange took place in October 1943.

A battered Red Cross liner named the *Atlantis* brought 790 blind
or wounded British prisoners of war and some internees to Liverpool in October 1943, and returned with 830 consular staff, merchant seamen and German prisoners of war. The next exchange
was not until June 1944, when a Swedish Red Cross ship, the
Drottnengholm, carried several hundred British women from France
via Lisbon and returned with single women from the Isle of Man.
The German U-boat threat had all but disappeared, but the Red
Cross made doubly sure by painting a warning on her side to let
her pass safely.

The *Reichsdeutschen* on the Isle of Man fell into two groups: those
who wished to go home at all costs, and those who were so dis-
couraged by the gloomy letters they had received about conditions
in Germany that they wanted to stay in Britain. Fehle discussed
the issue with his wife, but feared that anti-German feeling would
make life in Britain too uncomfortable. They were selected for one
of the last groups, due to leave at the end of May 1945. Three days
before their departure, Irmgard Fehle gave birth to a baby daughter. They were carried on to the *Drottnengholm* by stretcher and the
British escort asked the Red Cross for a receipt to acknowledge
that they had arrived in good health.

The Fehles arrived in southern Sweden two days later. Almost
all of Germany was occupied, and Bruno Fehle decided to go
ahead on reconnaissance. He sailed on a German ferryboat named
the *Telde* which took on several hundred badly harassed soldiers
of the German occupation forces from Denmark. Fehle learned
that his home town of Rathenow had been devastated, and that
several alternative destinations had also fallen to the Red Army.
He travelled instead to Flensburg in Schleswig-Holstein, occupied
by the British, where Flensburg's mayor billeted Fehle on a local
farm. Two months later, Irmgard Fehle and her three children
joined him. They decided to head for Brunswick, the home of
Irmgard's parents. They rode from Flensburg to Hamburg in a
train which consisted of cattle-trucks, save for one carriage reserved
for women and children. The waiting-room at Hamburg was full,
but a station official let them stay warm beside the fire in his office.
They caught a packed train to Brunswick in the middle of the

night and the following morning Irmgard's parents met them and
took them home.

Around the world, Britain's former internees came to terms with
their new lives. Returning Germans had to adjust to a country
divided and ravaged by defeat. Deportees who had chosen to stay
in Canada and Australia settled into their new countries. Internees
who had regained their freedom in Britain generally forgave the
British for what they saw as a moment of panic; few at any rate
have remained bitter to this day. The British government con-
gratulated itself for admitting its mistake and did not point to any
larger lessons; the episode was a mere aberration.

On 12 March 1946, Lord Vansittart opened a debate in the
Lords on 'Provisions for Security'. He complained that the government had 'thrown open this country to any displaced persons
who have relatives here who are willing to receive them and look
after them'. He conceded that this was 'a measure of humanity',
but asked that 'drastic restrictions should be applied to the intake
of aliens into this country . . . until we are in a position to cope
with an influx which otherwise might contain dangers'.

Lord Swinton was in the Lords that day. He rose to reassure his
'noble friend', Lord Vansittart. 'The question of aliens has been
debated a good deal,' Swinton commented; but he happened to
have had 'considerable responsibility and experience' in such matters, which he now imparted. 'The most dangerous man – it may
be the most dangerous woman too – is not always the most out-
wardly disreputable,' he advised. Swinton added: 'As for the scum,
quite rightly, we put lots of them inside at the critical time, but a
great many of them did not really matter very much.'

27 Journey's End

Nobby Fulford went to sea again with the Blue Star Line after the war, retiring to dry land in 1964. He became a wine waiter at the Royal Southampton Yacht Club, and was still working there when this book was completed in December 1979.

Serafino Pini returned to the restaurant business, retiring in the early 1970s and living in Golders Green, north London. He has remained closely linked with the story of the *Arandora Star*, campaigning to raise money for a memorial to the victims which was unveiled at the Italian Church in Clerkenwell in 1960, later helping to build a second memorial at the Italian town of Bardi, near Parma. It bore the names of forty-eight men from Bardi and the surrounding area who died with the *Arandora Star*.

Renate Scholem prospered as a professional actress, changing her name to Renée Goddard. In 1979 she returned to live and work for a spell in Germany.

Karl Wehner resumed his career as a journalist, becoming London correspondent for a number of German newspapers, and writing as a freelance until his retirement in 1977. In 1979, at the age of eighty-two, he was living in Streatham, south London.

Kurt Tebrich, who had changed his name to Clive Teddern on joining the British army, eventually became a teacher and in 1979 was careers master and department head at a comprehensive school in Fulham, west London.

Richard Broh worked for the post-war military administration in West Germany, helping to organize the Bavarian trade union movement under the auspices of the American Office of Strategic Services, forerunner of the CIA. He also helped to reeducate German prisoners of war. Once back in Britain, he resumed as a journalist until he retired in 1974. He has played cards with Karl Wehner every weekend since.

Hermann Bondi became Professor Sir Hermann Bondi, in 1979 Chief Scientist at the British Department of Energy.

Hellmuth Weissenborn married again and re-established himself as a successful lithographer, exhibiting regularly until 1979.

Michael Mellinger became an established actor, living in a comfortable house in Barnes, west London.

Erwin Frenkel, who stayed in Australia, had a variety of jobs, among them journalist, musician and businessman. In 1979 he was in Melbourne, running a tree-farming cooperative for small investors. He never saw his family again after leaving Vienna in 1938. All but his sister fled east, reaching Latvia before being shot. His sister headed west to France, and died in an internment camp in Nice.

Uwe Radok, who had started work as a technical assistant at Melbourne University in 1944, rose to become head of the university's department of meteorology in 1962. In 1977 he left Australia to take up a post as a senior research associate at the University of Boulder, Colorado. His brother Rainer had a variety of academic jobs in Australia and the United States, eventually setting up a research institute of oceanography in Adelaide. Jobst joined Volkswagen in Australia, and returned to Germany in the 1960s to become Volkswagen's manager of foreign operations. The three brothers met their parents for the first time after the war when they visited Australia from the United States in 1946.

Peter Jacobsohn went to Germany as an interpreter at the office of the US Chief of Counsel for the Nuremburg war-crime trials. He emigrated to the United States in 1948, and in 1979 was the publications editor at Harvard University's Center for International Affairs.

Franz Eichenberg left Australia for the United States in 1946. He settled in Portland, Oregon, where he changed his name to Frank Eaton and became Professor of German at Portland State University. He was still working part-time in 1979.

Leopold Kohn applied the skills he had learned in Suffolk by becoming a pastry cook in a Melbourne cake-shop. He later went into business on his own, and in 1979 his company, James King Enterprises, imported toys and fancy goods from the Far East. He also organized regular reunions for the *Dunera* men who stayed in Australia. His mother survived the war in Vienna, joining him in Melbourne in 1947.

Gerhard Miedzwinski changed his name to Mitchell. He went into business in Sydney and in 1979 was living in a beautiful house overlooking the Pacific Ocean close to Sydney Harbour.

Henry Teltscher graduated from his job as a technical assistant to become head of the Food Technology Department at the Royal Melbourne Institute of Technology, a position he held in 1979.

Bruno Fehle set up in the optical business in Germany again after the war. After his wife Irmgard died, he remarried and later retired to the small town of Erzingen in southern Germany. His son Gus emigrated to the United States in 1959. He married an Englishwoman and returned to Germany in 1964. In 1973, he and his wife visited the Isle of Man. 'We saw it at its worst,' Gus said later. 'The wind was blowing and it was pouring with rain. We decided this was where we wanted to live.' Gus took over his father's business and set it up in Ramsey. He was still living there in 1979.

Postscript

In October 1979, the British government published a Bill for the 'Protection of Official Information'. The Bill was to replace Section 2 of the Official Secrets Act, which forbade the disclosure of virtually any information about civil servants, including, it was often joked, how much sugar they took in their tea. Two recent cases had demonstrated the Act's ineffectiveness. In 1970, two journalists and an army officer were prosecuted for publishing a document about the Nigerian civil war; they were acquitted. In 1977, two radical journalists and a former British soldier were prosecuted for revealing details of electronic intelligence, including telephone tapping; the case against them collapsed into absurdity and all three left the court free men, two with conditional discharges, one with a suspended prison sentence.

The government tried to present its new Bill as a liberal measure: no longer would it be a crime to write about the culinary tastes of civil servants. But it would have had quite the opposite effect, for the blunderbuss of 1911, it was widely commented, would have been replaced by a 1980 Armalite rifle. The Bill created classes of protected information, which became protected on the unchallenged assertion of a government minister. The broadest category concerned 'security or intelligence'. This was defined as 'the work and activities of, and in support of, the security and intelligence services or any part of them, and references to information relating to security or intelligence includes references to information held or transmitted by those services or persons in support of them or any part of them'. Not only was the nature of security and intelligence work secret; even to refer to them would, it seemed, become illegal.

It is rare that governments are discomfited so neatly and totally as occurred a month after the Bill was published. Then it was revealed that Professor Sir Anthony Blunt, Adviser for the Queen's Pictures, had spied for the USSR before, during and probably after the war. In her pique, Britain's Prime Minister stripped Blunt of his knighthood. And as the press raked happily through the surrounding muck, much more was uncovered, not only about Blunt's sad past, but also about the behaviour of MI5 when Blunt had confessed to them in 1964. Blunt had received immunity from prosecution in return for everything he could relate about his activities, and probably for agreeing to act as a double-agent as well. MI5 had obeyed its standing instructions to inform the Home Secretary of some part of this – but only in such a way that neither he nor his permanent under-secretary perceived its full implications, while the Prime Minister, Lord Home, learned nothing of it at all. Not until 1967 were British Prime Ministers and Home Secretaries fully informed. Then, as one later implied, there was little to be done about so successful a *fait accompli*.

It should not have been surprising that the security service assumed for itself the power to determine Blunt's fate. It and the intelligence service had done the same in the Second World War, deciding which captured German spies should be turned round and which should face trial and execution. But it was soon realized that had the Protection of Official Information Bill been law, none of these issues could have been discussed in public. The constitutional relationship between the security service and the government's ministers would have remained a closed book.

The same would be true of much of the ground we have covered. The events of June 1940, in particular, when the Swinton Committee and MI5 enacted deportation so ruthlessly, would have become forbidden territory. So would the close links forged between these bodies and the politicians then arrogating increasing power. Of course, it could be argued then, and now, that such steps are necessary in times of crisis. But that is always the justification for attacking historical freedoms – and it is not a justification for preventing public debate. But then public discussion and freedom of information are the enemy of those who wish to subvert the liberty of the subject.

The Blunt affair brought the demise of the Protection of Information Bill, with the throng treated to the spectacle of their betters squabbling over who had really wanted the Bill in the first place. Ministers also paid lip-service to the desirability of open government, which fooled nobody. Whether or not a supposedly more palatable version of the Bill is devised, the trend is clear: towards greater secrecy, closer control of information, more power to the state. The individual can only defend himself by asserting his traditional rights. The price of liberty is eternal vigilance.

Source Notes and References

As the nature of our evidence has been so important a consideration when vital documents remained closed to us, we have frequently discussed our sources in the text. Where we have clearly
indicated the origin of our evidence, we have not duplicated this
information in these notes. The timing and sequence of events is
another important element of our story, and in most cases where
we have given the date and place of official statements in our text
we have not repeated them here. This is particularly true of statements in Parliament and discussions in Cabinet, and we have only
itemized these in our source notes where their dates are not clear:
their sources are, of course, *Hansard* and the Cabinet papers in the
British Public Record Office, Kew.

Researchers familiar with the notations of the PRO will readily
recognize which documents are to be found there. For others we
can briefly explain the initials which indicate a document has been
released to public access in the PRO, and its origin. They are:

ADM = Admiralty
Cab = Cabinet Office
DO = Dominions Office
FO = Foreign Office
HO = Home Office
MEPO = Metropolitan Police
WO = War Office

British ministry documents without these prefixes had not been released at the time of our research: in our case, this applies only to the Home Office, and we have discussed our dealings with them in the Introduction.

As stated in our text and listed in our acknowledgements (page ix), we conducted research in other libraries and archives: these should be clear in all cases in our text and/or source notes. Where other books were our source, we have keyed them by author, with full details in the Bibliography. Magazine articles consulted appear in the source notes.

In some cases where we have stated that we have made continuous use of a particular source, we have not keyed every reference from it, although we have been specific where doubt may arise and where alternative sources were used. In general, we have indexed particular folios or items only where the references appeared especially significant, or difficult for others to trace.

1   A Midsummer Morning

The sources for the sinking of the *Arandora Star* are discussed fully in the text of Chapter 17 and its source notes below.

2   The Health Resort

We have drawn on four Home Office files in the Public Record Office which cover internment in the First World War. HO 45 10946 and HO 45 10947 contain all official reports on conditions in the camps that we have cited, except as stated below. HO 45 10760 covers the formation and alteration of internment policy. HO 45 10756 deals with ancillary matters. Our account of life in internment also draws on the recollections of Karl Wehner, whom we interviewed in London in 1979.

page 8: the early history of internment is conveniently summarized by Sir Edward Troup in a letter to the War Office dated 20 October 1914 in HO 45 10760. The origin of MI5 (known first as M.O.5), the arrest of 'twenty known spies', and the Home Office boast are from Bulloch.

page 10: the altercation with Admiral Beresford is in HO 45 10756.

page 11: life in Olympia was described by Wehner.

page 12: the *Royal Edward*'s menu is in HO 45 10760.

page 14: Kitchener's letter is in HO 45 10760.

page 16: Asquith is cited in a letter from the Destitute Aliens Committee of the Home Office dated 18 May 1915, HO 45 10946.

page 16: the black market bacon, the stewed dog, and the Dualans are from Wehner.

page 20: the unpleasantness at the Hook is from Wehner.

3 The Home Office Need Not Be Informed

The main source for the formation and fluctuations of internment policy before the Second World War are the files which the Home Office opened to us in response to our request for all relevant files on internment. We have described our negotiations with the Home Office in the Introduction. Of the twelve files we saw, nine spanned the period May 1938 to August 1939, and we list them here. (The prefix HO 144 indicates that they have been sent to the Public Record Office but placed in a closed category there.) They are: HO 144 21254/700450/13 and 19; HO 144 21258/70463/2, 11, 12, 25, 40 and 41; HO 144 21262/700470. The remaining three files, pertaining to the war years, have been cited in the source notes to later chapters.

The history of Nazi Germany, the flight of refugees and their entry to Britain, is well-covered ground. We drew on: Bracher; Dawidowicz; Morse; Sherman; Stevens; Wasserstein.

The exceptions to these sources are as follows:

page 23: the 1923 CID meeting is referred to in FO 371 23939, which contains a Home Office memorandum summarizing repatriation policy.

page 29: the career of Kell is taken from Page, Leitch and Knightley; Bulloch; Cookridge (unreliable); Philby; and an interview with Sir Dick White in November 1979.

page 30: Hoare is minuted in HO 45 20206 (see source notes to page 119).

4 Essex by the Sea

Karl Wehner's memory of his internment during the Second World War was assisted from notebooks which he kept at the time. These included notes he made of his interrogation by MI5 (page 35). Corroborative details of life at Olympia and Clacton are in *The*

Protecting Power by Eugen Spier, a German who was interned at the start of the war; and in a manuscript account by the internee Dr Alex Natan (see page 32) which is in the Institut für Zeitgeschichte, Munich.

page 36: Kell's boast about the efficacy of his September round-up was cited by Bulloch. It was also reported to Cabinet by Anderson in his paper W.P.(G) (40) 131, dated 17 May, to be found in Cab 67/6 at the PRO, in which Anderson said: 'Widespread investigations by the Intelligence Service have not revealed any evidence of any plan for obtaining, in the event of an invasion, assistance from Germans and Austrians in this country... If there was any pre-arranged plan by which invaders were to be helped by Germans resident in this country, such a plan will have been disorganized completely by the measures already taken.'

5   Of Dubious Repute

The main source for the career and character of Sir John Anderson is the biography by John Wheeler Bennett.

In default of the Home Office itself, the best source for Home Office instructions to tribunals and related material is the US National Archives in Washington. On 11 February 1941, the US chargé d'affaires in London, Herschel Johnson, sent the State Department a set of thirty-five documents supplied to him by the Home Office. The documents and Johnson's covering letter are filed in the US National Archives Diplomatic Branch records under 740.00115 European War 1939/895.

page 44: our information about the use of Category 'B' comes from our interviews; Lafitte; 'Judex'; and material from Onchan Camp in the Department of Printed Books of the Imperial War Museum, IWM 536.131 K17362.
page 45: Lafitte, page 63, gives a table of the tribunals' allocation of categories. Anderson gave the current total to the Commons on 23 November 1939.

6   A World of its Own

The personal stories were obtained from the subjects themselves. We interviewed Peter Jacobsohn in Wayland, Massachusetts, in

February 1979; Franz Eichenberg (now Dr Frank Eaton) in Portland, Oregon, in April 1979; Erwin Frenkel in Melbourne in March 1979; Bruno Fehle in Erzingen, southern Germany, in May 1979. Bruno Fehle's recollections were assisted by those of his son Gus, whom we interviewed on the Isle of Man in November 1978 and who was most generous in his subsequent help. The portrait of camp life at Seaton was composed from these collective reminiscences. There are further details in Spier. There is one War Office file in the PRO to assist: WO 1693 which contains dates when various camps were opened and closed.

page 47: details of Ossietzky are taken from Grossmann; and Koplin.

page 58: Anderson announced the release statistics to the Commons on 1 February 1940.

7 The Bargaining Counters

The tortuous negotiations between Britain, France and Germany, mediated by the United States, can be traced in the PRO and the US National Archives. The British documents are in files FO 371 23929 and FO 371 23940; the most convenient source for the American documents are *Foreign Relations, 1939*, vol. I (Government Printing Office, Washington D.C., 1956) and *Foreign Relations, 1940*, vol. II (Government Printing Office, Washington D.C., 1957), which contain sections entitled 'Efforts of the United States to Secure the Repatriation of Civilian Enemy Aliens in Belligerent Countries'.

The exceptions are as follows.

page 62: the three Cabinet meetings were on 27, 28 and 30 September. The minutes do not specify that Churchill was opposing repatriation policy, merely reporting, on 27 September, 'some discussion as to the wisdom of this policy'. However, Maxwell made it clear that Churchill was objecting in a letter to Cadogan on 4 October 1939 (FO 371 23939 folio 98). Maxwell wrote: 'Urquhart of your Department telephoned to me last week and said that Mr Winston Churchill had raised at the War Cabinet some question about our policy of allowing Germans to return to Germany.'

page 64: that there was no Foreign Office section to deal with the

Red Cross is revealed by Sir Harold Satow in FO 916 8, folio 18.

page 64: American reports on Wülzburg are in National Archives Diplomatic Branch 740.00115 European War 1939, items 217 and 303.

page 65: E. N. Cooper of the Home Office referred to the women at a meeting of the 'Internment Camps Committee' at the Home Office on 20 October 1939. The committee itself seems to have been short-lived. It was intended as a sub-committee of the Aliens Advisory Committee, itself successor to the CID Committee for Control of Aliens in War Time (see page 25). In the event, the AAC seems to have taken over the ICC's functions.

page 67: the three Brazilian ships are referred to in Diplomatic Branch 740.00115 European War 1939/789. The *Asama Mahu* incident is covered in items 225, 230, 238, 239, 244, 245, 254, 263, 275, 281, 299, 300 and 301.

page 68: the memorandum to Long is in Diplomatic Branch 740.00115 European War 1939/403.

8   A Secret Weapon

Our sources for the Norwegian débâcle are Churchill; Liddell Hart; Taylor; Simon & Schuster; and Macintyre. The failure of military intelligence is copiously documented in the first volume of the official history of British intelligence (Hinsley *et al.*). Our newspaper research was conducted at the British Museum Newspaper Library at Colindale; the Wiener Library; the London Library; and the libraries of *The Times*, the *Sunday Times* and the Manx Museum.

page 70: Churchill's 'by all means and on every occasion' is in *The Second World War*, vol. I, p. 424.

page 73: Ed Murrow is cited by Knightley, p. 227.

page 73: the origin of the phrase 'Fifth Column' is discussed by Thomas (footnote on p. 470 of 1977 edition).

page 75: the source for Rothermere is Ferris.

page 77: Stowe's dispatch on 16 April 1940 was also published by the *Baltimore Evening Sun*. Stowe consolidated many of his reports into his book, *No Other Road To Freedom*. Stowe's remark about 'yellow-bellied pacifists' is from a letter to us, dated 31 August 1979. Stowe is also discussed by Knightley, pp. 226–8.

page 77: Dr Louis de Jong, who was director of the Rijksinstitut voor Oorlogsdocumentatie, Amsterdam, from 1945 to 1979, is also the author of the official Dutch war history, eventually to be published in twelve volumes. He dealt with the Fifth Column in vols II and III. These are not yet available in English, but Dr de Jong wrote to us on 11 October 1979: '. . . compared with what I wrote in my book on the German Fifth Column, there is no new information in volumes II and III of my main work'.

page 78: the Mass-Observation survey is in Lafitte, page 116.

page 80: Anderson's letters were quoted by Wheeler Bennett.

9   Backs Against the Wall

We again rely largely on Hinsley *et al.* for the failure of British intelligence before the Norwegian campaign. Our assessment of the JIC's members derives from a well-placed intelligence source who asked not to be named. He is also quoted on page 82.

page 81: the report of the 2 May JIC meeting is indexed C.O.S. (40) 315 (J.I.C.) in Cab 66/7.

page 87: the Chiefs of Staff meeting of 3 May is indexed W.P. (40) 143, Cab 66/7. The 4 May meeting is W.P. (40) 145/C.O.S. (40) 320, Cab 66/7.

page 88: the date of the third COS meeting is not clear, but the paper to which it led was ready for presentation to the War Cabinet on 10 May 1940 and is indexed as W.P. (40) 153/C.O.S. (40) 332 in Cab 66/7.

page 88: Churchill wrote of his 'profound relief' in *The Second World War*, vol. I, p. 526.

10   A Precautionary Measure

page 92: Newsam's observations are taken from his book, *The Home Office*. Newsam told Mrs Sylvia Sprigge on 7 July 1940 that 'he drafted *all* the Internment Orders'; Mrs Sprigge related this to Lafitte in a letter dated 13 November 1941.

page 94: Anderson described the events of 10 May in his Commons speech of 22 August 1940. Although Anderson did not give a date in that speech, a Foreign Office memorandum (FO 916 2580, folio 50) does. Newsam told the Foreign Office there had been a meeting with the 'Military Authorities' on the night of 10 May. FO 916 2580, folio 47, dated 11 May, refers to 'this morning's meeting of the Committee of Civil Defence' at which Anderson reportedly made his announcement. We have been unable to solve the problem that the minutes of the Cabinet's Civil Defence Committee ('CDC' – filed in Cab 73/1–8) do not show that it met that morning.

page 95: the first version of Newsam's telegram is in FO 371 25244, and the amendments in FO 916 2580.

page 95: we interviewed Leopold Kohn, who later became Jimmy King, in Melbourne in March 1979.

page 96: we interviewed Sir Hermann Bondi in London in May 1979.

page 97: we interviewed Kurt Tebrich, who changed his name to Clive Teddern in 1944, in London in May 1979.

page 97: the description of Huyton is based on our interviews; Lafitte; and Lord Snell's report to Cabinet dated 25 November 1940, indexed W. P. (40) 463 in Cab 66/13. We were aided by a set of photographs in the Fox Photo Library, London, which, although captioned 'The North of England' or 'Rochdale', were identified as Huyton by Rob Rohrer.

page 97: for the candid Home Office briefing, see the source notes to Chapter 5 above.

11   The Threat Below Stairs

The Bland Report and its progress are in FO 371 25189, which is also the source for the other documents and memoranda mentioned in this chapter, and the comments made by Jebb, Cavendish-Bentinck *et al.*

page 102: the Dutch diplomat was C. W. A. Schurmann, former Netherlands Ambassador to Britain, writing in *The Times* of 23 August 1972, following Bland's death. For the fall of Holland, we have again followed de Jong, aided by van Kleffens and Gerbrandy.

page 103: Home Office instructions to civilians, and the Air Ministry's alarm, are in FO 371 25189, folios 413 and 417.

page 104: Reynaud's claim and the German reaction are in US National Archives Diplomatic Branch 740.00114 European War 1939/68.

page 105: we interviewed Broh in London in March 1979.

page 109: for Sir Campbell Stuart, see his biography; and for the Coward episode, see Morley's biography.

page 110: the best source for the Ministry of Information is McLaine.

page 110: Bland's broadcast is in Lafitte, pp. 172–3.

page 112: Anderson's audience with King George VI is mentioned by Wheeler Bennett.

page 112: Anderson's report of 17 May is in W.P.(G) (40) 131 in Cab 67/6.

page 113: the modifications to the JIC paper by the Chiefs of Staff are listed by Anderson in his paper of 22 May, which was never presented and is in FO 371 25189, folio 447.

12   Britain Betrayed

We outline on page 112 the sources for re-examining the Kent/ Wolkoff affair. They are Jowitt, Chapters 5 and 6; Whalen, Chapter 12; the transcript of the trial, Rex v. Tyler Gatewood Kent, contained in the Charles B. Parsons Collection of the Historical Manuscripts Division at Yale University Library. (Parsons was a benefactor who sympathized with Kent and purchased a trial transcript from the British authorities. He released it to the Yale Library in 1963.) There is also US State Department Press Release No. 405, dated 2 September 1944, entitled 'The Trial of Tyler Kent'. All details of the MI5 inquiry and the 'set-up' of Kent and Wolkoff are taken from these, as are Kent's own quoted statements.

page 116: the Confidential Annex to the 22 May Cabinet meeting is in Cab 63/13. It bears the handwritten note: 'Copies sent to Prime Minister, Home Secretary.'

page 116: the post-war account is Firmin.

page 117: our sources for Mosley and the BUF are Skidelski; and Cross.

page 117: Ramsay's opinions are taken from Jowitt. Domvile's are in his book.

page 117: details of the Anglo-German Fellowship are taken from the *Anglo-German Review* filed by the Wiener Library. Lady Londonderry's article is in the issue of February 1937.

page 119: Anderson's report of 17 May, presented to Cabinet on 18 May, is indexed W.P.(G.) (40) 131 and is in Cab 67/6.

page 119: the best contemporary summary of the murky legal basis for mass internment was by E. Cohn, Modern Law Review vol. IV, 1941.

page 119: the history of Regulation 18B is contained in HO 45 20206 in the PRO.

page 121: the reaction of the Metropolitan Police and other details of the working of 18B are in MEPO 2 6433 in the PRO. There is a file about the November 1939 change to 18B in the Home Office's 700378/80.

page 125: Jowitt describes the problems of prosecuting under the Official Secrets Act on pp. 52–3 and reveals the crucial date of 9 April on p. 69.

page 127: for Ball's shadowy career, see Chester, Fay and Young; and Page, Leitch and Knightley. Harker's friendship with Ball was described to us by Sir Dick White.

page 127: Harker's views are in FO 371 25248, folio 417.

page 128: the Home Office deportation order is among the Kent case papers in Yale University Library.

page 128: Maxwell's letter is dated 14 June 1940, and is in MEPO 2 6433; so is his letter about pacifists, etc., dated 14 July 1940.

page 129: there is a copy of Anderson's paper dated 22 May in FO 371 25244, folio 147, marked 'to be returned to Mr Newsam HO'.

13   A Special Body

page 133: Maxwell's letter of 24 May 1940 and the explanatory memorandum are in FO 371 25244. The letter is also in the Johnson dispatch of 11 February 1941.

page 134: the story of the Fehle family follows our interviews with Bruno Fehle in Germany and Gus Fehle on the Isle of Man.

page 135: we interviewed Alec Clague in December 1978. Sergeaunt's letter appeared in the *Isle of Man Examiner*, 17 May 1940.

page 136: we interviewed Renate Scholem, who changed her name to Renée Goddard, in London in October 1978.

page 140: the figure of 823 men comes from the *Isle of Man Examiner*, 31 May 1940.

page 140: different versions of Kell's downfall are in Bulloch; and Page, Leitch and Knightley.

page 141: Harker's letter is to Gladwyn Jebb in FO 371 25193, folio 87 (see page 151).

page 141: the Chiefs of Staff paper is dated 25 May and indexed W.P.(40) 168/C.O.S. (40) 390, in Cab 66/7. The confidential discussion of 27 May is in Confidential Annex in Cab 65/13.

page 141: for Swinton's background see his own books; and Page, Leitch and Knightley.

page 142: the vital extract is in FO 371 25248, folio 416.

page 144: the Home Office letter of 31 May is in the Johnson dispatch of 11 February 1941.

14 'Collar the Lot!'

page 147: we interviewed Serafino Pini in London in January 1979. The background of the Fascio is from an account in FO 371 25210 by Professor Bruno Foa, pre-war legal advisor to the British Consul in Naples, and professor of law elect at Naples University.

page 149: Home Office file HO 144 21254 700450/21 contains a draft press notice which referred to 'All Germans, Austrians and Italians who do not intend to leave the country'.

page 149: the Cochis saga is in FO 371 24932.

page 151: Halifax mentioned his agreement with Anderson in a letter of 11 June, in FO 371 25192. Anderson's paper was that of 17 May – W.P.(G) (40) 131. Harker made his views known in a letter dated 27 May 1940 in FO 371 25193, folio 87. Cadogan's letter to Maxwell is folio 83.

page 152: the most valiant attempt to summarize the various understandings was made by Nigel Ronald of the Foreign Office in a memorandum dated 22 June 1940 in FO 371 25193, folio 101 *et seq*. It was Ronald who described the chaos over the Italian diplomatic list and who attributed to Churchill the phrase 'Collar the lot!'

page 154: Inspector Rogers's report is in FO 371 25193, folio 95; figures for arrests are in FO 371 25192, folio 221, and FO 371 25210, folio 81.

page 154: the Robert Mark incident is in his autobiography, pp. 30–31.

page 155: the anti-fascists are listed in letters and memoranda by Gillies in FO 371 25192.

page 155: the cases of Pacitto and Fiorini were described in the Commons on 8 October 1940. Alberto Loria and the man from Constantinople are in FO 371 25210.

page 156: details of Warth Mills are taken from Lafitte; our interview with Pini; a Red Cross report in FO 916 2576; and a report by Uberto Limentani in FO 371 25210. Warner's reaction is in FO 916 2576.

page 157: T. M. Snow provided information about Latham in a letter to us dated 14 December 1978, and there are more details in the 1965 Macrossan Lectures to the University of Queensland by Zelman Cowan. The Oldenzaal incident is in FO 371 24101. The first negotiations with the Home Office over French citizens are in FO 371 25244.

page 158: Latham wrote of 'panic alien restrictions' in FO 371 25246.

page 158: the MI5 bulletin and Cavendish-Bentinck's note are in FO 371 25193, folios 81 and 100.

page 159: minutes of the War Office meeting of 17 June and Farquhar's reaction are in FO 916 2580.

15   *Fait Accompli*

Our main British source for the story of deportation to the end of June 1940 is FO 916 2580. We were able to support our account from the Public Archives of Canada in Ottawa through Eric Koch, who gave generous assistance while writing his own book on the subject. There are further documents in DO 35 996 and the Australian Archives in Canberra, but we drew on these more copiously for later chapters.

page 162: Caldecote to Massey is in FO 916 2580.

page 162: the Canadian Cabinet meeting of 5 June is indexed PAC Canadian Privy Council Cabinet War Committee Minutes, RG2 7C. Canada's reply is in FO 916 2580.

page 163: Churchill's note to Bridges is in *The Second World War*, vol. II, p. 561.

page 163: Swinton's conversation with Chamberlain was reported by Lord Snell in his report to Cabinet dated 24 October 1940, indexed W.P.(40) 432, which we read in FO 371 25210.

page 163: General Panet's report and the new message to Massey are in Ottawa, PAC Department of National Defence, RG 24 C4.

page 164: Massey to Caldecote is in FO 916 2580. Massey

described the 10 June meeting in a further letter to Caldecote the same day, FO 916 2580, folio 376.

page 165: the Aliens Advisory Committee of 13 June is minuted in FO 371 25192; the War Office meeting of 17 June in FO 916 2580.

page 165: minutes of Aliens Advisory Committee 18 June are in FO 916 2580.

page 166: Australia's response is in Australian Archives, Canberra, Defence 36 (see source notes on Chapter 18 below). Other countries' replies are in FO 916 2580.

page 167: Foreign Office consternation is in FO 916 2580.

page 167: the British Cabinet discussed the evacuation of children on 17 June 1940.

page 167: Warner's note is in FO 916 2580.

page 167: Rucker's note of 20 June is in DO 35 996.

page 168: Maxwell's letter of 21 June is in the Johnson dispatch of 11 February 1941.

page 170: Tebrich – Clive Teddern – made his statement in his interview. Friemel's account is in FO 916 2581. Friemel named the British officer allegedly involved.

16   The Liverpool Train

The main source for deportations continues to be FO 916 2580.

page 173: there is a notorious lack of firm statistics on internment and releases. We have taken the figure of 27,200 as one of our bases as it was confided to the American Embassy by the Home Office in the February 1941 briefing (see page 97). It is quoted in Johnson's covering letter of 11 February 1941. (Indexed in the US National Archives Diplomatic Branch as 740.00115 European War 1939/895.)

page 173: we interviewed Professor François Lafitte, Head of the Department of Social Administration at Birmingham University, in October 1978.

page 176: the Onchan survey was published in an early issue of the *Onchan Pioneer* kept at the Department of Printed Books, Imperial War Museum. See also the 'Onchan Internment Camp' file (indexed IWM 536.131 K17362).

page 177: consultations over the weather are in FO 916 2580.

page 177: the weary memorandum was by Nigel Ronald (see source notes to page 152), and is in FO 371 25193, together with the reactions of Cadogan and Halifax.

page 178: the letter from Cross is in FO 371 25192.

page 178: the American end of the exchange is in US National Archives Diplomatic Branch 740.00115 European War. Hull's cable is item 425A. Kennedy's account of Achilles's conversation is item 424. Halifax's reply is in item 440. All were reprinted in *Foreign Relations, 1940*, vol. II (Government Printing Office, Washington D.C., 1957). The Special Division memorandum revealing Long's duplicity (page 180) is also in item 440. It was not reprinted.

page 181: the remarks by Moylan and Newsam are in FO 916 2580.

page 181: the Salerni saga is in FO 371 25192.

page 181: Farquhar described his meeting with Moylan in FO 371 25193.

page 182: selection procedures for the next sailing were described by Lord Snell in his report (see source note to page 261). But for statistics we have followed the embarkation list in FO 371 25210 (see footnote to Chapter 18, page 209).

17   The Last Torpedo

The information on the pre-war life of the *Arandora Star* is taken from brochures kindly made available by the Blue Star Line, Leadenhall Street, London E C 3; from an account of his voyages by Sir Montague Burton (*Globe Girdling*, privately published in 1937, generously supplied by his son Stanley Burton); from our interview with Nobby Fulford in Southampton in December 1978; and from an interview with former steward Ted Crisp in North Weald, Essex, in November 1978. Her wartime career is drawn from Taffrail; Roskill; FO 371 25096, which describes her part in the Gibraltar censorship fiasco; and the Naval War Diary, vol. XVII, 22–30 June 1940, kept at the Naval Historical Branch of the Ministry of Defence at Empress State Building, London S W 6. Our account of her sinking is based on our interviews with survivors (see page 193), supported by documents described on page 197. The names of casualties are taken from our interviews; Lafitte; Foreign Office documents; *Hansard*; and press reports.

page 186: a coal miner's wages are taken from Orwell, Chapter 3.

page 189: the *Arandora Star*'s armaments are described by Prien in his log (see note to page 191 below) and Bruno Fehle in his memorandum (see page 197).

page 190: we interviewed Gerhard Miedzwinski – now Gerhard Mitchell – in Sydney in March 1979.

page 191: Gunther Prien's log of the U–47 is in the Naval Historical Branch (see above), and is also kept in the Bundesarchivs-Militärarchiv, Freiburg, Germany.

page 191: Prien's background is in Costello and Hughes; Snyder; and McKee. The American journalist was William Shirer (Snyder, Chapter 7). The 'Happy Time' is described by Roskill; Macintyre; and Costello and Hughes.

page 197: the Admiralty casualty report, including de Wolf's account, is in ADM 199 2133, folio 96 *et seq.* and FO 916 2581, folio 449 *et seq.* in the PRO.

page 200: Maclean's article appeared in the *Daily Express*, 19 June 1960.

18   A Great Future Overseas

The main Foreign Office source is FO 371 2581, which takes over from FO 371 2580 at the beginning of July 1940. This chapter also contains some material from the Australian Archives in Canberra. It is convenient to list here all the files we consulted:

From the Attorney-General's Department:
W1193. Internees and Prisoners of War in United Kingdom – Transfer to Australia (1940).

From the Prime Minister's Department:
A20/1/3 Pt 1. Transfer of Internees to Australia from United Kingdom. Policy (1940–1942).

A20/1/3 Pt 2. Transfer of Internees to Australia from the United Kingdom. Policy (1942–1944).

D20/1/3. Internees from the United Kingdom – Personal effects (Claims, complaints, etc.) (1940–1941).

F20/1/3. Internees from United Kingdom – Wives and families of (1940–1941).

020/1/3. United Kingdom Internees. Enlistment in the Pioneer Corps of the British Army.

From the Department of Immigration:

47/3/3436. Internees from United Kingdom. Question of allowing some to remain in Australia.

From the Department of External Affairs:

Defence 36. Aliens – General – Internees transported from Countries – General (1940–1941).

Defence 36B. Aliens – General Internees transported from British countries (1941–1942).

43/40/7. Aliens transported from United Kingdom and British possessions – Individual cases.

From the Department of Defence:

54/301/217. Internees from United Kingdom.

page 203: Chamberlain's paper on deportations is indexed W.P. (G) (40) 170 in Cab 67/7.

page 204: the *Ettrick* details are from the War Diary of Captain E. Howell in WO 166 5982 in the PRO.

page 204: Dr Glucksmann's account is in the papers of Bishop Bell in the Lambeth Palace Library, London S E 1.

page 206: Massey's cable of 8 July is in Ottawa, PAC Department of National Defence, RG24 C4.

page 207: Maxwell's letters are in the Johnson dispatch of 11 February 1941.

page 208: the Foreign Office transactions with the American Embassy, the Red Cross, the Admiralty and the War Office are in FO 916 2581.

page 210: Whiskard to Menzies is in Canberra, A20/1/3, and Menzies's reply is cited in W1193.

page 210: we interviewed Henry Teltscher in Melbourne in March 1979.

page 211: the inducements to sail come from our interviews; an account by Walter Fliess in the Department of Sound Records of the Imperial War Museum; and letters in the files of Bishop Bell in Lambeth Palace Library. The Onchan telegram is in the 'Onchan Internment Camp' file in the Imperial War Museum.

page 213: Harms's diary of the U-56 is in the Naval Historical Branch, Ministry of Defence.

19   A Soldier's Letter

page 215: Merlin Scott's letter is in FO 371 25192, folio 241. Further information came in a letter to us from his father, Sir David Scott, dated 10 July 1979.

page 217: the Ronald draft is in FO 371 25192, folio 242 *et seq.*

page 217: Latham's memorandum is in FO 371 25247.

page 217: the Eggler/Schmid 'Catch-22' is described in FO 371 25189.

page 217: Farquhar wrote of his visit to MI5 in FO 371 25192, folio 223.

page 220: the Home Office file is HO 45 23514. It includes an account of the Home Policy Committee meeting of 18 July (see page 222).

page 221: Attlee's memorandum is W. P. (G) (40) 187 in Cab 67/7.

page 221: Anderson's reply is in FO 371 25192, folio 257.

page 222: for statistics, see source note to Chapter 16, page 173.

20   Regrettable Things Have Happened

Our picture of life in the Isle of Man is drawn from the *Isle of Man Examiner* and the *Isle of Man Weekly Times*; and interviews conducted on the Isle of Man in December 1978. Life in the camps comes from our interviews; copies of the *Onchan Pioneer* and the Onchan camp file in the Imperial War Museum (see source notes to Chapter 16, page 176).

page 227: we interviewed Dorothea and Klaus Marx in London in February 1979.

page 231: Churchill made his statement to the Commons on 15 August 1940.

page 231: the first fifty releases were reported by the *News Chronicle* on 6 August 1940.

page 231: Herbert Morrison gave a full list of committees to the Commons on 20 November 1940.

page 232: Latham fulminated in FO 371 25248, folio 369. Cavendish-Bentinck's note of 29 July is on folio 366.

page 234: the briefing is that to Johnson, described in his letter of 11 February 1941.

page 235: Latham resumed the attack in FO 371 25210. FO 371 25210 and FO 371 25192 contain records of the Loraine Committee.

page 235: Anderson expressed his desire to Cabinet on 1 August 1940.

21   A Cynical Excuse

An important source for events in Canada is the Paterson Report, described on page 267 and in the source notes to Chapter 24 below. Other material comes from our interviews; DO 35 996; Bishop Bell's files in Lambeth Palace Library; Spier; an article by Barbara Moon in *Maclean's* magazine of 10 February 1962; and personal communication from Eric Koch. There is also material in the Diplomatic Branch of the US National Archives.

page 237: the news reports and the protest by Haccius are in FO 916 2581.

page 239: Panet's note is in Ottawa, PAC Department of National Defence, RG 24 C4. His letter is in the Paterson report.

page 239: for Ritchie's comment, see his diary.

page 239: Massey's letter to Caldecote, Caldecote's reply and the Home Office memorandum are in DO 35 996.

page 240: the US intervention is in US National Archives Diplomatic Branch 740.00114 European War 1939, items 137, 187, 237 and 249.

page 242: there is a memorandum of a Home Office meeting on 4 November 1940 in the J. D. Layton file in the Department of Documents in the Imperial War Museum (IWM 79/22/1). It refers to an earlier meeting on 15 October. See page 255 for more information on Layton. There is an account of Paterson's East End work in the University College Oxford *Record*, 1979.

22   'Drown Like Rats!'

Harms never knew the name of the liner he attacked. His log, like that of Gunther Prien, was captured by the British after the war and kept in the naval archives of the Ministry of Defence. In September 1979, the ministry's naval archivist, R. M. Coppock, searched all the U-boat logs for 12 July and found Harms's entry. Harms described his target as a 'passenger liner, one funnel', and from his position, and the timing and description of the encounter, Coppock told us that he was convinced that Harms was the *Dunera*'s attacker. The calculations leading to the conclusion that Harms's torpedoes missed by 100 to 200 metres were performed by Uwe Radok. In a letter dated 17 November 1979, he estimated his accuracy as 'no more than 50% . . . so anything between 50 and 300 metres is quite consistent with the information'. Although he did not dismiss an actual impact Radok recalled that the noise came from the *Dunera*'s port side, and preferred the theory that the torpedo had exploded shortly after passing ahead.

In *The Dunera Internees*, Benzion Patkin wrote that the U-boat that fired on the *Dunera* was commanded by one S. C. Clerque. According to Patkin, Clerque saw people jumping overboard from the *Dunera* and believed that a mutiny had broken out. He did not fire again, but sent out sailors in rubber boats to pick up survivors. They found suitcases floating on the water containing letters written in German. Clerque deduced that the *Dunera* carried German prisoners of war and radioed to other U-boats not to molest her. This fanciful account is not supported by the available documents. In a letter dated 17 September 1979, R. M. Coppock told us that he had been unable to trace any U-boat captain or officer named Clerque or anything similar.

As we remark on page 244, there is no shortage of evidence about the *Dunera*. We introduce the Dunera Statement on page 245 and discuss it more fully on page 255. We obtained a copy from Henry Teltscher; there is one in the Australian Archives, Canberra. Other information comes from our interviews. There is also no shortage of accounts of the Australian camps. As well as our interviews, we have drawn on the following published Australian sources:

Konig, Walter, SJ, 'Internment in Australia', *Twentieth Century*, Spring 1963 (Melbourne).
Encel, Sol, 'These Men are Dangerous', *Nation*, 18 September 1965 (Melbourne).
Loewald, Klaus, 'A Dunera Internee at Hay, 1940–41', *Historical Studies*, 1968 (Melbourne).

We have cited the main Australian documentary sources under Chapter 18 above. The main British source for events in pages 250–1, including the negotiations with New Zealand, is FO 916 2581, supported by DO 35 996.

page 252: the Kisch story is told by Ward.
page 253: the remarkable Scott document is in Canberra, D.20/1/ 3.
page 255: we interviewed Julian Layton in April 1979. His memory was amply supported by his diary and documents, which have

now been lodged in the Department of Documents at the Imperial War Museum.

23   The Other Side of the Hill

We have again used material about Onchan from the Onchan file at the Department of Printed Books at the Imperial War Museum. For Anderson's departure from the Home Office, we have followed Wheeler Bennett.

page 261: Lord Snell's report on the *Arandora Star* was eventually published in 1940 (HMSO Cmd 6238) with all references to MI5 bowdlerized.

page 262: Farquhar complained of the whitewash in FO 371 25210, folio 312.

page 262: Clayton's minute and the comments added are in HO 144 21262, which was shown to us at the Home Office but which is in the PRO.

page 263: Peake told the Commons about the 100,000 letters on 22 August 1940.

page 263: the War Office file is WO 32 10671. The Home Office response is in HO 144 21262.

page 266: the problem of the espionage dropouts is also in WO 32 10671.

24   Dear Breck

The Paterson Report is in both DO 35 996 and HO 45 23145, which we saw at the Home Office. The Home Office file includes the comments by Morrison and Newsam. We obtained further information in an interview with Chaim Raphael in November 1979. Raphael wrote about the abortive negotiations with the United States in Appendix C to the Paterson Report and in his own book. The relevant US documents are in National Archives Diplomatic Branch 740.00115 European War 1939/801.

page 270: the barriers Bondi encountered are Section 3 of the 1917 Immigration Act and Section 17 of the 1924 Immigration Act.

page 274: the Louisiana Bill was indexed HR 4873. The June Act was HR 4983, and captioned 'To Authorize the Refusal of Visas to Aliens whose admission into the United States Would Endanger the Public Safety'.

page 274: the Johnson dispatch, so frequently cited, of 11 February 1941.

page 274: the 3 March 1942 cable is in US Diplomatic Branch 740.00115 European War 1939/2121.

page 275: details of the internment of Japanese and Japanese descendants are taken from the US Supreme Court judgment of 18 December 1944, which is published in *United States Reports*, vol. 323 (Government Printing Office, Washington D.C., 1945).

page 275: the Draper incident is from the Paterson Report and Raphael.

page 276: the statistics are from Moon's article in *Maclean's*, verified by Eric Koch.

25   Ten Thousand Miles from Home

The sources are largely those for Chapters 18 and 22 above.

page 279: Serafino Pini gave us a claim form.

page 280: we interviewed Michael Mellinger in London in October 1978.

26   Colonel Scott's Diary

page 285: Scott's diary is in the Department of Documents at the Imperial War Museum, item 69/66/1. Other material comes from our interviews.

page 288: Fehle described the handiwork scheme and the well-stocked shops of Port Erin.

page 288: there is abundant material about the treatment of British internees in France and Germany in FO 916 6, 7, 8 and 11; and in the US National Archives Diplomatic Branch European War 1939.

page 289: there are photographs and captions of the *Atlantis* exchange in the Department of Photographs at the Imperial War Museum, items H 33707–10.

Postscript

page 295: the 1970 case was that against the editor of the *Sunday Telegraph*, Brian Roberts, the journalist Jonathan Aitken, and Colonel Douglas Cairns. That of 1977 was the so-called 'ABC'

case. The three who stood trial were Crispin Aubrey, John Berry
and Duncan Campbell.

page 296: the Home Secretary was Henry Brook, the Permanent
Under-Secretary, Sir Charles Cunningham. On 17 November
1979, Lord Brook told the *Sunday Times* that he was not aware
of any 'confession or pact'. Sir Charles said he had not been
aware of the Blunt case 'in the context in which it later emerged'.
The former Prime Minister, Lord Home, told the BBC on 15
November that he had not known of Blunt's confession. The
Prime Minister who remarked that when he was told about
Blunt's immunity, there was little he could do, was Edward
Heath, in the Commons on 21 November.

Bibliography

Ashton, H. S., *The Netherlands at War*, Routledge & Kegan Paul, London, 1941.

Barwick, John, *Alien Internment Camps in the United Kingdom*, YMCA, London, 1941.

Birkenhead, Earl of, *Halifax*, Hamish Hamilton, London, 1965.

Bracher, Karl Dietrich, *The German Dictatorship*, Weidenfeld & Nicolson, London, 1971.

Bulloch, John, *MI5*, Arthur Barker, London, 1963.

Caine, Hall, *The Woman of Knockaloe*, Cassell, London, 1923.

Calder, Angus, *The People's War*, Jonathan Cape, London, 1969.

Chester, Lew, Fay, Stephen and Young, Hugo, *The Zinoviev Letter – A Political Intrigue*, Heinemann, London, 1967.

Churchill, Winston S., *The Second World War* vol. I: *The Gathering Storm*; vol. II: *Their Finest Hour*, Cassell, London, 1948, 1949.

Costello, John and Hughes, Terry, *The Battle of the Atlantic*, Collins, London, 1977.

Cowen, Zelman, *Sir John Latham and other Papers*, Oxford University Press, Melbourne, 1965.

Cross, Colin, *The Fascists in Britain*, Barrie & Rockliff, London, 1961.

Dawidowicz, Lucy S., *The War Against the Jews 1933–1945*, Bantam Books, New York, 1975.

De Jong, Louis, *The German Fifth Column in the Second World War*, Routledge & Kegan Paul, London, 1956.

Dilkes, David (ed.), *The Diaries of Sir Alexander Cadogan 1938–45*, Cassell, London, 1971.

Domvile, Sir Barry, *From Admiral to Cabin Boy*, Boswell Publishing Company, London, 1947.

Donoughue, B. and Jones, G. W., *Herbert Morrison, Portrait of a Politician*, Weidenfeld & Nicolson, London, 1973.

Farago, Ladislas, *The Game of the Foxes*, David McKay Company, New York, 1971.

Ferris, Paul, *The House of Northcliffe*, Weidenfeld & Nicolson, London, 1971.

Firmin, Stanley, *They Came to Spy*, Hutchinson, London, 1946.

Fraser, Charles F., *The Control of Aliens in the British Commonwealth of Nations*, The Hogarth Press, London, 1940.

Gilbert, Martin, *The Roots of Appeasement*, New American Library, New York, 1966.

——*Britain and Germany Between the Wars*, Longman, London, 1964.

Gladwyn, Lord, *Memoirs*, Weidenfeld & Nicolson, London, 1972.

Grossmann, Kurt R., *Ossietzky: Ein Deutscher Patriot*, Kindler, Munich, 1963.

Harrisson, Tom, *Living Through the Blitz*, Collins, London, 1976.

Himsley, F. H., *et al.*, *British Intelligence in the Second World War*, vol. I, HMSO, London, 1979.

Jones, R. V., *Most Secret War*, Hamish Hamilton, London, 1978.

Jowitt, The Earl, *Some Were Spies*, Hodder & Stoughton, London, 1954.

'Judex', *Anderson's Prisoners*, Gollancz, London, 1940.

Knightley, Phillip, *The First Casualty*, Deutsch, London, 1975.

Koplin, Raimund, *Carl von Ossietzky als politischer Publizist*, Annelore Leber, Frankfurt, 1964.

Lafitte, F., *The Internment of Aliens*, Penguin Books, Harmondsworth, 1940.

Laurent, Livia, *A Tale of Internment*, Allen & Unwin, London, 1942.

Liddell Hart, B. H., *History of the Second World War*, Cassell, London, 1970.

Lomnitz, Alfred, *'Never Mind Mr Lom!'*, Macmillan, London, 1941.

Macintyre, Donald, *Narvik*, Evans Bros., London, 1959.

——*The Battle of the Atlantic*, B. T. Batsford, London, 1961.

Mark, Sir Robert, *In the Office of Constable*, Collins, London, 1978.

Masterman, John C., *The Double-Cross System in the War of 1939–45*, Yale University Press, 1972.

McKee, Alexander, *Black Saturday*, Souvenir Press, London, 1966.

McLaine, Ian, *Ministry of Morale*, Allen & Unwin, London, 1979.

Montgomery Hyde, H., *Neville Chamberlain*, Weidenfeld & Nicolson, London, 1976.

Morley, Sheridan, *A Talent to Amuse*, Heinemann, London, 1969.

Morse, Arthur D., *While Six Million Died*, Secker & Warburg, London, 1968.

Newsam, Sir Frank, *The Home Office*, Allen & Unwin, London, 1954.

Orwell, George, *The Road to Wigan Pier*, Gollancz, London, 1937.

Page, Bruce, Leitch, David and Knightley, Phillip, *Philby: The Spy Who Betrayed a Generation*, Deutsch, London, 1968.

Parrish, Thomas, and Marshall, S.L.A. (eds), *Encyclopedia of World War II*, Simon & Schuster, New York, 1978.

Patkin, Benzion, *The Dunera Internees*, Cassell, Melbourne, 1979.

Philby, Kim, *My Silent War*, Granada Publishing, London, 1969.

Pryce-Jones, David, *Unity Mitford – a Quest*, Weidenfeld & Nicolson, London, 1976.

Public Record Office Handbook, *The Second World War: A Guide to Documents in the PRO*, HMSO, London, 1972.

Raphael, Chaim, *Memoirs of a Special Case*, Chatto & Windus, London, 1962.

Ritchie, Charles, *The Siren Years – A Canadian Diplomat Abroad*, Macmillan, Toronto, 1974.

Roskill, Captain S. W., *The War at Sea 1939–1945*, vol. I, HMSO, London, 1954.

Stowe, Leland, *No Other Road to Freedom*, Faber & Faber, London, 1942.

Stuart, Sir Campbell, *Opportunity Knocks Once*, Collins, London, 1952.

Sherman, A. J., *Island Refuge*, Paul Elek, London, 1973.

Skidelsky, Robert, *Oswald Mosley*, Macmillan, London, 1975.

Snyder, Gerald S., *The Royal Oak Disaster*, William Kimber, London, 1976.

Spier, Eugen, *The Protecting Power*, Skeffington, London, 1951.

Stevens, Austin, *The Dispossessed – German Refugees in Britain*, Barrie & Jenkins, London, 1975.

Swinton, Earl of, *Sixty Years of Power*, Hutchinson, London, 1966.

—— *I Remember*, Hutchinson, London, 1947.

'Taffrail', *Blue Star Line at War*, Foulsham, London, 1973.

Taylor, A. J. P., *The Second World War*, Hamish Hamilton, London, 1975.

Theimer, W., *The Penguin Political Dictionary*, Penguin Books, Harmondsworth, 1939.

Thomas, Hugh, *The Spanish Civil War*, new edn, Hamish Hamilton, London, 1977.

Van Kleffens, E. N., *The Rape of the Netherlands*, Hodder & Stoughton, London, 1940.

Ward Price, G., *I Know these Dictators*, Harrap, London, 1937.

Ward, Russel, *Australia, a Short History*, Ure Smith, Sydney, 1969.

Wasserstein, Bernard, *Britain and the Jews of Europe 1939–1945*, Clarendon Press, Oxford, 1979.

Whalen, Richard, *The Founding Father*, Hutchinson, London, 1965.

Wheeler Bennett, John W., *John Anderson, Viscount Waverley*, Macmillan, London, 1962.

Index